ASIAN
AMERICANS
AND
PACIFIC
ISLANDERS
IN HIGHER EDUCATION

NASPA
Student Affairs Administrators
in Higher Education

ASIAN AMERICANS
AND
PACIFIC ISLANDERS
IN HIGHER EDUCATION

Research and Perspectives on
Identity, Leadership, and Success

Edited by
Doris Ching and Amefil Agbayani
Foreword by Bob H. Suzuki

NASPA
Student Affairs Administrators
in Higher Education

Asian Americans and Pacific Islanders in Higher Education:
Research and Perspectives on Identity, Leadership, and Success

Published by
NASPA–Student Affairs Administrators in Higher Education
111 K Street, NE,
10th Floor
Washington, DC 20002
www.naspa.org

Additional copies may be purchased by contacting the NASPA publications department at 301-638-1749 or visiting http://bookstore.naspa.org.

NASPA does not discriminate on the basis of race, color, national origin, religion, sex, age, gender identity, gender expression, affectional or sexual orientation, or disability in any of its policies, programs, and services.

Library of Congress Cataloging-in-Publication Data

Asian Americans and Pacific Islanders in higher education : research and perspectives on identity, leadership, and success / edited by Doris Ching and Amefil Agbayani. — 1st ed.
    p. cm.
  Includes bibliographical references and index.
  ISBN 978-0-931654-60-2
  1. Asian American college students. 2. Pacific Islanders—Education (Higher)—United States. 3. Asian American college teachers. 4. Minorities in higher education—United States. 5. Asian Americans—Ethnic identity. 6. Pacific Islanders—United States—Ethnic identity. I. Ching, Doris (Doris M.) II. Agbayani, Amefil, 1943-
  LC2633.6.A85 2012
  378.1'982995073—dc23
              2011051746

Printed and bound in the United States of America
FIRST EDITION

Contents

PART I
AAPI Background and Statistics

PART II
AAPI Racial Identity Formation

PART III
Strengthening AAPIs through Organizations and Leadership

PART IV
Working with AAPI College Students

PART V
AAPI Role Expectations

PART VI
Looking Forward

Foreword

Bob H. Suzuki

It is a great pleasure for me to write the foreword to what I believe will become a groundbreaking book. The contributing authors are all experienced practitioners and leaders in higher education student affairs. The editors, Doris Ching and Amy Agbayani, have done a superb job not only in bringing together this outstanding team of writers but also in coordinating a rather complex book project and keeping it on track.

In my first reading of the chapters, I was struck by the tremendous diversity and comprehensiveness of the topics, as well as the diversity of the authors, many of whom delve into areas never before explored and analyzed so deeply in writing. I was also struck by the fact that many of the authors were not content to simply expound on theoretical concepts, statistical analyses, and historical events but also expressed, often with passion, a desire to translate theory into practice and to engage in efforts to promote social justice for Asian Americans and Pacific Islanders (AAPIs) and other minorities. Because such an orientation strongly resonated with my own perspectives and career path, I thought I might share some of my experiences during my 40-year career as a faculty member and administrator. Many of these experiences relate directly to several of the themes and concepts articulated by the authors, and they show that one can be deeply engaged in social activism as well as in one's professional career.

After completing my PhD in 1967, I obtained my first job as an assistant professor of aerospace engineering at the University of Southern California (USC). At the time, my most ambitious long-term goal was to become a full professor with tenure. However, it was the late 1960s, and social unrest was rampant throughout the country: urban riots, civil rights protests, anti-Vietnam War demonstrations, assassinations of political leaders, and the emergence of social activism by AAPIs. USC was not immune to these social forces: the Watts riot in Los Angeles had occurred not far from the campus. Before long, my wife Agnes and I found ourselves deeply involved, first with Blacks and Latinos in various civil rights and political activities, and later increasingly with the emerging Asian American movement.

Among numerous other activities, I helped lead a national campaign to repeal the Emergency Detention Act of 1950, a law that essentially legalized actions such as those taken by the government to incarcerate Japanese Americans during World War II. I was strongly motivated to become involved in this repeal effort because of my own experience as a young boy in one of the internment camps and my conviction that such actions should never again be used against any group. After an almost three-year campaign, the law was repealed in 1971.

Agnes and I also became involved in the desegregation of the Pasadena public schools, the first school district outside of the South to be court-ordered to desegregate. I served as vice chair of the Community Advisory Committee for the Desegregation of the Pasadena Schools. In this role, I discovered that AAPIs were recognized neither as minorities nor as nonminorities and were not considered for participation in the federal Emergency School Assistance Program, which was funding the desegregation activities of the school district. I wrote to the Department of Health, Education and Welfare (HEW) to request that AAPIs be specifically designated as a protected group—along with African Americans, Latinos, and Native Americans—in the federal legislation and Executive Order that mandated affirmative action. With the help of a key White House staff assistant, William (Mo) Marumoto, we accomplished this goal. Even with this specific designation, it has been difficult to have AAPIs recognized for inclusion in affirmative action programs at many higher education institutions; without the designation, they might have been ignored entirely.

I mention these activities for two reasons. First, they show that academicians can be effectively involved in the political arena and can have an impact on bringing about social change. Second, these activities taught me many skills that have been valuable and helpful in my academic career, especially as an administrator, and provided valuable experience for dealing with the often intense political climate on many campuses. In addition to honing my political skills, I learned important leadership skills, especially in the repeal campaign: When you work with volunteers, you quickly learn that you cannot order them around but need to motivate and inspire them to action. Faculty are much like volunteers; they enjoy a high degree of independence and freedom of action, especially if they are tenured.

As a result of my deep involvement in these activities, I decided to change my professional field and devote myself full time to work that more directly addressed pressing societal problems. After exploring a number of possible options, I accepted an offer to join the faculty as an associate professor in the School of Education at the University of Massachusetts in Amherst. I arrived there in the fall of 1971 planning to teach courses in science and math education, Asian American studies, and urban education.

This switch in fields may seem drastic and risky, but I have always been willing to take risks in my career to pursue my interests and passions. I have often told graduating students at commencements that they should not believe that their career options are limited to the field in which they majored; rather, they should view their major as a foundation on which to build a career in which they will likely have to change jobs and fields several times. I hope student affairs practitioners, especially in career centers, are helping students develop this mindset. It has certainly had a positive effect on my own career.

Two months after I arrived at UMass, the dean asked me to take the position of assistant dean for administration in the School of Education. Although I had never served as an administrator, the dean thought I could do the job, amazingly enough, because of my engineering background! After serving in this capacity for more than 3 years, I resigned in December 1974 to return to fulltime teaching and research. During my 10 years at UMass, I continued my social activism as an integral part of my academic career development. Among other activities, I developed one of the first multicultural education programs in the country. As I wrote in an article published in 1984, after I left UMass, the conceptualization of the program was different from that of most other multicultural programs. In particular, it provided a broader framework that addressed the impact of racism, sexism, and class inequality on the educational process, thus overcoming the criticisms leveled against such programs in the chapter by Sumun Pendakur and Vijay Pendakur in the second section of this book.

The other activity I'd like to mention is the organization of the Asian Faculty Association. When I learned that two Asian colleagues in other departments were being denied tenure, I called a meeting at my home with these colleagues and about six other AAPI faculty to discuss the issue. We discovered that all of these faculty members had faced or were facing similar negative personnel actions but felt powerless to do anything about them. We decided to call a larger meeting of all the Asian faculty on campus; a meeting that led to the formation of the Asian Faculty Association (AFA), which included about 30 of the 40 or so Asian faculty we could identify on the campus. The AFA filed a discrimination complaint with the U.S. Office of Civil Rights in Boston, which decided to investigate the matter. This put a lot of pressure on the university to settle the complaint and led to the awarding of tenure to the two faculty facing denial, and later to turning around negative personnel actions facing a number of other AAPI faculty.

When word got out around the campus about AFA's actions, the two other minority faculty organizations—the Black Faculty Association and the Hispanic Faculty Association—approached the AFA about forming a coalition organization, the Minority Faculty Association. The MFA became quite active in influencing not only personnel actions affecting minority faculty, but also searches for various administrative positions on campus, including the chancellorship.

All these activities took place on a predominantly White campus, where minority faculty and students comprised a small percentage of the total faculty and student population. My experience shows what can be accomplished when people organize and make unified efforts to bring about change; individuals acting alone usually feel impotent and are powerless to do anything about their circumstances. The lesson to student affairs practitioners who wish to promote social justice should be clear: organize, organize, organize!

After 10 years at UMass, I was a tenured full professor and was beginning to think that I would be spending the rest of my career there. However, an African American friend and colleague was asked by a childhood friend, who had just become a university president in California, to recommend people for a number of administrative positions he was trying to fill. My friend convinced me to apply, which I did half seriously, thinking it was improbable that I would be selected. Much to my surprise, I was selected and then had to decide whether to give up the comfort and security of my full professorship and tenure and accept an administrative position with no job security.

Partly because Agnes and I had always wanted to return to California, I accepted the offer to become dean of graduate studies and research at California State University, Los Angeles. During my 4 years at Cal State LA, under the strong leadership of a dynamic African American president, James Rosser, I learned a great deal about how to promote diversity in a university. Among many other activities, I served on the steering committee for the Minority Biomedical Research Support Program funded by the National Institutes of Health. This program was highly successful in sending minority students on to PhD programs in the biomedical sciences, as well as medical, dental, and pharmacy programs.

With the president's support, I was also able to initiate the Asian American theater program in the Department of Theater. The late Nobu McCarthy, a well-known actress, was hired as the first instructor. She turned out to be a natural and enthralling teacher who lured many AAPI students—mostly math, science, and business majors—into performing in plays written by Asian American playwrights. It was probably the first time that any AAPI students on that campus had ever participated in a theater program.

Up to this point, my academic career had developed through a series of accidents. It was not guided by a purposeful goal. I had never considered pursuing a career in administration and certainly never thought I could be a university president. However, my experience at Cal State LA changed my outlook. With constant encouragement from my wife and the support and role-modeling provided by Dr. Rosser, I began to believe I could pursue a career in administration and, for the first time, decided to seriously seek a higher level administrative position.

After applying and interviewing for a number of academic vice presidencies, I was offered and accepted the position of vice president for academic affairs at California State University, Northridge (CSUN), a large urban university of about 30,000 students in the San Fernando Valley. Although I had always been a strong advocate for diversity, my experience at Cal State LA had better prepared me and put me in a position with more influence and authority to promote diversity programs.

CSUN had one of the largest counseling centers in the CSU system, employing around 30 professional counselors. However, although about 15% of the students at CSUN were AAPIs (the largest minority student group on campus), there was not a single AAPI counselor on the center's staff. When I asked why the center had not hired any AAPI counselors, I was told they were difficult to find. Besides, I was told, almost no AAPI students ever came to the center, leading some counselors to conclude that AAPI students were so well adjusted that they had no need for counseling!

I didn't believe that rationale and kept putting pressure on the center. After about 2 years of prodding, the center hired its first AAPI counselor.

Within 6 months, this counselor was overloaded with AAPI students who flocked to see her. By the end of the year, she was so backlogged that she had to stay into the evening hours to counsel all the students who wanted to see her.

At that point, she went to the center director and told him, "I can't continue with this workload. You either have to hire another Asian counselor, or you're going to have to let me cross-train some of the other counselors." He couldn't hire another counselor right away, because a search that could take several months had to be conducted first, so they decided on the latter course of action. The AAPI counselor proceeded to cross-train a number of the other counselors, helping them understand the kinds of problems faced by AAPI students and how to counsel them. She then distributed her backlog of students to these other counselors. Interestingly enough, the other counselors were able to work with these students almost as effectively as the AAPI counselor. The point is that even a small increase in the diversity of the counseling staff made a huge difference in improving and extending the services provided by the center and, at the same time, increasing the competence of the counseling staff.

This example could apply to any other racial or ethnic group, and what was true for that counseling center is probably true for many other units in a university. Diversity does matter and can have a significant effect on improving services to students and enhancing their education.

In my position as vice president for academic affairs, I was able to take the initiative in numerous areas; for example, persuading the Department of Foreign Languages to hire its first tenure-track faculty member to teach and expand classes in Asian languages, and instituting an Asian American Studies Department. I could never have successfully undertaken these initiatives if I had not been the vice president, which is why I believe that it is important to increase the number of AAPIs in higher level administrative positions.

After serving in the vice presidency for 6 years, I was selected as the fourth president of the California State Polytechnic University, Pomona (Cal Poly Pomona), a campus of around 20,000 students. By the time I became president, Proposition 209—California's initiative to ban affirmative action—had passed, so programs to promote diversity became much more difficult to implement. I remember talking to a group of faculty about the need to diversify our faculty. Even though students of color comprised about 70% of the total student body, faculty of color comprised less than 20% of the total faculty, and women comprised less than 30% of the faculty. During the discussion, an angry White faculty member said, "I've always been very supportive of minority students on this campus. Are you now telling me there's no place for me in this push to diversify the faculty?" My response to him was "Quite the contrary." And I went on to tell him the story about my experience with the counseling center at CSUN. As a result of diversifying the counseling staff there, I told him, the entire staff was able to broaden their skill sets and provide more effective counseling to a wider range of students. "In the same way," I told him, "you'll be able to become a more effective teacher to a wider range of students." I don't know whether I convinced that faculty member or not, but efforts to diversify the faculty proved to be much tougher than at my previous institution. I believe this was partly because Cal Poly Pomona, owing to its history as a polytechnic university, was a more conservative campus, and partly due to the passage of Proposition 209.

When I assumed the presidency, I was already known as a strong advocate for diversity, so expectations ran high among people of color on campus that I would institute significant changes. There is a curious and commonly observed phenomenon that high expectations often trigger more complaints and protests than low expectations. It is easy to understand, because people are more likely to complain or protest when they believe they will be heard and something will be done. That was certainly my experience.

Early in my tenure, a group of Latino students staged a protest, taking over my office suite and demanding that I establish a special campus center to serve Latino students. I was sympathetic to their concerns, but I was not about to establish a special center exclusively for Latino students. Instead, I decided to establish a multicultural center by converting an old building into several offices for a variety of ethnic and cultural groups. We had offices for Latino, African American, AAPI, and Native American students, as well as offices for the Re-entry and Women's Resource Center and for the Pride Center, which served gay and lesbian students.

In establishing these offices, I emphasized two expectations: First, every office had to be open to all groups, regardless of ethnic background; second, the offices were encouraged to work with each other by sharing resources and supporting each other's activities. At first, some White students felt excluded and were quite resentful of the multicultural center. However, as time went on, most of these students came to accept the center because they saw that it was, indeed, open to all.

What was most heartening to me was to see the various offices working together and supporting each other's activities. For example, every year the African American Center would sponsor a parade on campus to celebrate the birthday of Dr. Martin Luther King, Jr., and students from all ethnic backgrounds would participate. It was truly multiculturalism at its best.

Finally, I want to mention the Leadership Development Program in Higher Education (LDPHE), which was established in 1995 and designed to prepare and motivate more AAPIs to aspire to leadership positions in higher education. At the time, I was the only AAPI president among the 23 campuses of the CSU system and one of perhaps a dozen nation-wide. AAPIs were clearly the most severely underrepresented minority in higher education CEO positions. Because I had personally seen the positive impact that AAPIs in leadership positions could have, I believed it was urgent that efforts be made to begin remedying the situation. I was, therefore, quite grateful to J. D. Hokoyama, the president of Leadership Education for Asian Pacifics (LEAP), when he agreed to have LEAP develop a program for this purpose. He called on Audrey Yamagata-Noji and Henry Gee, both community college vice presidents for student affairs, to lead this effort. They have done a superb job in conducting the program, and they chronicle the development of the LDPHE in considerable detail in the chapter they have written for this book. They are prime examples of AAPIs who are not only accomplished student affairs leaders but also social activists, working to provide greater opportunities and equity for AAPIs in higher education.

I have tried to describe experiences that have some relevance to the issues, problems, and concerns likely to arise in student affairs. I could relate many other experiences, and they are by no means all success stories; I have experienced many failures. Promoting diversity is always a high-risk endeavor, but people should not be discouraged from taking actions that fail as long as they are willing to learn from their mistakes.

I have been a strong supporter and proponent of diversity because I believe the diversity of American society is one of our country's most valuable cultural assets. I believe that diversity, nurtured in an environment that supports individual freedom and expression, is the basic source of American creativity and ingenuity, which have enabled the United States to lead the world in innovation and inventiveness. Tapping diversity is a way of improving what we do.

The stories I have told are quite personal, but I hope my experiences will provide context and additional validity to the views expressed by the authors of this book. Although the book is intended to give visibility and voice to the issues, problems, and concerns facing AAPI student affairs professionals, it also offers valuable insights and lessons for *all* student affairs professionals and higher education leaders in general.

Although we are still far from realizing the democratic ideals of our society, promoting social justice in the ways suggested by the authors can help us attain this goal, as long as they and other allied student affairs professionals continue to take the risks and actions necessary to bring about needed changes in our educational institutions. I hope this book will be a catalyst for making that happen.

Introduction

Amefil Agbayani and Doris Ching

As the first Asian American and first woman of color to be elected to the position of president of NASPA–Student Affairs Administrators in Higher Education, and after having spent decades working in academia to prevent racial inequity and discord on university campuses, co-editor Doris Ching was nevertheless shocked by the following personal incident in 1997:

> The tall, slender, young Asian American turned to me. I was taken aback at his look of grave concern. The lobby of the large hotel in Chicago was abuzz with the excitement of hundreds of student affairs professionals, cheerfully greeting and embracing colleagues they had not seen since the last conference. It was my first day as the president-elect of NASPA. Amidst the hubbub of friendship renewals, conference registration, and anticipation of the 3-day conference, I clearly heard the voice of the young professional.

"You have to help us," he pleaded. "We feel so isolated and discriminated against on our campuses."

If Asian American and Pacific Islander (AAPI) student affairs professionals are experiencing isolation and racial discrimination at their institutions, what does that mean for AAPI students? Are campuses and communities aware of the increase in the AAPI student population? Colleges and universities rely on student affairs professionals to help *all* students achieve their educational goals, career aspirations, and personal transformation as they become contributing members of the community. It seems incongruous that professionals whose job is to enhance student success would themselves be encountering a lack of encouragement and recognition in the work environment. Although this is not a pervasive circumstance on campuses across the nation, it is disconcerting that any student affairs professional does not feel supported by his or her institution.

Unintentional benign negligence and erroneous "model minority" myths may be partially responsible for a campus environment that is unwelcoming to AAPI professionals and students. An AAPI student at Arizona State University said, "Arizona doesn't even see us. And when they do see us, I think it's a stereotype of, 'All Asians are intelligent and succeed,' and therefore they don't need any type of encouragement or counseling or tutoring and the like" (Nakagawa, 2008, p. 39). Isolation, discrimination, and lack of understanding of AAPI student affairs professionals and students, and those of other ethnic groups at colleges and universities, are unacceptable and must be corrected. The AAPI community must provide information to ensure accurate perceptions of AAPIs in higher education and diminish misconceptions among college and university officials and the public.

A 2007 report from the Higher Education Research Institute states that more Asian American students are experiencing difficulties attaining academic success in colleges and universities than in the past. Asian American freshmen are socially better prepared for college and more engaged in civic and community concerns than in previous years but are less likely to be skilled in applying to college and more likely to face hardships in finances and use of the English language. With the antici-pated rapid growth of the AAPI population by 2050, higher education institutions across the country are projected to see an exponential increase in the number of AAPI students. It is imperative that higher education decisions on policies, funding, and program development are informed by updated information and insights. Colleges and universities that are more aware and understanding of this rapidly growing student population will be better prepared and more successful in addressing these students' diverse and complex needs.

Researchers, accrediting agencies, and higher education institutions are realizing the effectiveness of holistic learning, transformative education, experiential learning, collaboration of academic affairs and student affairs, and outcomes-based assessment. The involvement of student affairs pro-fessionals in students' academic achievements is more pronounced than it has been in the past. Arthur Sandeen wrote:

> Professors, department chairs, and deans no longer are the sole sources of the learning experiences that undergraduate students benefit from on our campuses. Recent years have seen the growth or expansion of a wide variety of out-of-the-classroom supplements to classroom education.... Central to many of the new learning venues that have blossomed over the past decade or two are student affairs professionals. (Sandeen, 2004, p. 28)

In higher education institutions, the amount of money spent on students is not as important as how it is spent. For example, research has shown that effective institutions allocate a higher proportion of funds to academic and student support (Ewell, 2003). In addition, the research suggests a positive correlation between spending on student support services and higher levels of degree attainment (Kelly & Jones, 2005).

Very little has been published on AAPIs in higher education student affairs. A few publications include AAPIs in limited ways. For example, *Working with Asian American College Students* (McEwen, Kodama, Alvarez, Lee, & Liang, 2002) focuses primarily on Asian American students' college experiences with references to the work of student affairs professionals in higher education. This book includes the chapter *Revisiting the Model Minority Stereotype: Implications for Student Affairs Practice and Higher Education* (Suzuki, 2002), which retrospectively analyzes the model minority stereotype of Asian Americans 25 years after the author wrote the seminal article that debunked this stereotype. A chapter on Asian American students in *Understanding College Student Subpopulations* (Bonner, Jennings, Chen, & Singh, 2006) presents a demographic and historical background of Asian American college students, the model minority and other myths, and related topics. In a section titled "The Asian American Client" in *Counseling American Minorities* (Atkinson, Morten, & Sue, 2004, pp. 217–239), the authors provide a brief practical history and overview of the physical and mental health of Asian Americans. Another resource is *Asian American Dreams: The Emergence of an American People* (Zia, 2000). Although these publications highlight issues of importance to AAPIs in higher education, none focuses on the primary AAPI student affairs issues.

Two recent monographs in the *New Directions for Institutional Research* series deliberate more deeply on AAPI college student experiences and concerns. *Conducting Research on Asian Americans in Higher Education* (Museus, 2009) strongly reinforces previous challenges to the false and distorted perception that Asian American student success in higher education justifies the lack of data and attention by researchers on this population. In *Using Mixed-Methods Approaches to Study Intersectionality in Higher Education* (Griffin & Museus, 2011), three of the eight chapters include discussions of issues related to AAPI students in higher education.

The title of this book uses the Asian Americans and Pacific Islanders (AAPI) designation. The federal government, researchers, media, community advocates, individuals, and authors of chapters in this book use various terminologies, including Asians and Pacific Islanders (APIs), Asian and Pacific Islander Americans (APIAs), Asian Americans (AAs), and others. A few authors refer to Asian and Pacific Islanders and Desi Americans (APIDAs)—*desi* refers to a diasporic South Asian group.

There is no consistency in the terminology used, and some of the terms are interchangeable. The data are also defined, collected, and presented in a variety of ways.

In 2009, U.S. President Barack Obama reestablished the President's Advisory Commission and White House Initiative on Asian Americans and Pacific Islanders, 10 years after it was established by President Bill Clinton. In 2007, the U.S. Department of Education provided funding for new minority categories, including Asian American, Native American, and Pacific Islander-Serving Institutions (AANAPISIs), which are institutions of higher education with student enrollments of at least 10% AAPI and at least 50% students eligible to receive Pell grants (Asian Pacific Islander American Association of Colleges and Universities, 2011). In 2011, AANAPISI was included in the official list of categories of minority-serving institutions eligible for at least 42 federal programs representing $500 million in funding.

In 1997, the U.S. Office of Management and Budget (OMB) required federal agencies to use the categories "Asian" and "Native Hawaiian or Other Pacific Islander." A sixth category ("some other race") was approved for the 2000 and 2010 census. The census allows individuals to check more than one category. In 2010, 97% reported only one race: White, 223.6 million (72%); Black or African American, 38.9 million (13%); American Indian or Alaskan Native, 2.9 million (0.9%); Asian, 14.7 million (5%); Native Hawaiian and Other Pacific Islander, 0.5 million (0.2%); and some other race, 19.1 million (6%). Hispanic or Latino persons, 50.5 million (16%), are included as a separate concept from race (U.S. Census Bureau, 2011a, 2011b). Although some scholars, individuals, and community groups make a strong distinction between the terms *race* and *ethnicity*, the co-editors of this book do not.

The U.S. Census counts AAPIs in two major race categories: (1) Asian and (2) Native Hawaiian and Other Pacific Islanders. At least 24 separate groups have been identified for each category, for a combined total of 48 ethnic groups. The Asian American ethnic categories include Bangladeshi, Bhutanese, Burmese, Cambodian, Chinese, Filipino, Hmong, Indian, Indo

Chinese, Iwo Jiman, Japanese, Korean, Laotian, Malaysian, Maldivian, Nepalese, Okinawan, Pakistani, Singaporean, Sri Lankan, Taiwanese, Thai, Vietnamese, and other Asian. The Pacific Islander ethnic categories include Carolinian, Chamorro, Chuukese, Fijian, Guamanian, I-Kiribati, Kosraean, Mariana Islander, Marshallese, Native Hawaiian, Ni-Vanuatu, Palauan, Papua New Guinean, Pohnpeian, Saipanese, Samoan, Solomon Islander, Tahitian, Tokelauan, Tongan, Yapese, Polynesian, Micronesian, and Melanesian.

In the 10 years between the 2000 and 2010 censuses, the nation's Asian population grew faster than that of any other major race group, increasing by 43% (U.S. Census Bureau, 2011a). The Asian population increased from 4% to about 5% of the total U.S. population (10.2 million to 14.7 million), the largest increase of any group. According to the Census Bureau, an estimated 17.3 million persons (5.6% of the population) includes Asians who reported a specific Asian group (14.7 million) and those who reported a particular Asian group in combination with one or more other Asian groups or races (2.6 million). The largest groups are Chinese Americans (3.8 million), Filipinos (3.2 million), Asian Indians (2.8 million), Vietnamese (1.7 million), Korean (1.6 million), and Japanese (1.3 million). By the year 2050, Asians or Asians in combination with one or more other races are projected to be 9% of the U.S. population (40.6 million). Asian Americans' projected percentage increase is 161%, compared with a 44% increase in the population as a whole (U.S. Census Bureau, 2011b).

The Census Bureau further identified 1.2 million persons (0.4% of the total population) as Native Hawaiian and Other Pacific Islanders, either alone or in combination with one or more other races (U.S. Census Bureau, 2011b). More than half (56%) reported multiple races. California had the largest Asian population (5.6 million), followed by New York (1.6 million). In Hawai`i, Asians made up the highest proportion of the total population (57%); Hawai`i also had the largest population of Native Hawaiians and Other Pacific Islanders (356,000, or 26% of the state population).

Although there are good reasons to use a pan-ethnic category (e.g., AAPI), it is inaccurate to consider this category as homogeneous. There is great diversity within the AAPI category. In this book, some authors refer to a pan-Asian identity or group, while others disaggregate the term or focus on one of the groups. The use of categories broader than one ethnic group or country of origin began in the 1960s. Espiritu (2008) wrote: "Pan-ethnic identities are self-conscious products of political choice and actions, not of inherited phenotypes, bloodlines, or cultural traditions." She identifies "the twin roots of Asian American pan-ethnicity" as "the racialization of Asian national groups by dominant groups and Asian Americans' responses to those constructions" (p. 119). Some ethnic-specific Asian groups, such as Japanese and Chinese, saw similarities in their history and minority status in the United States and established pan-ethnic organizations. As a result, Asian American became a common term in the mid-1970s and began to be used by student and community groups, media, and some government agencies (Espiritu, 2008).

Asian Americans understood that there was strength in numbers and that a pan-Asian category was not only relevant but also potentially more politically powerful than multiple Asian categories. Because government often treated Asian Americans as a single administrative unit in distributing economic and political resources, a group response was useful. Pan-ethnic and ethnic-specific organizations were successful in demanding separate individual group categories as well as a total API pan-ethnic count for the 1980 and 1990 censuses. As Espiritu wrote, many ethnic-specific and pan-ethnic groups were protesting against "the *absence* of subgroup categories, not against the *presence* of the pan-Asian category" (p. 123). Pan-Asian identity and activism were clearly demonstrated in 1982, when Chinese-American Vincent Chin was beaten to death by two White men who allegedly mistook him for Japanese. The tragedy united Asian Americans from all walks of life, ethnic origins, and political lines. Today, it is speculated that we might see a resurgence of anti-Asian violence as China and India grow in economic and political importance (Espiritu, 2008).

The AAPI category raises two competing challenges for the AAPI community, researchers, media, and policymakers. Some see the need for a visible and effective single group in a multiethnic and multiracial community and nation, while others identify with only one ethnic group or country of origin. Some individuals and groups resent being part of a larger group that includes historical enemies or groups that are considered privileged. Others see the need to disaggregate information for more accuracy and to understand and respond to the many differences of the subgroups. In Hawai`i, where AAPIs comprise two thirds of the state population, the term AAPI is rarely used. Native Hawaiians (the indigenous population) are comfortable identifying their mixed heritage and generally do not use pan-ethnic terms.

These two competing challenges can be and have been addressed in a creative and productive way. Many advocates and researchers who use AAPI terminology and aggregate data also disaggregate data for analysis, policy recommendations, and advocacy. A large national survey in 2000 found that "Although most prefer an ethnic-specific rather than a pan-ethnic identity, the majority of the respondents are also amenable to the pan-ethnic Asian American label under certain contexts" (Espiritu, 2008, p. 126). Many people are comfortable with a specific ethnic identity, such as Korean American, and also accept being referred to as AAPI. The heterogeneity of groups compels disaggregating the AAPI data while simultaneously retaining a pan-Asian category (e.g., AAPI).

The National Commission on Asian American and Pacific Islander Research in Education (CARE) has presented data that challenge the model minority myth, which assumes that AAPI students attend highly selective 4-year institutions and are academically successful in science, technology, engineering, and mathematics (CARE, 2008, 2010). CARE principal investigator Robert Teranishi (who co-authors the opening chapter of this book with Howard Wang) emphasizes the incredible heterogeneity of AAPIs as a group. In contrast to the model minority myth, the data show that nearly half of AAPI students attend community colleges rather than Ivy League schools. In addition, when AAPI student data are disaggregated, some of these students have among the lowest rates of high school graduation and college degree attainment in the United States.

In reality, there is no such thing as one Asian American and Pacific Islander composite, especially when there are more differences than similarities between the many groups designated by the federally defined categories of "Asian American" and/ or "Pacific Islander." Although there are varied and historical reasons for reporting these groups under one umbrella, it is critical for educators and policymakers to recognize that there are numerous Asian American and Pacific Islander ethnicities, many historical backgrounds, and a full range of socioeconomic spectra, from the poor and underprivileged to the affluent and highly educated. There is no simple description that can characterize Asian American and Pacific Islander students or communities as a whole. (CARE, 2008, p.15)

The following statement in a recent article of the Association of American Colleges and Universities' (AAC&U's) *Diversity & Democracy* excludes AAPI students. Unfortunately, this exclusion is by no means unique; many other analysis and policy recommendations also exclude AAPI students—as though they are invisible—in discussions on equity and access in higher education.

Educational opportunity yields a broad array of benefits to both individuals and society. Reports . . . have consistently shown that going to college has far-reaching and quantifiable personal and national benefits . . . higher education advocates . . . articulate the need for individuals and society to invest in higher education. Yet, despite these efforts, access and success within higher education remains unequal. Many students— particularly those who are black, Latino/a, first generation, and low income—face numerous challenges throughout their educational journeys that obstruct their paths to and through college. In order to meet current national goals for increased access and completion, higher education leaders must clear these pathways so all students can succeed. (Cooper, 2010, p. 1)

For multiple reasons—including a national effort to meet President Obama's goal that the United States will have the highest proportion of college graduates in the world by 2020—it is imperative to increase the public's understanding and the understanding of college and university faculty, staff, and administration of the challenges and strengths of diverse AAPI students in higher education. As a group, AAPI students are growing in size and heterogeneity, and they are not adequately researched.

The importance of postsecondary education, for individual well-being and for the public good, is generally acknowledged. However, it is an unfortunate fact that college access and success are unequal. To educate all students, the higher education community must engage in self-study and must be inclusive. We need to understand the issues facing higher education, including those that affect AAPI students and professionals, who must be included in the national discourse. AAPIs in higher education, including all the various groups in this category, can and must contribute to local and national efforts to improve educational quality and equity.

Frank Chong, president of Santa Rosa Junior College and former deputy assistant secretary for community colleges in the U.S. Department of Education Office of Vocational and Adult Education, unequivocally stated,

> Higher education policy needs to be better informed about the experiences of all American students if we are going to meet President Obama's goal of having the highest proportion of college graduates in the world by 2020. . . . Our higher education needs resources to better equip all Americans, including AAPI students, with the right skills to pursue high-paying and fulfilling careers . . . the largest segment of AAPI undergraduate enroll-ment (47.3 percent) is at community colleges. (Chong, 2011)

This book provides information, analysis, and a voice for AAPI students and AAPI student affairs professionals. The authors present narratives to counter the lack of information and misinformation about themselves. As a group, AAPIs are a minority in numbers and status in the nation and in higher education institutions. Similarly, student affairs professionals are the minority in numbers and have a subordinate status compared with academic instructional and research faculty. Although women are the majority among student affairs professionals, women generally hold a minority status on and off campus. With the exception of Robert Teranishi, who is an academic faculty member, the authors are double minorities as AAPIs and student affairs professionals, and some are triple minorities as AAPIs, student affairs professionals, and women.

This book presents research and stories that give voice and visibility to AAPI students and AAPI student affairs professionals in the context of racial history, power, and hierarchy in society and campuses consistent with Critical Race Theory and race formation scholarship. Not all of the authors use these theories explicitly or implicitly, but nonetheless the book is a counternarrative to correct misinformation, provide different information, and empower subordinate groups. Student affairs professionals play an important role in the educational success of students. While they are a small and underrepresented group, their services, responsibilities, and contributions reach every corner of college and university campuses. AAPI student affairs professionals are eager to be understood, supported, and recognized for their service and leadership contributions. This book is an invaluable guide to inform decisions by faculty, administrators, and educational policymakers who seek to strengthen the position of AAPI student affairs professionals as well as the learning outcomes for students of all ethnicities. The book is a compilation of statistical reports, research findings, and experiential accounts by academic and student affairs professionals, many of whom work directly with students. The authors are from various parts of the United States—eastern, southeastern, midwestern, northwestern, western, and Hawaiian Islands—and represent a wide range of institutional experiences. They serve or have served at public and private community colleges, comprehensive 4-year colleges and universities, and Research I institutions.

The talents, distinction, and competence of the contributing authors are a major strength of the book. They are men and women of East Asian American, Filipino American, Native Hawaiian, South Asian American, and biracial backgrounds. Some are foreign-born, while others are from second- to fourth-generation American families. They are former and current college and university presidents, vice presidents, researchers, faculty, psychologists, counselors, practitioners, and administrators whose successful contacts with college students and decades of dedicated high-quality education, service, and programs to help students attain their academic and personal goals are enlightening and inspiring. They are innovators and visionary leaders in institutional administration and various areas of cocurricular activities, student leadership development programs, multicultural resource centers, lesbian/gay/bisexual/transgender resource centers, and other programs at community colleges and private and public universities. Most important, they promote the development of the whole person and address the need for success of AAPIs and students of all other ethnic groups on their campuses and in the community.

The six parts of the book present a range of statistical information, research studies, personal experiences, observations, and reflections. Part I provides statistical data, general background, and an analysis of reports and perspectives of the representation and inclusion of AAPI students, faculty, staff, and student affairs professionals in primary, secondary, and higher education. Part II describes personal experiences and theoretical models of AAPI racial identity formation. Part III covers organizational structures that promote and develop leadership among AAPIs. Part IV focuses primarily on issues related to AAPI college students in Greek letter organizations, Native Hawaiian student success, and AAPI student mental health. Part V focuses on the personal experiences of AAPI student affairs professionals related to their perceived role expectations. Part VI expresses the hopes, dreams, and goals of new AAPI professionals and lessons learned from senior administrators.

The authors' insights are invaluable to understanding the diverse issues and characteristics that affect AAPI student affairs professionals and AAPI students' learning and educational success. The authors' research, personal encounters, reflections, and analyses have implications for the student affairs profession and can inform decisions and policy development in higher education.

References

Asian Pacific Islander American Association of Colleges and Universities. (2011, July). *Asiance: Connecting Asian American women to the world.* Retrieved from http://www.asiancemagazine.com/node/16357

Atkinson, D. R., Morten, G., & Sue, D. W. (2004). *Counseling American minorities.* New York, NY: McGraw-Hill.

Bonner, F. A., Jennings, M. E., Chen, Y. H., & Singh, S. M. (2006). Asian American students. In L. A. Gohn & G. R. Albin (Eds.), *Understanding college student subpopulations: A guide for student affairs professionals* (pp. 387–410). Washington, DC: National Association of Student Personnel Administrators.

Chong, F. (2011, May 24). Increasing access to higher education for AAPI students [Web log post]. Retrieved from http://www.whitehouse.gov/blog/2011/05/24/increasing-access-higher-education-aapi-students

Cooper, M. A. (2010). Investing in education and equity: Our nation's best future. *Diversity and Democracy, 13*(3), 1–4.

Espiritu, Y. L. (2008). Asian American panethnicity: Challenges and possibilities. In P. M. Ong (Ed.), *The state of Asian America: Trajectory of civic and political engagement* (pp. 119–136). Los Angeles, CA: LEAP Asian Pacific Public Policy Institute.

Ewell, P. (2003). *Do DEEP institutions spend more or differently than their peers?* Boulder, CO: National Center for Higher Education Management Systems.

Griffin, K. A., & Museus, S. D. (Eds.). (2011). *Using mixed-methods approaches to study intersectionality in higher education* (New directions for institutional research, no. 151). San Francisco, CA: Jossey-Bass.

Higher Education Research Institute. (2007, October). *Beyond myths: The growth and diversity of Asian American college freshmen: 1971–2005* (HERI Research Brief). Los Angeles, CA: Author.

Kelly, P. J., & Jones, D. (2005). *A new look at the institutional component of higher education finance: A guide for evaluating performance relative to financial resources.* Boulder, CO: National Center for Higher Education Management Systems. Retrieved from http://www.nchems.org/pubs/docs/Policy Guide Jan2007.pdf

Museus, S. D. (Ed.). (2009). *Conducting research on Asian Americans in higher education* (New directions for institutional research, no. 142). San Francisco, CA: Jossey-Bass.

McEwen, M., Kodama, C. M., Alvarez, A. N., Lee, S., & Liang, C. T. H. (Eds.). (2002). *Working with Asian American college students* (New directions for student services, no. 97). San Francisco, CA: Jossey-Bass.

Nakagawa, K. (2008). Moving beyond the model minority myth. *The State of Asian Americans and Pacific Islanders in Arizona.* Retrieved from Arizona State University, Asian Pacific American Studies Program website: http://apas.clas.asu.edu/research/apazi.shtml

National Commission on Asian American and Pacific Islander Research in Education (CARE). (2008). *Asian Americans and Pacific Islanders, facts, not fiction: Setting the record straight.* Retrieved from http://professionals.collegeboard.com/profdownload/08-0608-AAPI.pdf

National Commission on Asian American and Pacific Islander Research in Education (CARE). (2010). *Federal higher education policy priorities and the Asian American and Pacific Islander community.* Retrieved from http://apiasf.org/CAREreport/2010_CARE_report.pdf

Sandeen, A. (2004). Educating the whole student: The growing academic importance of student affairs. *Change, 36*(3), 28.

Suzuki, B. H. (2002). Revisiting the model minority stereotype: Implications for student affairs practice and higher education. In M. McEwen, C. M. Kodama, A. N. Alvarez, S. Lee, & C. T. H. Liang (Eds.), *Working with Asian American college students* (New directions for student services, no. 97, pp. 21–32). San Francisco, CA: Jossey-Bass.

U.S. Census Bureau. (2011a). *Overview of race and Hispanic origin: 2010* (2010 Census Briefs). Retrieved from http://www.census.gov/prod/cen2010/briefs/c2010br-02.pdf

U.S. Census Bureau. (2011b). *Facts for features: Asian/Pacific American Heritage Month*. Retrieved from http://www.prnewswire.com/news-releases/us-census-bureau-facts-for-features-asianpacific-american-heritage-month-may-2011-120597214.html

Zia, H. (2000). *Asian American dreams: The emergence of an American people*. New York, NY: Farrar, Straus, and Giroux.

PART I

AAPI Background and Statistics

CHAPTER ONE

AAPI Background and Statistics

Perspectives on the Representation and Inclusion of AAPI Faculty, Staff, and Student Affairs Professionals

Howard Wang and Robert T. Teranishi

In the 19th century, Asian Americans and Pacific Islanders (AAPIs) faced social, educational, and immigration discrimination in the United States. As a group, AAPIs were treated as undesirable and portrayed as the "Yellow Peril" (Feagin, 2008). Chinese children attended segregated schools, as chronicled by Victor Low's 1982 book *The Unimpressionable Race*. The 1882 Chinese Exclusion Act, the 1924 Immigration Act, and the 1942 internment of Japanese American citizens reflect a history of discrimination against AAPIs. Currently, there seems to be a resurgence of the "perfidious foreigner" fear, generally triggered during wars and economic downturns, even as the model minority stereotype of the 1960s continues into the

21st century (Suzuki, 2002). An introduction to the 2008 CARE report (National Commission on Asian American and Pacific Islander Research in Education [CARE]) provides a succinct summary of the implications of the model minority stereotype on educational practices; for example, placing students in the wrong grade or inappropriately placing them in bilingual classes; treating all AAPI students as a homogeneous group without regard to the high poverty levels and academic barriers some of them have faced; and lack of disaggregated data used in research to inform policies or create programs and services for Asian American students. Projected AAPI population growth by 2020 will have policy implications for K–12 as well as higher education. Because AAPI students are the fastest growing subgroup in the country, attention must be given to curriculum reform to ensure cultural sensitivity not only in the historical context but also as a contemporary reality. Research is needed to address issues such as school climate, teacher recruitment, training and professional development, language needs, AAPI student support services, and AAPI parental involvement (Teranishi, 2010). The increase in enrollment of AAPI students in U.S. higher education may generate debates over emerging issues such as the perception of their "overrepresentation" in the top national universities and colleges, changes in admission criteria, affirmative action, and retrenchment of institutional resources leading to the displacement of financially needy AAPI students from selective 4-year institutions to less expensive ones and 2-year colleges (Leadership Education for Asian Pacifics [LEAP] Asian Pacific American Public Policy Institute and UCLA Asian American Studies Center, 1993, pp. 25–59).

Popular beliefs include an exaggerated perception that AAPI students are "taking over" U.S. colleges and universities. In fact, between 1987 and 2004, the increase in AAPI students in higher education paralleled increases of students in other ethnic groups. The CARE report showed that in 2000, two thirds of AAPI students were enrolled in only 200 institutions in just eight states.[1] The perception that AAPI students are most likely to attend

---

[1] There are 4,182 Title IV degree-granting higher education institutions (National Center for Education Statistics [NCES], 2010a).

private 4-year institutions is also incorrect. In 2000, only 12.4% of AAPIs were enrolled in private 4-year institutions, while 87.6% were enrolled in public 2-year and 4-year institutions. For all 4-year institutions, 78% of AAPIs were enrolled in public institutions and 22% in private institutions. Not only are AAPI students not taking over U.S. higher education, especially the elite institutions, their enrollment in public 2-year institutions increased 73.3% between 1990 and 2000 (CARE, 2008, pp. 4–6, 9, 13). The CARE report also showed that, contrary to popular beliefs, Asian students are not necessarily likely to major in math or science. AAPI students had a variety of academic interests. Among degrees awarded to AAPIs, 28.8% were in business/management, 26.1% were in social sciences/humanities, 14.2% were in education/library science, 21.8% were in engineering/math/computer science, 7.3% were in health sciences, and 6.2% were in biological/life/physical science.

The AAPI population is ethnically diverse, composed of at least 48 ethnic categories[2] plus multiethnic and multiracial combinations, along with more than 200 spoken languages and dialects. Immigration histories and various socioeconomic and cultural backgrounds are contributing factors that challenge how educators should view issues such as college admissions and affirmative action for AAPIs. These same factors support the need to ensure that AAPI faculty, staff, and administrators be placed in key decision-making positions to serve as mentors and role models who understand the unique and diverse needs of AAPI ethnic groups and are willing to act as advocates for the underserved AAPI students (CARE, 2008, pp. 7, 16–29).

A literature review of comparative studies cited in a national demographic study of student affairs administrators at Historically Black Colleges and Universities (HBCUs) (Harper, 2005) strongly suggested

---

[2] Asian American ethnic categories include Bangladeshi, Bhutanese, Burmese, Cambodian, Chinese, Filipino, Hmong, Indian, Indo Chinese, Iwo Jiman, Japanese, Korean, Laotian, Malaysian, Maldivian, Nepalese, Okinawan, Pakistani, Singaporean, Sri Lankan, Taiwanese, Thai, Vietnamese, and other Asian. Pacific Islander ethnic categories include Carolinian, Chamorro, Chuukese, Fijian, Guamanian, I-Kiribati, Kosraean, Mariana Islander, Marshallese, Native Hawaiian, Ni-Vanuatu, Palauan, Papua New Guinean, Pohnpeian, Saipanese, Samoan, Solomon Islander, Tahitian, Tokelauan, Tongan, Yapese, Polynesian, Micronesian, and Melanesian.

that HBCUs had "more positive, profound, and enduring effects on African American student outcomes and satisfaction than do PWIs [predominantly White institutions]" (p. 9). A review of other studies pointed to the contention that "the underrepresentation of African Americans and other racial/ethnic minority students in graduate preparation programs poses negative implications for the multiethnic composition of the profession and the administrative pipeline" (p. 11). We might posit that AAPI student outcomes and satisfaction also depend on successful role modeling by AAPI teachers, faculty, and administrators. Asian American and Native American Pacific Islander-Serving Institutions (AANAPISIs), much like HBCUs, could play a key role in improving AAPI student retention, graduation, and satisfaction. In his 2010 book *Asians in the Ivory Tower: Dilemmas of Racial Inequality in American Higher Education*, Robert Teranishi challenged the notion that "educational attainment tells a full story about AAPI access to and participation in U.S. higher education." Teranishi noted that the stereotype of AAPI success "is often driven by false assumptions of AAPI overrepresentation in higher education as a whole." In addition to simply noting AAPI participation in higher education and degree attainment, research is needed on the representation and recruitment of AAPI teachers and leaders in the K–12 sector as well as AAPI faculty, staff, and administrators in higher education.

In this chapter, we discuss the proposition that inadequate presence of AAPI teachers, staff, and administrators may have contributed to the lack of a pipeline and, therefore, role models, in leadership positions in higher education. To address these pipeline concerns and issues, we will explore AAPI participation as students and staff in K–12 and higher education, and in key student affairs and related academic administrative positions.

AAPIs in Public Schools

Of the total fall 2008 student enrollment of 48.4 million in U.S. public schools, 55.8% of students were White, 17% Black, 21.2% Hispanic, 1.2%

American Indian/Alaska Native, and 4.8% (2.35 million) AAPI (National Center for Education Statistics [NCES], 2007–08b). Among slightly more than 3.4 million teachers in all U.S. public schools, 83.1% were White; 7% Black; 7.1% Hispanic; 0.9% non-Hispanic, two or more races; 0.5% American Indian/Alaska Native; and only 1.4% (48,320) were AAPI teachers. Diversity among students was not reflected in diversity among teachers. The disparity between the representation of AAPI students and AAPI teachers is expected to increase: Public school enrollment is projected to increase by 2014 to 50 million, whereas the number of teachers is projected to remain at about 3.4 million (NCES, n.d.a).

In academic year 2007–08, close to 6.3 million students were enrolled in California public schools, of whom 11% were Asians (including Filipinos) and 1% Pacific Islanders (Chang, 2010). Asians, Filipinos, and Pacific Islanders made up 5% to 7% of all K–12 personnel in the state of California but only 4.8% of school administrators. A majority of the administrators (67%) were White. The gaps are even more apparent within each race/ethnic group:

- 8.4% of K–12 students are Asian, but only 5.3% of teachers are Asian (3.7% administrators, 5.1% pupil services, and 5.1% certificated staff).
- 2.7% of K–12 students are Filipino, but only 1.5% of teachers are Filipino (0.9% administrators, 2.4% pupil services, and 1.5% certificated staff).
- 0.6% of K–12 students are Pacific Islanders, but only 0.3% of teachers are Pacific Islanders (0.2% administrators, 0.4% of pupil services, and 0.3% of certificated staff).

Similar results are reflected in the NCES *Schools and Staffing Survey* (2007–08a), which showed that out of almost 91,000 public school principals, 80.9% were White and only 2% were considered as "other"—this category included principals of "Non-Hispanic, American Indian/Alaska Native, Asian, Native Hawaiian or Other Pacific Islander, or two or more of the above races."

Table 1

Average Years of Teaching Experience for Regular Full-Time Public School Teachers and Percentage Who Have <3 years of Teaching Experience, by Race/Ethnicity Concentration of School, 2007–08

Race/ethnicity concentration of school	Average years of teaching experience	% teachers with <3 years of experience
Total[a]	13.5	11.5
White enrollment ≥50%	14.1	10.0
Black enrollment ≥50%	13.1	12.9
Hispanic enrollment ≥50%	12.4	15.4
Asian/Pacific Islander enrollment ≥50%	12.5	15.7!
American Indian/Alaska Native enrollment ≥50%	13.1	13.8

[a]Total includes all regular full-time public school teachers.

! Interpret data with caution.

Note: Race categories exclude persons of Hispanic ethnicity. From U.S. Department of Education, National Center for Education Statistics, Schools and Staffing Survey, Public School Teacher and Public School Data Files, 2007–08, Table 9.2.

In addition to the gap between K–12 teacher/administrative leaders and students of the same race/ethnic group, teachers in schools with 50% or more AAPI enrollment tend to have fewer years of experience (NCES, 2007–08c) as shown in Table 1. Teachers in schools with 50% or more AAPI enrollment had an average of only 12.5 years of teaching experience, while teachers in schools with 50% or more White enrollment had 14.1 years of experience. Schools with 50% or more AAPI student enrollment also had a higher percentage of teachers with fewer than 3 years of experience (15.7%) compared with schools with at least 50% White enrollment (10%). These findings correspond to Teranishi's analysis of NCES 2000 data (Teranishi, 2005, p. 133), which showed that public school AAPI teachers had an average of 12.1 years of experience, compared with 15.1 years for White teachers (see Table 2). Furthermore, a much higher percentage of AAPI teachers (21.6%) had 3 or fewer years of experience compared with White teachers (14.9%).

Table 2

Average Years of Teaching Experience Among Public School Teachers by Race, 2000

	Average years of experience	Years of teaching experience		
		≤3 years	4–5 years	≥5 years
AAPI	12.1	21.6%	13.9%	64.5%
Black	14.6	18.9%	10.3%	70.8%
White	15.1	14.9%	8.7%	76.4%
Latino	11.0	26.0%	11.8%	62.2%
All teachers	14.8	16.0%	9.1%	75.0%

From R. T. Teranishi, *Asians in the Ivory Tower: Dilemmas of Racial Inequality in American Higher Education,* Teachers College Press, Columbia University, New York and London, 2005, p. 133.

Using data from the 2008 NCES *Schools and Staffing Survey,* Teranishi showed that 45.2% of AAPI teachers left their teaching positions in 2004–05 to pursue another career, whereas smaller percentages of teachers from other ethnic groups did so (Teranishi, 2005, pp. 133–134). The NCES data showed that 26% of AAPI teachers returned to graduate school to pursue studies outside the education field, whereas much smaller percentages of teachers from the other ethnic groups did so. AAPI teachers seem to be leaving their teaching positions entirely to pursue opportunities other than education.

The lack of all kinds of diversity among teachers and administrators, and the low retention rate for AAPI teachers in public schools, are worth noting. The California data also support Teranishi's contention that "there are significant gaps in the representation of different AAPI ethnic groups among teachers, which result in gaps in language and cultural resources for subpopulations of AAPI students" (2005, p. 133). It is important for all students, regardless of their ethnic backgrounds, to be cognizant of how the United States relates to the rest of the world and to "learn to make connections between their community, national, and global identities" (Teranishi, 2005, p. 135). Without an adequate number of AAPI teachers, such connections are unattainable. School administrators, school districts, and policymakers must also be aware of the trends in student and teacher demographics as well as the inherent value of diversity in the U.S. education system. Lack of diversity among teachers and administrators, as well as the limited experience of AAPI teachers, could be the result of an inadequate effort to encourage students to major in education fields. With so few AAPI teachers, and even fewer AAPIs in key decision-making positions, it is important to conduct further research studies, using disaggregated data, on the effect of the lack of recruitment and retention of AAPI teachers, educators, and educational policymakers on the next generation. Community activism and legislative action can influence national policies to provide immediate assistance to underserved AAPI communities.

Following the release of its 2008 report, CARE worked with community advocacy groups, policy centers, and higher education scholars, and released another report in 2010. This report, *Federal Higher Education Policy Priorities and the Asian American and Pacific Islander Community*, facilitated a dialogue among communities, educators, and federal officials to address issues in three areas: (1) education and workforce development needs of AAPIs; (2) AAPIs in community colleges; and (3) how legislation aimed at Asian American and Native American Pacific Islander-Serving Institutions (AANAPISIs) could provide an opportunity and strategy to help underserved AAPI students become part of a pipeline to access higher education.

AAPIs in Higher Education

The situation with AAPI faculty and administrators in higher education is not much better. Stronger interest among AAPI freshmen in business and science majors and in careers in engineering and health-related fields (rather than in humanities and social sciences such as education) has negative implications for creating a pipeline of AAPI graduates to serve as teachers, faculty, and administrators in leadership roles.

Table 3 shows that in a survey of the top 10 probable major

fields for AAPI freshman students, only 2.2% of the men surveyed in 1971 chose education (ranked 9th), compared with 30.4% who chose engineering (ranked 1st) (Chang, 2007). For women, 7.1% chose education (ranked 4th), while 21.2% chose health professional (ranked 1st). In a 2005 survey—34 years later—engineering was still the top choice among men (22.8%), while only 1.5% chose education (ranked 10th). The top choice among AAPI women was still health professional (19.9%), while only 4% chose education (ranked 8th).

Table 3
Preference for Majors Among AAPI Freshmen, 1971 and 2005

Men	1971 (%)	Men	2005 (%)
1. Engineering	30.4%	1. Engineering	22.8%
2. Health professional	14.3%	2. Business	20.1%
3. Business	8.3%	3. Biological science	13.4%
4. Social sciences	7.5%	4. Health professional	11.6%
5. Biological science	6.7%	5. Fine arts	4.1%
9. Education	2.2%	10. Education	1.5%
Women	**1971 (%)**	**Women**	**2005 (%)**
1. Health professional	21.2%	1. Health professional	19.9%
2. Social sciences	15.2%	2. Business	17.6%
3. Fine arts	9.3%	3. Biological science	16.3%
4. Education	7.1%	4. Social sciences	7.4%
5. Mathematics or statistics	6.2%	5. Fine arts	5.0%
9. English	3.9%	8. Education	4.0%

From Mitchell J. Chang et al., *Beyond Myths: The Growth and Diversity of Asian American College Freshmen, 1971–2005,* Higher Education Research Institute, UCLA, 2007.

AAPI freshmen also were surveyed regarding their career aspirations (see Table 4). In 1971, teacher or administrator (secondary) was the top choice among women (7.3%), while men preferred engineer (23.6%) or physician (14.2%). However, in 2005, being a teacher or administrator (elementary) ranked as the 9th choice among women (2.5%), while 13.5% selected physician as their top career choice. AAPI men ranked engineer (16.1%), business executive (11.2%), and physician (11.2%) as their top three career choices in 2005. The results of this survey paralleled the data from an NCES report (Ramani, 2007) that showed many more bachelor's degrees granted in 2003–04 to AAPIs in business (24.1%), social sciences and history (12.2%), and computer and information sciences (9.2%) than in education (1.9%). Likewise, in an American Council on Education (ACE) report, AAPIs showed great increases between 2000–01 and 2001–02 in degrees awarded in business (up by 11.2%) and social sciences (up by 5.3%), and a decline in health professions and biological/life sciences degrees (Harvey, 2005, pp. 33, 81, 85). Bachelor's degrees awarded in education showed an insignificant gain of 0.8%. However, master's degrees in education showed a gain of 9.3%, similar to the gain in business (9.2%) and health professions (10.5%). Still, a decline or lack of interest in undergraduate education majors may have led to the lack of a pipeline to graduate studies in teacher education or education administration, thus exacerbating the shortage of AAPI teachers in public schools and possibly of AAPI student affairs faculty, staff, and administrators on college and university campuses.

Table 4
Career Aspirations Among AAPI Freshmen, 1971 and 2005

Men	1971 (%)	Men	2005 (%)
1. Engineer	23.6%	1. Engineer	16.1%
2. Physician	14.2%	2. Business executive	11.2%
3. Scientific researcher	8.6%	3. Physician	11.2%
4. Business executive	6.8%	4. Pharmacist	4.8%
5. Military service (career)	4.3%	5. Business owner	4.0%
8. Teacher or administrator (secondary)	1.8%	6. Computer programmer or analyst	3.7%
Women	1971 (%)	Women	2005 (%)
1. Teacher or administrator (secondary)	7.3%	1. Physician	13.5%
2. Physician	7.2%	2. Business executive	8.8%
3. Pharmacist	6.3%	3. Pharmacist	7.4%
4. Scientific researcher	5.5%	4. Nurse	5.9%
5. Teacher or administrator (elementary)	5.1%	9. Teacher or administrator (elementary)	2.5%

From Mitchell J. Chang et al., *Beyond Myths: The Growth and Diversity of Asian American College Freshmen, 1971–2005,* Higher Education Research Institute, UCLA, 2007.

Teranishi's review of one of the research studies in his book showed that "there is a lack of faculty and administrators of color in higher education despite the fact that the number of doctoral degrees awarded to students of color, particularly in the field of education, has increased significantly over the past 3 decades" (Teranishi, 2005, p. 136). Among 42,858 AAPI faculty members in 2005, most were at public 4-year institutions (60.8%), rather than private 4-year (29.3%) or public 2-year (24.5%) institutions. The larger proportion of AAPI faculty working in public 4-year institutions is similar to that of other racial groups. Analyzing the 2005 data from NCES, Teranishi (2005, pp. 136–137) showed that AAPI faculty represented 7.2% of the total full-time faculty at all Title IV degree-granting institutions, compared with 4.4% for Latino and 5.3% for Black faculty members.

Table 5

Percentage Distribution of Students Enrolled in Degree-Granting Institutions by Race/Ethnicity, Selected Years, Fall 1976–Fall 2007

Race/ethnicity	Institutions of higher education			Degree-granting institutions						
	1976	1980	1990	2000	2002	2003	2004	2005	2006	2007
Total	100	100	100	100	100	100	100	100	100	100
White	82.6	81.4	77.6	68.3	67.1	66.7	66.1	65.7	65.2	64.4
Total minority	15.4	16.1	19.6	28.2	29.4	29.8	30.4	30.9	31.5	32.2
Black	9.4	9.2	9.0	11.3	11.9	12.2	12.5	12.7	12.8	13.1
Hispanic	3.5	3.9	5.7	9.5	10	10.1	10.5	10.8	11.1	11.4
AAPI	1.8	2.4	4.1	6.4	6.5	6.4	6.4	6.5	6.6	6.7
American Indian, Alaskan Native	0.7	0.7	0.7	1.0	1.0	1.0	1.0	1.0	1.0	1.0
Nonresident alien	2.0	2.5	2.8	3.5	3.6	3.5	3.4	3.3	3.4	3.4

Note: Race categories exclude persons of Hispanic ethnicity. Data through 1990 are for institutions of higher education, while later data are for degree-granting institutions. Degree-granting institutions grant associate or higher degrees and participate in Title IV federal financial aid programs. The degree-granting classification is very similar to the earlier higher education classification, but it includes more 2-year colleges and excludes a few higher education institutions that did not grant degrees. Numbers may not sum to totals because of rounding. From National Center for Education Statistics, U.S. Department of Education, *Digest of Education Statistics, 2008* (NCES 2009-020), 2009, Table 226.

Tables 5 and 6 show the gap between AAPI student enrollment and the presence of AAPI senior administrators. Table 5 shows that, in 2007, U.S. college enrollment included 6.7% AAPI students (compared with 6.5% in 2005), 11.4% Hispanic, and 13.1% Black (NCES, 2009). Table 6 shows that, of almost 1.4 million full-time faculty and instructional staff in 2007, only 5.7% (78,593) were AAPIs, 3.8% Latino, and 6.4% Black. Clearly, the increase in diversity of enrolled students from 2005 to 2007 was not reflected in a corresponding increase in minority faculty. Table 6 also shows that (1) there were close to 195,000 AAPI employees, about 5.5% of the total 3.56 million professional and nonprofessional employees; (2) of the AAPI employees, 80.5% were considered to be professional, which includes executive/administrative/managerial, faculty, graduate assistants, and other professional; (3) of the 217,518 senior positions (i.e., executive/administrative/managerial), 80% were occupied by Whites (173,948), compared with 9.7% by Blacks (21,047), 4.6% by Hispanics (10,074), 2.99% by AAPIs (6,517), and 0.6% by American Indian/Alaska Natives (1,221); and (4) among all employees from all institutions occupying all positions (3,267,989 excluding resident aliens and persons whose race/ethnicity is unknown), 5.3% of White employees were in senior positions, 0.6% of Blacks, 0.3% of Hispanics, 0.2% of AAPIs, and 0.04% of American Indian/Alaska Natives (NCES, 2010b).

Table 6

Employees in Degree-Granting Institutions, by Race/Ethnicity and Primary Occupation, Fall 2007

Primary occupation	Total[a]	Race/ethnicity				
		White	Black	Hispanic	Asian/ Pacific Islander	American Indian/ Alaska Native
Total, all institutions		2,496,754	353,146	202,098	194,934	21,057
Professional staff	2,629,401	1,894,641	191,204	110,052	156,969	13,501
Executive/administrative/ managerial	217,518	173,948	21,047	10,074	6,517	1,221
Faculty (instruction/ research/public service)	1,371,390	1,038,982	87,107	51,660	78,593	6,934
Graduate assistants	328,979	169,028	12,634	11,548	24,712	1,299
Other professional	711,514	512,683	70,416	36,770	47,147	4,047
Nonprofessional staff	932,027	602,113	161,942	92,046	37,965	7,556

[a] Total includes figures for nonresident aliens and persons whose race/ethnicity is unknown: 3,561,428 staff.

Note: Degree-granting institutions grant associate or higher degrees and participate in Title IV federal financial aid programs. Race categories exclude persons of Hispanic ethnicity. From National Center for Education Statistics, U.S. Department of Education, Digest of Education Statistics, 2009 (NCES 2010-013), 2010, Table 246.

In California's Community College (CC) system, 2,051 (8.0%) educational and 1,544 (8.5%) classified administrators were "Asian," which included "Asian, Pacific Islander, and Filipino," although total CC enrollment of AAPI students was 16% for the 2008 fall semester (Chang, 2010, pp. 17–22). In the California State University (CSU) system, of a total of 1,540 employees in the management personnel plan (i.e., campus executives, deans, personnel officers, and other managers and supervisors), 9% were considered AAPIs, although total AAPI enrollment in the CSU system was 18% (pp. 23–27). Finally, in the University of California (UC) system, of 8,948 employees in the senior management (SMG) and management and senior professional (MSP) classifications, AAPIs held only 16% of the positions, although 38% of total UC system enrollment was AAPIs (pp. 28–35). The management personnel plans for both CSU and UC systems include frontline managers, supervisors, and professional staff members whose positions are not necessarily senior-level positions. Disaggregated data would likely show an even lower percentage of AAPI staff among senior administrators.

Although the poor representation of AAPIs among California's higher education personnel is significant, they are even more poorly represented in the most senior higher education leadership positions across the United States. Using ACE data, Teranishi showed that, in 2003, there were 145 (4.5%) Latino college presidents, 213 (6.7%) Black, 33 (0.9%) AAPI, and 18 (0.6%) Native American (see Table 7). Additional analysis of the data showed that even though community colleges enrolled the bulk of AAPI students, only nine CCs had AAPI presidents (six men and three women) (Teranishi, 2005, p. 141).

Table 7
College Presidents by Race and Institutional Type, 2003

	2-year institutions	4-year institutions	All institutions
White	1,011 (87.5%)	1,770 (87.8%)	2,781 (87.7%)
Black	76 (6.5%)	137 (6.8%)	213 (6.7%)
Latino	60 (5.1%)	85 (4.2%)	145 (4.5%)
AAPI	9 (0.8%)	24 (1.2%)	33 (0.9%)
Native American	12 (1.0%)	7 (0.3%)	18 (0.6%)

Note: Data are for Title IV degree-granting institutions in the United States and Puerto Rico. From American Council on Education, ART corporate database.

At an ACE roundtable in 2009, discussion revealed that the percentage of AAPI presidents remained at 0.9% (4.6% Latino and 5.8% Black). At the meeting, Frank Chong, then president of Laney College in Oakland, California, and currently president of Santa Rosa Junior College, said, "Among the reasons for the dearth of Asian presidents is the longstanding stereotype of Asians as being hard workers but too quiet to be charismatic, effective leaders" (Lum, 2009, p.1). At the same meeting, Ding-Jo Currie, former chancellor of the Coast Community College District in Costa Mesa, California, said, "The fact that many of us are viewed as modest, reserved, and nonconfrontational does not mean we are not leadership material" (p. 1). The 2010 CARE report said that lack of representation at the most senior administrative level of an institution would mean "fewer opportunities for bringing attention to the needs of the AAPI student population" (p. 11). Many presidents have served as faculty members—a lack of AAPI representation at the faculty level is bound to affect pipeline and professional development/mentorship issues facing AAPI educators. As a result of the roundtable discussions, ACE officials understood the need to form a pipeline of Asian Americans into the most senior administrative levels of higher education. In addition, AAPI provosts and chief academic officers must be given the opportunity to participate in leadership development programs (Lum, 2009).

Using data from a 2005 ACE report (Harvey, 2005), Table 8 shows that in 1993 Asian Americans constituted only 1.6% of full-time administrators in the United States. In the same report, aggregate data showed a 57.9% gain in Asian American administrators, from 1.6% in 1993 to 2.4% in 2001. In 1994, 1.2% (38) of all presidents in U.S. colleges and universities were Asian Americans; in 2004 the figure was 1.5% (57), a gain of 50% (19 presidents) over 10 years. Despite the purported gains, all percentages for administrators and presidents were below the percentages of AAPI population estimated by the U.S. Census in 1990 and 2000 (4.2% and 4.4%, respectively). Table 8 also shows that, according to a CSU system employee profile (CSU, 2006), 7.6% (75) of fall 2001 full-time managerial positions were occupied by Asian Americans. Asian American managers increased by 9.7% (to 146) by fall 2006, a gain of 95%. However, systemwide managerial positions for all ethnic groups increased by 54% during that 5-year period. In a similar report (CSU, 2009) comparing the employee profiles for fall 2004 and fall 2009, the systemwide increase in managerial positions was 10.5%, while AAPIs in those positions showed a gain of 27%. The managerial group might include office managers, directors, or administrators, so it is unknown how many of these Asian American managers were senior administrators. The total percentage gains might seem impressive on paper, but their significance cannot be known until AAPI personnel data are disaggregated to show the number of AAPIs who are in decision-making positions.

Table 8

AAPI Administrators and Presidents in Higher Education

	Administrators[a]		Presidents[a]		CSU Managers[b]
1993	2,243 (1.6% of total)	1994	38 (1.2% of total)	2001	75 (7.6% of total)
2001	3,541 (2.4% of total)	2004	57 (1.5% of total)	2006	146 (9.7% of total)
Gain	1,298 (+57.9%)	Gain	19 (+50%)	Gain	71 (+95%)

CSU = California State University
[a] W. B. Harvey & E. L. Anderson, *Minorities in Higher Education,* American Council on Education, Washington, DC, 2005.
[b] CSU, Profiles of CSU Employees, 2006, http://www.calstate.edu/hr/employee-profile/archive.shtml.

AAPIs as Student Personnel Administrators

Data in the previous sections highlighted the underrepresentation of AAPI teachers and administrators in public schools and in higher education, especially in senior-level positions, including an inadequate number of AAPI presidents of universities and colleges. In this section, we examine the number of AAPIs in senior-level student affair administrative positions. In an online survey of a randomly racially stratified sample (n = 1,694) of American College Personnel Association (ACPA), NASPA–Student Affairs Administrators in Higher Education, and Asian Pacific Americans in Higher Education (APAHE) members, Sunny Park Suh (2005) showed in her dissertation that earlier literature on AAPI administrators—specifically in student affairs—was limited. Most of the literature, including dissertations and papers presented at conferences, pertained to general issues facing minorities; minority women; women academics; the model minority myth; foreigner stereotypes; career aspirations; the glass ceiling; workplace racism; lack of leadership skills; lack of campus advocates, mentors, and role models; and being relegated to minority-related tasks, positions, and issues. Suh showed that the positions of AAPI student personnel administrators tended to cluster around certain minority function areas, had less supervisory and budgetary responsibilities, and were located mainly in large research universities. She reported that AAPIs held significantly fewer senior administrative positions (e.g., dean of students, vice president, chancellor, provost) (16.2%), compared with Whites (27.5%) and others (including Blacks and Hispanics) (29.2%). The senior AAPI administrators were less experienced (11.88 years) overall in their current positions compared with Whites (13.77 years) and others (13.06 years). More Whites (37.2%) and others (32.4%) had more than 16 years of experience in student affairs compared with AAPIs (24.3%).

In an attempt to determine the types of administrative positions members of NASPA currently hold, the authors of this chapter analyzed the association's membership database (NASPA, 2010), with identifying membership information removed. Of more than 12,000 records, 7,891 contained entries in the ethnicity data field. We used 7,762 records, reflecting only institutions in the United States, for the analyses. Table 9 shows the distribution of NASPA members who self-identified their ethnicity[3] across institutions grouped by student FTE (full-time equivalent) enrollment. Of the 7,762 members, 61% were Caucasian, 16% African American, 8% Hispanic, 4% Asian Pacific Islander (331), and 1% Native American. Three percent of the members specified "multiracial," 359 members specified "other" (5%), and 180 chose "prefer not to answer" (2%).

---

[3] Almost 5,000 of the approximately 12,000 members did not complete the "ethnicity" data field when they registered for NASPA membership. Of the 7,762 members who did complete the field, 539 responded with either "other" (n = 359) or "prefer not to answer" (n = 180).

Table 9

Distribution of NASPA Members in Administrative Positions by Ethnicity and Full-Time Equivalent Institutional Enrollment

Self-reported ethnicity	<8,000 FTE	%	8,000–19,999 FTE	%	>20,000 FTE	%	Total by Ethnicity	% of Total
Caucasian	1,803	38%	1,801	38%	1,117	24%	4,721	61%
African American	366	30%	510	42%	347	28%	1,223	16%
Hispanic	158	25%	263	41%	222	35%	643	8%
Asian Pacific Islander	78	24%	138	42%	115	35%	331	4%
Multiracial	83	33%	94	37%	75	30%	252	3%
Native American	16	30%	19	36%	18	34%	53	1%
Other (unspecified)	133	37%	133	37%	93	26%	359	5%
Prefer not to answer	91	51%	71	39%	18	10%	180	2%
Total by institutional FTE	2,728	35%	3,029	39%	2,005	26%	7,762	100%

FTE = full-time equivalent
From authors' analyses of NASPA Membership Database.

Of the 331 members who identified themselves as AAPIs, a majority (42%) work in mid-sized institutions (FTE 8,000–19,999), 35% in large institutions (FTE >20,000), and 24% in small institutions (FTE <8,000). For this analysis, categorization by institutional enrollment was based on referencing and matching as closely as possible to the Carnegie Classification on "Size and Setting" (Carnegie Foundation for the Advancement of Teaching, 2010). Similar distributions were found among Hispanic members in mid-sized, large, and small institutions (41%, 35%, and 25%, respectively) and among African American members (42%, 28%, and 30%, respectively). A smaller percentage of Caucasian members (24%) are employed at large institutions (FTE >20,000), while their employment at small and mid-sized institutions is equally distributed (38%). Slightly more than 40% of AAPIs, Hispanics, and African Americans were found to be working at mid-sized institutions.

Among the 331 AAPI NASPA members, 180 positions carry titles[4] that can be considered entry- or mid-level, and 134 members did not give their job titles. Of the remaining 17 positions (5.1% of all AAPIs and 2.5% of all members with senior-level job titles), the position titles were those of senior administrators. Seven AAPI members were deans of students or academic deans; this is 2.1% of all AAPI members and 3.9% of all dean positions. Four AAPI members were assistant vice chancellors or assistant vice presidents; this is 1.2% of all AAPI members and 4.3% of all assistant vice chancellor or assistant vice president positions. Four AAPI members were associate or senior associate vice chancellors or associate vice presidents; this is 1.2% of all AAPI members and 3.6% of all associate vice chancellor or vice president positions. Finally, two AAPI members were in the highest category (vice chancellor, vice president, provost, or president); this is 0.6% of all AAPI members and 0.7% of all of the senior titles in this category. Even though AAPIs constituted 4% (n = 331) of the 7,762 members studied, they held only 17 senior administrative positions, which is only 2.5% of all senior-level administrative positions (see Table 10).

---

[4] Almost 41% (n = 134) of 331 AAPI members left the job title data field blank.

Table 10

Senior Administrative Positions Held by NASPA Members (Academic or Student Affairs) by Ethnicity

	Total Member	Dean	%	Asst. VC/VP	%	Assoc./Sr. Assoc. VC/VP	%	President, VC/VP, or provost	%	Total senior positions	%	% of all senior positions
Caucasian	4,721	119	2.5%	58	1.2%	74	1.6%	211	4.5%	462	9.8%	67.1%
African American	1,223	29	2.4%	18	1.5%	26	2.1%	54	4.4%	127	10.4%	18.4%
Asian Pacific Islander	331	7	2.1%	4	1.2%	4	1.2%	2	0.6%	17	5.1%	2.5%
Hispanic	643	9	1.4%	6	0.9%	4	0.6%	9	1.4%	28	4.4%	4.1%
Native American	53	0	0.0%	0	0.0%	0	0.0%	2	3.8%	2	3.8%	0.3%
Multiracial	252	1	0.4%	1	0.4%	2	0.8%	2	0.8%	6	2.4%	0.9%
Other	359	8	2.2%	5	1.4%	2	0.6%	13	3.6%	28	7.8%	4.1%
Prefer not to answer	180	6	3.3%	0	0.0%	0	0.0%	13	7.2%	19	10.6%	2.8%
Total	7,762	179	2.3%	92	1.2%	112	1.4%	306	3.9%	689	8.9%	100.0%

Dean = dean of students or academic dean

Asst. VC/VP = assistant vice chancellor or assistant vice president

Assoc./Sr. Assoc. VC/VP = associate or senior associate vice chancellor or vice president

VC/VP = vice chancellor or vice president

Note: Column percentages represent % within each ethnic group. Percentages in the last column represent % of all senior-level positions.

From authors' analyses of NASPA Membership Database.

Finally, when institutions in the NASPA membership database were cross-referenced with the list of 116 institutions that are eligible to apply for Title III Asian American and Native American Pacific Islander-Serving Institution (AANAPISI) grants, Alaska Native and Native Hawaiian-Serving Institution (ANNH) grants, or Title V Hispanic-Serving Institution (HSI) grants, 16 institutions are AANAPISI-eligible, 3 are ANNH- and AANAPISI-eligible, and 7 are HSI- and AANAPISI-eligible (Congressional Research Service, 2009). A total of 26 AANAPISIs represented membership institutions that have enrollments of at least 10% AAPIs, the requisite enrollment of needy students, low educational and general expenditures, and at least 50% of enrolled students on federal financial aid programs. Of the 17 AAPI senior administrators, only 1 currently holds a position in one of the 26 AANAPISI-eligible institutions listed in the NASPA membership database (although these numbers are underestimated owing to blank data fields in the database and the fact that not all 116 AANAPISIs are members of NASPA).

Recommendations for Action

Creating a pipeline into the workforce may be one of the most urgent challenges facing the United States, especially during the ongoing economic downturn. Historical discrimination against AAPIs, the model minority myth, and the "perfidious foreigner" perception are obstacles to access by underserved AAPIs to higher education and the workforce. Lack of adequate numbers of AAPI teachers in public schools, of faculty and staff in higher education, and especially of student affairs administrators to serve as role models, mentors, decision makers, and advocates are additional factors that community leaders, educators, scholars, researchers, and policymakers must consider.

The 2010 CARE report suggested several actions that can be taken to overcome these obstacles; for example, (1) higher education and the AAPI community need to reduce and ultimately eliminate equity gaps by enhancing postsecondary access, degree attainment rates, and workforce skills of the AAPI population; (2) a more accurate and reliable information base must be established through sustainable higher education research that uses disaggregated data by race, ethnicity, gender, and generational status to identify key areas of concern and to inform policymakers; and (3) awareness of AAPIs needs to be increased in the context of U.S. higher education policy priorities by sharing research findings, showcasing best practices, sharing well-planned strategies, and establishing benchmarks.

Researchers, think tanks and policymakers, community-based advocacy organizations, and elected officials should work together to address issues facing AAPIs in higher education relative to federal policy priorities. These efforts could include creating more AANAPISIs, establishing an AANAPISI grant program, encouraging eligible higher education institutions to apply for funding to improve services and academic programs provided to AAPIs, and ensuring a way to disaggregate all AAPI data to get more specific information on AAPI ethnic subgroups (CARE, 2010, p. 31).

References

Asian and Pacific Islander American Scholarship Fund (APIASF). (2010). *2010 APIASF Higher Education Summit.* Retrieved from http://www.apiasf.org/higher_ed.html

California State University (CSU). (2006). *Profiles of CSU employees 2006.* Retrieved from California State University: http://www.calstate.edu/hr/employee-profile/archive.shtml

California State University (CSU). (2009). *Profiles of CSU employees 2009.* Retrieved from California State University: http://www.calstate.edu/hr/employee-profile/2009

Carnegie Foundation for the Advancement of Teaching. (2010). *2010 Carnegie Classification; National Center for Educations Statistics, IPEDS fall enrollment (2009).* Retrieved from http://classifications.carnegiefoundation.org/summary/size_setting.php

Chang, M. J., Park, J. J., Lin, M. H., Poon, O. A., & Nakanishi, D. T. (2007). *Beyond myths: The growth and diversity of Asian American college freshmen, 1971–2005.* Retrieved from Higher Education Research Institute website: http://www.heri.ucla.edu/PDFs/pubs/briefs/AsianTrendsResearchBrief.pdf

Chang, M. J., Fung, G., Nakanishi, D., Ogawa, R., Um, K., Takahashi, L., Cruz-Viesca, M., Shek, Y. L., Kuo, A., & Russ, L. (2010, September). *The state of Asian American, Native Hawaiian, and Pacific Islander education in California.* Retrieved from The California State University website: http://www.calstate.edu/externalrelations/documents/API-Education-MRP-Report.pdf

Congressional Research Service. (2009). *2009 report on and list of potentially eligible AANPISIs.* Retrieved from http://www2.ed.gov/about/inits/list/asian-americans-initiative/potentially-eligible.pdf

Feagin, R. S. (2008). *The myth of the model minority: Asian Americans facing racism.* Boulder, CO: Paradigm Publishers.

Harper, S. R. (2005, Spring). Staffing practices, professional preparation trends, and demographics among student affairs administrators at historically black colleges and universities (HBCUs): Implications from a national study. *NASAP Journal, 8*(1), 8–25.

Harvey, W. B., & Anderson, E. L. (2005). *Minorities in higher education: Twenty-first annual status report.* Retrieved from College of Lake County website: http://clcpages.clcillinois.edu/home/res213/MinoritiesReport.pdf

Leadership Education for Asian Pacifics (LEAP) Asian Pacific American Public Policy Institute and UCLA Asian American Studies Center. (1993). *The state of Asian Pacific America: A public policy report, policy issues to the year 2020.* Los Angeles, CA: Author.

Low, V. (1982). *The unimpressionable race.* San Francisco, CA: East/West Publishing Company, Inc.

Lum, L. (2009, October). Asian-Americans hope to build pipelines to college presidencies. *Diverse Issues in Higher Education.* Retrieved from http://diverseeducation.com/cache.print.php?articleId=13097

National Association of Student Personnel Administrators (NASPA). (2010, October). NASPA Membership Database. Composite report provided with permission by NASPA.

National Center for Education Statistics (NCES). (2007–08a). *Schools and staffing survey.* Retrieved from U.S. Department of Education, Institute of Education Sciences: http://nces.ed.gov/surveys/sass/tables/sass0708_2009321_s1s_03.asp

National Center for Education Statistics (NCES). (2007–08b). *Status and trends in the education of racial and ethnic minorities.* Retrieved from U.S. Department of Education, Institute of Education Sciences: http://nces.ed.gov/pubs2010/2010015/tables/table_7_2.asp

National Center for Education Statistics (NCES). (2007–08c). *Status and trends in the education of racial and ethnic minorities.* Retrieved from U.S. Department of Education, Institute of Education Sciences: http://nces.ed.gov/pubs2010/2010015/tables/table_9_2.asp

National Center for Education Statistics (NCES). (2009). *Fast facts: 1976–2007 college enrollment.* Retrieved from U.S. Department of Education, Institute of Education Sciences: http://nces.ed.gov/fastfacts/display.asp?id=98

National Center for Education Statistics (NCES). (2010a). *Digest of education statistics.* Retrieved from U.S. Department of Education, Institute of Education Sciences: http://nces.ed.gov/programs/digest/d10/tables/dt10_005.asp?referrer=list

National Center for Education Statistics (NCES). (2010b). *Fast facts: Fall 2007 employee diversity.* Retrieved from U.S. Department of Education, Insitute of Education Sciences: http://nces.ed.gov/fastfacts/display.asp?id=61

National Center for Education Statistics (NCES). (n.d.a). *Projections of education statistics to 2014.* Retrieved from U.S. Department of Education, Institute of Education Sciences: http://nces.ed.gov/programs/projections/projections2014/sec_1b.asp

National Center for Education Statistics (NCES). (n.d.b). *Projections of education statistics to 2014.* Retrieved from U.S. Department of Education, Institute of Education Sciences: http://nces.ed.gov/programs/projections/projections2014/sec_5b.asp

National Commission on Asian American and Pacific Islander Research in Education (CARE). (2008). *Asian Americans and Pacific Islanders, facts, not fiction: Setting the record straight.* Retrieved from http://professionals.collegeboard.com/profdownload/08-0608-AAPI.pdf

National Commission on Asian American and Pacific Islander Research in Education (CARE). (2010). *Federal higher education policy priori-*

ties and the Asian American and Pacific Islander community. Retrieved from http://apiasf.org/CAREreport/2010_CARE_report.pdf

KewalRamani, A., Gilbertson, L., & Fox, M. A. (2007). *Status and trends in the education of racial and ethnic minorities.* Retrieved from U.S. Department of Education, National Center for Education Statistics website: http://nces.ed.gov/pubs2010/2010015.pdf

Suh, S. P. (2005). *Characteristics of Asian Pacific American student affairs administrators: Implications for practice in higher education* (Doctoral dissertation). Retrieved from Columbia University Teachers College Dissertations & Theses: The Humanities and Social Sciences Collection. (Publication No. AAT3175732).

Suzuki, B. H. (2002). Revisiting the model minority stereotype: Implications for student affairs practice and higher education. In M. McEwen, C. M. Kodama, A. N. Alvarez, S. Lee, & C. T. H. Liang (Eds.), *Working with Asian American college students* (New directions for student services, no. 97, pp. 21–32). San Francisco, CA: Jossey-Bass.

Teranishi, R. T. (2010). *Asians in the ivory tower: Dilemmas of racial inequality in American higher education.* New York, NY: Teachers College Press.

PART II

AAPI Racial Identity Formation

CHAPTER TWO

Let's Get Radical

Being a Practitioner-Ally for Asian Pacific Islander American College Students

Sumun Pendakur and Vijay Pendakur

Asian Americans are made, not born.[1]

This powerful epigraph from Frank Wu calls attention to the notion that Asian Americans, and Asian America, do not exist outside historical and political contexts. The authors of this chapter were born as second-generation members of the Indian diaspora. Through the history and politics of racism and White hegemony, as well as the history and politics of resistance and the struggle for social justice, we have been made into Asian Americans. We open with these words to ask you to shift your

---

[1] From F. H. Wu, *Yellow: Race in America beyond Black and White*, Basic Books, New York, 2002, p. 307.

31

thinking from popular paradigms of Asian-ness that centralize ethnicity and culture to a counternarrative construction of Asian Pacific Islander American (APIA) political race. This chapter is not about food, language, holidays, or other popular markers of Asian-ness. It is about reframing and repositioning. In the following pages, we call for a reframing of how race is understood in student affairs practice and the repositioning of APIA college students. We wish to provide you with the tools to be successful in this project to reframe and reposition, and engage you in the movement to better support APIA college students, as student affairs practitioner-allies.

The chapter is divided into four sections; each offers a different set of tools through which to advocate for APIA college students. The first section is an overview of two key theoretical lenses. The lenses of racial formation and Critical Race Theory are not new, but they are not yet canonical in student affairs scholarship and practice. We begin with theory because we strongly believe that these lenses are critical to the process of reframing APIA identity and because these lenses can be applied to subsequent sections of the chapter. This section is followed by a brief, empirical capture of the numerous ways in which APIA college students experience risk. We offer practitioners both quantitative and qualitative data to use in their arguments to include APIA students in the larger conversation on students of color at predominantly White institutions by demonstrating that APIA students, too, are at risk.

The last two sections offer two sets of tools through which student affairs educators can effect change on college campuses. First, we review the three major tropes through which APIAs are racialized, marginalized, and silenced in our society. Instead of limiting our analysis of these dominant tropes to the theoretical, we examine them through a process of counternarrative history in which we role-model the critical thinking process we suggest for practitioner-allies. Rooting an analysis of race in counternarrative history is a crucial step in repositioning the APIA community on college campuses. Finally, we offer recommendations for practice and institutional reform in response to the need for a conceptual shift in how we think about APIA students and a transformation in the way we educate, engage, and serve these students on college campuses.

Bifocal Lenses: Racial Formation and Critical Race Theory

In the 1980s and 1990s, scholars concerned with race and racism in the United States began to articulate a set of arguments that claimed that race, as opposed to gender and class, had been undertheorized in the American academy (Ladson-Billings and Tate, 1995). Two bodies of theory emerged to meet this need: Omi and Winant's (1994) *Racial Formation in the United States: From the 1960s to the 1990s* and Critical Race Theory (CRT). First published in 1986, Omi and Winant's work offers scholars a robust theorization of race and racism in the context of American capitalist hegemony, a form of dominance and subordination based on consent. CRT—particularly the work on CRT in the field of education—gives us a set of challenging conceptual guidelines and counterhegemonic ethical convictions through which to systematically analyze the experience of people of color in American education. We briefly review Omi and Winant's central contribution—their theory of racial formation—as well as five key tenets of CRT in the field of education. We then discuss how racial formation and CRT inform our approach to critically examining the APIA experience in higher education.

Omi and Winant argued that "race is a concept which signifies and symbolizes social conflicts and interest by referring to different types of human bodies" (1994, p. 55). This definition of race is particularly potent because it balances the ideological nature of race as a social construct with the material reality that race is ascribed onto human bodies. Omi and Winant challenged us to think of race as neither an essential category nor a total illusion. The authors stated that racial formation is the "sociohistorical process by which racial categories are created, inhabited, transformed, and destroyed (p. 55)." Key elements in this notion of racial formation are that race is a process—one that is inextricably embedded in social and historical realities.

Omi and Winant wrote that their theory of racial formation has two central parts that are crucial to understanding this process. First, they argued that racial formation happens in a series of racial projects ("historical projects") in which both the ideological and structural components are organized and assigned to certain human bodies. They noted, however, that racial projects are intimately connected to "[efforts to] . . . reorganize and redistribute resources along particular racial lines" (p. 56). This link between race and resources is a doorway to understanding the second part of their theory, which claims that the process of racial formation and its attendant racial projects are tied to the maintenance of hegemony. Omi and Winant not only offered critical theorists a way to think about race in historical, material, and ideological terms, they also positioned race in the scholarship on hegemony. Racial formation challenges us to think about how race has been constructed to support the maintenance of hierarchical power relations and the elite in American society.

CRT is the second major theoretical influence on how we conceptualize race. Historically, CRT emerged from Critical Legal Studies (CLS), a branch of legal scholarship that developed along with the civil rights movement to critique the legal system for its role in maintaining oppression (Yosso, Parker, Solórzano, & Lynn, 2004). CLS placed a heavy emphasis on examining the law as a representation of the liberal state, but many scholars of color found CLS lacking in its account of race (Bell, 1980; Delgado, 1987). These scholars began to write about the law, using a framework that centralized race and racism in problematizing the traditional legal system. Although often misunderstood as being oppositional to CLS, these critical race theorists sought to extend the analysis of CLS in the post-civil rights era (Tate, 1997, p. 206). As a result of this historical context, the initial body of CRT scholarship is heavily focused on issues of race and racism in legal analysis. By the mid-1990s, another set of scholars concerned with race and racism in the field of education decided to formally articulate the utility of CRT for educational scholarship. These bridge-builders and border-crossers developed a set of central tenets (which we will review) that make CRT valuable for theorizing race and racism in U.S. education, both historically and in the present (Ladson-Billings & Tate, 1995; Tate, 1997).

Tate (1997) writes that racism is endemic in American society. For CRT in the field of education, this situation calls for a focus on how racism legally, culturally, and psychologically limits opportunities for students of color. CRT also challenges education scholars to be pragmatically transdisciplinary in their approach to emancipatory scholarship. Rather than adhering to one ideological stance, CRT calls for scholars to use the best theoretical tools to accomplish their task; this approach lends itself to broad interdisciplinary practice. CRT strongly problematizes a civil rights-based legal approach to addressing inequity because of the conviction that legal reforms are undermined before they can become effective. In the field of education, this conviction presents a potent challenge to the multiculturalism movement, a liberal framework closely tied to the civil rights movement and the demand for incremental legal reform. Ladson-Billings and Tate (1995) articulate this multiculturalist paradox as "the difficulty of maintaining the spirit and intent of justice for the oppressed while simultaneously permitting the hegemonic rule of the oppressor" (p. 62). This is an important contribution from CRT to the field of education, as multiculturalism remains the dominant paradigm in the field for understanding race, power, and oppression.

Tate also sharply questions epistemic claims of "neutrality, objectivity, color blindness, and meritocracy" (p. 235), and calls for educators to problematize research that adheres to these flawed constructs, as they serve as veils for dominant interests. In parallel with rejecting classic academic notions of objectivity and neutrality, CRT centralizes the stories and the act of story-telling by unearthing the lived experience of people of color. Ladson-Billings and Tate explain, "For the critical race theorist, social reality is constructed by the formulation and exchange of stories." Not only are the stories themselves important, the act of storytelling can serve as "medicine to heal the wounds of pain caused by racial oppression" (p. 57). Finally, CRT asserts that history and context are crucial to addressing the experience of people of color. In educational praxis and educational research, this final challenge is a reminder that we must not ignore the crucial role of history in shaping our understanding and experience of race, as well as the integral nature of class, gender, and other social identities, as contextual to our experience in U.S. education.

Omi and Winant's theory of racial formation and the scholarship on CRT in education provide a theoretical foundation for this chapter. Omi and Winant offered a comprehensive theorization of race that is embedded in U.S. history, as well as an understanding of U.S. capitalist hegemony. This perspective is crucial to our examination of APIA racial identity, as we argue that this identity has been constructed as a racial project and reconstructed over time in response to sociopolitical agendas. We also link APIA racial formation to the needs of the U.S. state as a capitalist and imperialist hegemonic system.

CRT, particularly the scholarship that bridges this framework into education, helps us shape our examination of the APIA student experience in higher education. Our emphasis on history and context comes directly from CRT, and we strongly believe that one cannot understand APIA identity without these pieces. CRT in education offers a strong challenge to multiculturalism; our conviction is that the multiculturalist paradigm cannot sufficiently explain the oppression faced by APIA students in higher education, nor does it offer us tools to address the existing inequity. CRT centralizes stories and storytelling as a way to bring the experience of people of color into account, and we employ "story" in this chapter by using fictional vignettes and historical stories to humanize the APIA experience in our analysis and challenge hegemonic constructions of objective scholarship in the process.

Students at Risk and Universities in Deficit: The APIA College Experience

The following two vignettes are fictional representations, created by the authors for educational purposes.

Keiko Matsuda is a yonsei, a fourth-generation Japanese American. She grew up in Orange County in Southern California, and both of her parents have master's degrees. Her father is a biochemistry researcher at a pharmaceutical research and development laboratory and her mother is an architect. In the fall of 2011, Keiko will be traveling to the Midwest for her first year of college. She will be attending a private Catholic university on the north side of Chicago and participating in the pre-medical program. Keiko is a college student at risk.

Bao Nguyen is a second-generation Vietnamese American. He grew up in Minneapolis, Minnesota, and his parents have different levels of educational attainment. Bao's father worked on a small farm in Vietnam and doesn't speak any English. Bao's mother obtained a degree from a 2-year program to work as a nurse's assistant, and her English is proficient. Bao's family was relocated out of a refugee camp in Thailand to Minneapolis. His father does odd jobs in the Vietnamese refugee community, mostly day labor for cash. In the fall of 2011, Bao will be attending a community college in Minnesota with the hope of transferring to the University of Minnesota after two years. Bao would like to major in computer science. Bao is a college student at risk.

It is our conviction that the social and historical construction of APIA racial identity actually produces unique forms of risk for APIA college students. As these areas of risk are well-documented in the broader literature on APIA college students, we present only the major risk archetypes for APIA college students here and provide citations for further exploration of these issues. The fictional vignettes feature APIAs who embody these unique risk formations. How does the dominant APIA racial construction engender risk for these college students, including the Keikos and Baos on your campus? What tools do you have, as a practitioner-ally, to reposition and reframe APIA identity in ways that counter the current hegemonic construction?

- The model minority mythology positions APIAs as well-adjusted, well-mannered, smart, hardworking, and from financially well-off families, cloaking the very real struggles and challenges these students face on college campuses (Choi, Rogers, & Werth, 2007; Yeh, 2002, 2004).

- The model minority mythology also makes APIAs targets for hate crimes and intergroup violence, while simultaneously denying them the experience of race by positioning them as "honorary Whites" (Alvarez, 2002; Alvarez, 2009; Alvarez & Helms, 2001). Moreover, the ongoing arrival of new Asian immigrants, along with the racial construction of APIAs as "forever foreign," positions APIA college students to be especially vulnerable to xenophobia and anti-immigrant politics (Alvarez & Yeh, 1999; Ancis, Sedlacek, & Mohr, 2000; LeSure, 1994; Mack, Tucker, & Cha, 2000).

- APIA college students exhibit low help-seeking behaviors and, in conjunction with model minority stereotyping, are chronically underserved on college campuses because they are perceived as not needing any help (Choi et al., 2007; Yeh, 2002).

- Barely 1% of articles published in the most widely read peer-reviewed higher education journals focus specifically on APIA college students (Museus & Kiang, 2009), and some often-used canonical texts on college students of color claim that APIAs do not need special services (Astin, 1982; Ogbu, 1978).

- APIA college students are particularly susceptible to suicidal ideation and gesture; recent studies have found APIA students more than 1.6 times more likely than White students to consider suicide (Choi et al., 2007; College Board, 2008).

- APIA pan-ethnicity and the umbrella term *Asian American* obscure critical differences in the APIA community. In many areas of the country, large populations of Filipino, Hmong, Laotian,

Cambodian, Vietnamese, and other Asian groups are greatly under-served because institutions classify all APIA students similarly. These APIA subgroups, and others, often include large numbers of low-income and first-generation college student representation, but are rarely provided with the appropriate services to mitigate these academic risks, owing to the perception that all Asians are model minorities (Ngo & Lee, 2007; UCLA, 2006).

Keiko and Bao are APIA college students, and they are at risk. Higher education institutions in this country are either incapable of or unwilling to address the needs of their APIA students, whether through student support services, programs, or theory development and application. APIA students are held up as models and obscured as not needing attention at the same time. They find themselves in this liminal position just when they are supposed to be exploring their multiple identities, finding a vocation, developing the ability for critical thinking, and stepping into adulthood.

Higher education is failing its APIA students in multiple ways, rendering them further at risk. This is the crux of the issue. The following three key areas are selected from numerous areas that deserve consideration:

- *Gateway programs.* Often, African American and Latino students are offered a variety of bridge, mentoring, community-building, and comprehensive studies programs. APIAs are not considered as a target recruitment population, even though they consistently earn below-average verbal SAT scores (Escueta & O'Brien, 1995). In addition, the APIA community has increased dramatically—more through immigration than through natural increase (birth in the United States)—so many students are bilingual or have limited English proficiency. Thus, institutional expectations regarding the social or cultural capital APIA students possess are challenged by issues of language acquisition and immigrant/first-generation college student status.
- *Academic and career advising.* APIA college students sometimes

must juggle the stereotype-driven assumptions of professors as well as familial (and often internalized) pressure to succeed and excel (Lowe, 2009). Moreover, these students walk the fine line between collectivism and individualism. Lowe (2009) says many APIA college students report "struggling to find a path consonant with their family's goals for them, but also something they feel is a good fit with their personality" (p. 465). Academic advisors and career counselors who have not received critical training and who do not consider factors such as race, ethnicity, culture, immigrant status, and socioeconomic status when working with their APIA students are missing a large piece of the puzzle.

- *Counseling and psychological services.* McEachern and Kenny (1999) note that "evidence suggests that Asian college students may be at even higher risks of stress and psychological disturbance than their White American counterparts" and that they "experience value conflicts, loneliness, passivity, conformity, deference, and reserve with greater frequency than White students" (p. 307). Tewari (2009) says that counseling APIA students with knowledge and theory based on studies of White students may not be effective: "Overall, an absence of culturally sensitive, ethnically or racially similar personnel and a scarcity of practitioners trained in language-specific services are believed to contribute to the overall low rates of mental health service utilization for Asian Americans" (p. 580). Are counselors on your campus prepared to deal with APIA issues that range from the exploration of racial/ethnic identity development and the effect of racism on the psyche to gender, achievement-stress, sexuality, and suicidal ideation?

The literature on APIA student success and risk is a key tool for student affairs practitioner-allies in the struggle for social justice. It is time to think about how APIA students are positioned at universities and to use the data presented here and elsewhere to begin new conversations or inform current ones regarding APIA students.

Counternarrative History

Counternarrative storytelling is a powerful tool that emerges from CRT. Counternarrative history subverts the dominant narrative—the traditional narrative framed as objective, neutral, and value-free. Solórzano and Yosso (2002) simply and eloquently define counterstorytelling:

> We define the counter-story as a method of telling the stories of those people whose experiences are not often told (i.e., those on the margins of society). . . . Counter-stories can shatter complacency, challenge the dominant discourse on race, and further the struggle for racial reform. (p. 32)

We aim to build a lens through which to understand and problematize the APIA experience, drawing on multiple sources of data, from the personal to the empirical. Counternarrative history is useful to reposition Asian American identity, shifting it from the margins of American racial discourse. Hegemonic racialized processes have masked Asian American racial identity, leaving even those who identify as APIAs in the dark about their own communities, histories, and stories. We offer these examples of counternarrative history to inspire your own critical thinking processes and support your work in dismantling hegemonic tropes that oppress the APIA community.

Traditionally, Asian American history has been understood as the movement of people from Asia to the United States in three distinct waves. Many historians, including Takaki (1993, 1998) and Chan (1991), have complicated that understanding with nuanced portrayals of the varied struggles and successes of Asian immigrants and Asian Americans. From a political economy perspective, the construction of the Asian American community in the United States has largely been predicated and triangulated on U.S. labor needs and U.S. foreign policy. The rapid shift in identity from coolie to model minority is directly linked to changes in U.S. immigration policy specifically based on evolving labor needs and a selection bias (Junn, 2007). Before World War I, the domestic policy of growth and westward expansion required vast amounts of unskilled labor. Corporations recruited large numbers of Asian laborers to come to the United States to work in heavy industry: mining, railroads, and plantations. A dramatic shift occurred during the Cold War after the 1965 Hart-Celler Immigration Act. The selection bias of the decades since then—for highly skilled, educated workers—has led to a unique construction of racial tropes that continue to affect APIA community identity development.

Many historians, political scientists, and sociologists have used the traditional model of waves of immigration to elucidate key theoretical concepts (Chan, 1991; Junn, 2007; Takaki, 1993; Wu, 2002); we will use storytelling to present three case studies. These case studies illustrate the dominant themes that affect the treatment of the APIA community and the internalization of racial mythologies by Asian Americans.

Hegemonic Trope 1: Forever Foreigner

This trope positions APIAs as eternally not-American. Taken literally, it erases APIA history in the United States by continually positioning the community as having just arrived. At the same time, it casts APIAs as *essentially* un-American, unassimilable, and critically different. This positioning of APIAs outside normative American-ness allows for the constant questioning of APIA national loyalty by invoking the unspoken question of whether APIAs are more American or more Asian.

Counternarrative 1: From World War II to the War on Terror

In 1942, Executive Order 9066 changed the fate of the Japanese American community overnight. Most know the story: Already suspicious of the nearly 120,000 Japanese and Japanese Americans on the West Coast, the government used the bombing of Pearl Harbor, overt racism, and wartime hysteria as catalysts to enact mass internment (Chan, 1991). More than 60% of those interned were U.S. citizens. Not one internee was ever found guilty of treason. The Japanese and Japanese Americans were forcibly imprisoned by their own government and lost almost everything: homes, businesses, even sentimental items. The internees' loyalty was constantly questioned—the controversial "loyalty questions" in the internment camps were a source of strife within families (Chan, 1991; Kurashige, 2001).

Flash forward through the killing of Vincent Chin, the false treason case against Wen Ho Lee, and the murder of Balbir Singh Sodhi, all of which exemplify the tendency in American culture to question the loyalty and American-ness of those considered foreign and unassimilable. Decades after the mass incarceration of innocent Americans of Japanese descent, we witnessed the post-9/11 targeted deportations and incarcerations of South Asians/South Asian Americans and Arabs/Arab Americans. The perception that these APIAs are more Muslim/other than American has created the latest xenophobic hysteria, which has resulted in civil liberties and human rights being placed on the back burner in the name of national security (Sekhon, 2003). Counterstorytelling enables us to displace traditional narratives of patriotism, nationalism, and security, and to question the actions of a nation that breed fear and xenophobia and the continued "foreignness" of APIA students.

Hegemonic Trope 2: Model Minority

This trope positions APIAs as being different from people of other color groups by rendering them as homogenously successful. Through careful erasure of history and APIA heterogeneity, the image of the Indian doctor or the Chinese astrophysicist is deployed with the question "Why do Asians do so well, while African Americans and Latinos do so poorly?" This trope not only divides people of color, thereby weakening their unified demand for social justice, it also dehumanizes APIAs by casting them as dutiful, academically gifted robots.

Counternarrative 2: Constructed Communities

From the 1800s through the early 1900s, Asian immigrants were perceived as dirty, uneducated, criminal, job-stealing, and opium-addicted. They were the laboring class, imported to fulfill the westward expansion goals of the U.S. government (Junn, 2007). In 1924, the Asian Exclusion Act banned virtually all immigration from Asia. The act was fueled by a variety of factors, including nativism, xenophobia, and fears of Asian world powers; it was the culmination of numerous exclusionary immigration laws specifically targeting Asians (Takaki, 1998; Wu, 2002).

Less than 50 years later, the picture changed dramatically. The 1960s brought a new demand for labor from Asia. The Cold War, especially the rise of the USSR's scientific prowess, embodied in the Sputnik launch, pushed the U.S. government to enact the 1965 Hart-Celler Immigration Act. This act allowed for more immigration from Asia, on the basis of specific desirable selection characteristics such as education and profession (Chan, 1991; Junn, 2007; Takaki, 1998; Wu, 2002). The influx of educated, professional/student immigrants led to an artificial construction of community, one that does not include Asian laborers, the uneducated, or the poor. Also in the 1960s, the federal government launched the War on Poverty, further stigmatizing the African American population. Piercing a dagger in the heart of civil rights work and the goals of coalitional solidarity, the popular media began to use the term "model minority" in 1966 (Kim, 1999; Ng, Lee, & Pak, 2007; Petersen, 1966; "Success Story", 1966; Wu, 2002). The model minority label was used to describe this artificially constructed community of Asian immigrants and their offspring, in contrast to "troublesome" minorities such as African Americans, who were demanding their civil and human rights.

Referring again to Omi and Winant's (1994) racial formation theory, we see how the model minority stereotype was constructed and reconstructed as a racial project. Counterstorytelling enables us to deconstruct cultural explanations of success and build cross-racial coalitions.

Hegemonic Trope 3: Pan-ethnicity

This trope is complex: It offers both a utility for social justice work and a myriad of problems for the APIA community. "Asian American" is a pan-ethnic term that seeks to encompass and politicize the relationship between people in the Asian diaspora and those in the U.S. state. The term functions as a powerful umbrella for coalition building and for exerting a larger, collective voice. However, unexamined use of the term can peripheralize and obscure critical heterogeneity within the APIA community. Finally, this trope contributes to the dominant stereotype that all Asians look alike, which results in various APIA groups experiencing nativism, xenophobia, and racism in confusing and misdirected ways.

Counternarrative 3: Problematic Pan-ethnicity

The model minority trope is all-encompassing, but it does not speak to the diversity of experience within the APIA community, from the trauma experienced by Southeast Asian refugees to the aftereffects of colonialism and militarism experienced by Pacific Islanders. A mass influx of refugees from Cambodia, Laos, and Vietnam after 1975 changed the face of Asian America. Many of these refugees experienced "significant trauma, including torture, witnessed killings, and starvation" (Wong, Kinzie, & Kinzie, 2009, p. 441). Many lived for years in refugee camps abroad and in the United States, resulting in multigenerational trauma. Pacific Islanders, an extremely diverse community, "face incredible challenges in the balancing of American and Pacific Islander belief systems, practices and rules" (Pacific Islander Health Careers Pipeline Program, 2009, p. 8).

Both the forever foreigner and the model minority tropes affect all Asian Americans and Pacific Islanders, in individual and institutionalized ways. However, pan-ethnicity, while a powerful tool, must be balanced with nuance and disaggregation. If college campuses have not disaggregated their data by ethnicity, students can be lost in the context of the dominant, hegemonic myth. At the same time, students from marginalized communities face the burden of demanding equitable programs and policies. The problems of pan-ethnicity demonstrate the importance, yet again, of the centrality of history and context to individual and collective experiences.

What does all this mean for student affairs and higher education practice today? The fact that this history and counternarrative have been hidden affects how we work (or do not work) with APIA students on our campuses. We have been systematically trained to treat APIA students, from a service and dialogue perspective, as White. We discussed this lack of complexity—and the failings in the American education system regarding teaching about race, differences, power, and access—in the first section, along with the fact that APIA students are at risk in multiple directions. The second section, focused on racial formation theory and counterstory-telling, gave us the opportunity to shift the narrative to empower the prac-titioner-ally. We will close with specific recommendations for campuses to consider as they aim for equitable, race-conscious policies that enable all students to succeed.

Recommendations for Campus Practice

We hope that the following questions and suggestions will be the basis of campus conversations among practitioners, administrators, and all those who care about countering hegemonic practices at higher education insti-tutions and ensuring student success. The suggestions are not intended to be comprehensive; they may spark ideas or generate valuable changes or enhancements for your campus context. Most important, we hope this chapter will help you challenge dominant, normative thought about APIA students on your campus and serve as strong advocate-allies.

- **Disaggregation:** The first step toward unmasking the prob-lematic aspects of pan-ethnicity is the disaggregation of data. Knowing who your students are is essential to being able to accurately gauge their needs, offer programs, and enhance campus culture. When students apply to your college or uni-versity, do they have the option of checking off a variety of ethnicities on the application form, or can they only check "Asian"? Collecting data from the moment students consider applying gives you the power to determine programming and resource allocation. Disaggregation allows for distinctions, such as understanding the possible experiential differences between middle-class Indian American students and low-income Bangladeshi American students.

- **Admissions:** Disaggregation is also key to the admissions process. If admissions staff are using a model minority lens through which to understand the diversity of APIA experience, many students will be lost in that filter. A data-driven, race-conscious approach allows for nuance, helping the admissions officer understand the specificity of the second-generation Cambodian American experience in contrast to the fourth-generation Japanese American experience.

- **Outreach and bridge programs:** Knowing the specifics of the members of the local community will enable you to advocate for increased outreach programs to APIA students. Use the quantitative and qualitative data provided in this chapter, and in other excellent research, to make the case for bridge programs that include APIA students, especially those from low-income households and those who are first-generation students. If a campus program uses the term "underrepresented," question whether the program is truly inclusive of all who are underrepresented or the word is being used as a substitute for African American, Latino, and Native American.

- **Academic and career advising:** Do the academic advisors on your campus undergo training at the beginning of each year that prepares them for the multiplicity of APIA student experiences? Recommend it or, if you are an academic advisor, offer a professional development workshop on the topic to your colleagues. Does your career center staff reflect the diversity of the student body or at least have a breadth and depth of cultural competence regarding APIA community complexity and needs? Ask these questions of applicants for career center positions.

- **Staff and faculty:** Do student affairs staff and the faculty at your institution reflect the diversity of the student body? For example, are Asian/Asian American faculty only found in the STEM (science, technology, engineering, and medicine) disciplines? Does your campus offer strong ethnic studies programs, including Asian American studies? If you serve on hiring or curriculum committees, you can ask these questions; they are vitally important to enable institutions to counter hegemony and oppression.

- **Programming:** Particularly for student affairs practitioners, this is a key area in which to offer empowerment-oriented measures. Does programming on your campus mostly rely on events or one-time activities (such as speakers, films, or performers)? Are concrete short- and long-term programs in place that enable APIA students to navigate the institution, access key resources, explore self in context, and free themselves from the chains of U.S. hegemony and imperialism, in which they and their agency are invisible? Are there programs that create the space for APIA and non-APIA students to critically engage with and learn about one another, so as to dismantle systems of oppression? As a practitioner-ally, you have the opportunity to benchmark what your campus is doing against other campuses, celebrate what you are doing well, and continuously evolve and improve, so as not to perpetuate institutional policies and behaviors of dominance that render APIA students at risk.

These questions and suggestions are not intended to be comprehensive. We hope they will spark dialogue and action on your teams, units, and campuses to initiate change.

Connecting the Personal to the Political: The Struggle To Be Practitioner-Allies

This has been a highly personal topic to write about. And, in the same vein that we wrote about students, we could write a parallel chapter on higher education professionals who are APIAs. According to CRT and racial formation, we are also a group at risk. We are often not visible or fully understood. We juggle our ethnic and pan-racial identities. And we bear multiple roles in our relationships with APIA students, and with non-APIA students and colleagues. In our work, we are called upon to be social justice educators about race, class, ethnicity, sexuality, ability, and power, while we ourselves are marginalized by racialized and systemic structures.

We are APIA practitioner-allies who exist in very different spaces. Multiple factors affect our own journeys. One of us works in the Midwest in a multicultural retention and student success department at a private Catholic university. The other works at a private secular university on the West Coast, in an APIA empowerment department that focuses on cross-cultural engagement. There are rewards and challenges in both environments. Both of us are using all the recommendations we have offered in this chapter, because we have seen that they are effective. The chapter, while grounded in research, is not solely about the theoretical; it is also a reflection of our own complicated lived experiences. We both must navigate multiple processes of "deracination," in which some question our racialized experiences and identities. On both campuses, the APIA experience is often marginalized or miscast as a White experience. In departments and committees where it really matters (admissions, financial aid, curriculum development), APIA students often are not considered when decisions about minority students or students of color are made.

At our institutions, we try to draw attention to the risks our APIA students face, advocate for their needs, and offer viable programs that benefit them. At the same time, we invest in challenging the universities in which we serve, while we face the same risk our students do every day. Being a practitioner-ally to one another, supporting and empowering one another, is just as important as advocating for students and changing campus culture. Delving into our own hidden histories motivates us to counter the master narrative in our daily lives and invest in our abilities to serve as critical practitioner-allies for all students. In our cases, turning the intimately personal into the deeply political is a potent source of empowerment that sustains us and inspires us in our journeys in higher education.

Conclusion

In this chapter, we offered empirical evidence demonstrating how APIA college students are at risk in multiple directions. In addition, we highlighted the ways higher education institutions are currently failing their APIA students because their practices and policies are guided by dominant myths and hegemonic assumptions. We have attempted to move beyond problematizing the APIA experience by reframing and repositioning race and community construction and shifting/countering the narrative. By integrating two potent theoretical frameworks—racial formation and CRT—we are offering tools that might help you as a practitioner-ally in this underresearched, underserved community. Developing a keen understanding of the American racial project, as well as of the importance of history and context, is essential to being a practitioner-ally.

At times, dominance can seem overwhelming and efforts to counter it futile. However, incorporating boundary-crossing theories and the power of counter-storytelling into our student affairs and higher education practice can be revelatory and empowering. Furthermore, taking action by engaging practical questions and recommendations that can be immediately implemented on your campus can lead to much-needed change. As our field continues to evolve and increase its responsiveness, our students and our future demand systemic change. You are a part of that journey.

References

Alvarez, A. N. (2002). Racial identity and Asian Americans: Supports and challenges. In M. McEwen, C. M. Kodama, A. N. Alvarez, S. Lee, & C. T. H. Liang (Eds.), *Working with Asian American college students* (New directions for student services, no. 97, pp. 33–44). San Francisco, CA: Jossey-Bass.

Alvarez, A. N. (2009). Racism: "It isn't fair." In N. Tewari & A. N. Alvarez (Eds.), *Asian American psychology: Current perspectives*. New York, NY: Lawrence Erlbaum Associates.

Alvarez, A. N., & Helms, J. E. (2001). Racial identity and reflected appraisals as influences on Asian Americans' racial adjustment. *Cultural Diversity and Ethnic Minority Psychology. 7*(3), 217–231.

Alvarez, A. N., & Yeh, T. L. (1999). Asian Americans in college: A racial identity perspective. In D. Sandhu (Ed.), *Asian and Pacific Islander Americans: Issues and concerns for counseling and psychotherapy* (pp. 105–119). Commack, NY: Nova Science.

Ancis, J., Sedlacek, W., & Mohr, J. (2000). Student perceptions of campus cultural climate by race. *Journal of Counseling and Development, 78*(2), 180–185.

Astin, A. W. (1982). *Minorities in American higher education.* San Francisco, CA: Jossey-Bass.

Bell, D. A. (1980). *Race, racism and American law* (2nd ed.). Boston, MA: Little, Brown.

Chan, S. (1991). *Asian Americans: An interpretive history.* New York, NY: Twayne Publishers.

Choi, J. L., Rogers, J. R., & Werth, J. L., Jr. (2007). Suicide-risk assessment with Asian American college students: A culturally informed perspective. *The Counseling Psychologist, 20*(10), 1–31.

College Board and National Commission on Asian American and Pacific Islander Research in Education. (2008). *Asian Americans and Pacific Islanders; facts, not fiction: Setting the record straight.* Retrieved from http://professionals.collegeboard.com/profdownload/08-0608-AAPI.pdf

Delgado, R. (1987). The ethereal scholar: Do critical legal studies have what minorities want? *Harvard Civil Rights-Civil Liberties Law Review, 22,* 301–322.

Escueta, E., & O'Brien, E. (1995). Asian Americans in higher education: Trends and issues. In D. Nakanishi & T. T. Nishida (Eds.), *The Asian American educational experience: A sourcebook for teachers and students* (pp. 259–272). New York, NY: Routledge.

Junn, J. (2007). From coolie to model minority: U.S. immigration policy and the construction of racial identity. *Du Bois Review, 4*(2), 355–373.

Kim, C. (1999). The racial triangulation of Asian Americans. *Politics and Society, 27*(1), 105–138.

Kurashige, L. Y. (2001). Agency, resistance, and Manzanar protest. *Pacific Historical Review, 70*(3), 387–418.

Ladson-Billings, G., & Tate, W.F., IV. (1995). Toward a Critical Race Theory of education. *Teachers College Record, 97*(1), 47–68.

LeSure, G. (1994, August 22). *Ethnic differences and the effects of racism on college adjustment.* Paper presented at the annual convention of the American Psychological Association, Toronto.

Lowe, S. M. (2009). A frank discussion on Asian Americans and their academic and career development. In N. Tewari & A. N. Alvarez (Eds.), *Asian American psychology: Current perspectives* (pp. 463–481). New York, NY: Lawrence Erlbaum Associates.

Mack, D., Tucker, T., & Cha, S. (2000, August 4–8). *Inter-ethnic relations on campus: The color of hatred*. Paper presented at the annual conference of the American Psychological Association, Washington, DC.

McEachern, A. G., & Kenny, M. C. (1999). Sexual abuse in Asian and Pacific Islander populations: Current research and counseling implications. In D. S. Sandhu (Ed.), *Asian and Pacific Islander Americans: Issues and concerns for counseling and psychotherapy* (pp. 301–318). Commack, NY: Nova Science Publishers, Inc.

Museus, S. D., & Kiang, P. N. (2009). Deconstructing the model minority myth and how it contributes to the invisible minority reality in higher education research. In S. D. Museus (Ed.), *Conducting research on Asian Americans in higher education* (New directions for institutional research, no. 142, pp. 5–15). San Francisco, CA: Jossey-Bass.

Ng, J. C., Lee, S. S., & Pak, Y. K. (2007). Contesting the model minority and perpetual foreigner stereotypes: A critical review of literature on Asian Americans in education. *Review of research in education, 31*, 95–130.

Ngo, B., & Lee, S. J. (2007). Complicating the image of model minority success: A review of Southeast Asian American education. *Review of Educational Research, 77*(4), 415–453.

Ogbu, J. U. (1978). *Minority education and caste: The American system in cross-cultural perspective*. New York, NY: Academic Press.

Omi, M., & Winant, H. (1994). *Racial formation in the United States: From the 1960s to the 1990s*. New York, NY: Routledge.

Pacific Islander Health Careers Pipeline Program. (2009). Orange County Asian and Pacific Islander Community Alliance. Retrieved from http://www.ocapica.org/documents/PipelineReport.pdf

Petersen, W. (1966, January 9). Success story, Japanese-American style. *New York Times*, pp. 20–43.

Sekhon, V. (2003). The civil rights of "others": Antiterrorism, the Patriot

Act, and Arab and South Asian American rights in post-9/11 American society. *Texas Forum on Civil Liberties & Civil Rights, 8*(1), 117–148.

Solórzano, D. G., and Yosso, T. J. (2002). Critical race methodology: Counter-storytelling as an analytical framework for education research. *Qualitative Inquiry, 8*(23), 23–44.

Success story of one minority group in U.S. (1966, December 26). *U.S. News and World Report,* pp. 73–78.

Takaki, R. (1993). *A different mirror: A history of multicultural America.* Boston, MA: Little, Brown.

Takaki, R. (1998). *Strangers from a different shore: A history of Asian Americans.* Boston, MA: Little, Brown.

Tate, W. F., IV. (1997). Critical race theory and education: History, theory, and implications. *Review of Research in Education, 22,* 195–247.

Tewari, N. (2009). Seeking, receiving, and providing culturally competent mental health services: A focus on Asian Americans. In N. Tewari & A. N. Alvarez (Eds.), *Asian American psychology: Current perspectives* (pp. 575–606). New York, NY: Lawrence Erlbaum Associates.

UCLA Asian American Studies Center, Census Information Center. (2006). Pacific Islanders lagging behind in higher educational attainment. Retrieved from http://www.aasc.ucla.edu/archives/PIEducationAttainBrief.pdf

Wong, E. C., Kinzie, J. D., and Kinzie, J. M. (2009). Stress, refugees, and trauma. In N. Tewari & A. N. Alvarez (Eds.), *Asian American psychology: Current perspectives* (pp. 441–462). New York, NY: Lawrence Erlbaum Associates.

Wu, F. H. (2002). *Yellow: Race in America beyond Black and White.* New York, NY: Basic Books.

Yeh, T. L. (2002). Asian American college students who are educationally at risk. In M. K. McEwen, C. M. Kodama, A. N. Alvarez, C. Liang, & S. Lee (Eds.), *Working with Asian American college students* (New directions for student services, no. 97, pp. 61–72). San Francisco, CA: Jossey-Bass.

Yeh, T. L. (2004). Issues of college persistence between Asian and Asian Pacific American students. *Journal of College Student Retention, 6*(1), 81–96.

Yosso, T. J., Parker, L., Solorzano, D. G., & Lynn, M. (2004). From Jim Crow to affirmative action and back again: A critical race discussion of racialized rationales and access to higher education. *Review of Research in Education, 28*, 1–25.

CHAPTER THREE

Asian American
Identity Consciousness
A Polycultural Model

Mamta Motwani Accapadi

An understanding of the racial identity exploration process is fundamental to the development of authentic, inclusive environments for
students of color (Patton, McEwen, Rendón, & Howard-Hamilton, 2007).
Using racial identity exploration as the central point of entry for student
empowerment, educators can create programs that positively affect the
student's experience (Baxter Magolda, 2003). A comprehensive body of
research has contributed to an understanding of the identity exploration
journey for Asian Americans (Alvarez & Kimura, 2001; Chen, LePhuoc,
Guzman, Rude, & Dodd, 2006; Ibrahim, Ohnishi, & Sandhu, 1997; Kim,
2001; Koshy, 2001; Min & Kim, 1999; Sandhu, 1997; Teranishi, 2002;
Tse, 1999; Uba, 2002; Yeh & Huang, 1996). These studies have repeatedly

emphasized the importance of recognizing a unique, complex, and multi-faceted Asian American identity exploration process, and they are a solid foundation from which we can engage in a deeper inquiry of how Asian American students negotiate identities as people of color in relation to the other social identities that inform their identity exploration journey. In this chapter, I propose an Asian American Identity Consciousness Model informed by Critical Race Theory and polyculturalism. I coined the acronym APIDA (Asian/Pacific Islander/Desi American) to be more inclusive of the diversity of Asian American communities. I introduced this acronym at the National Conference on Race and Ethnicity in 2006, after having used it on my own campus.

The most significant, transformative, and empowering experience for me as an undergraduate student was my involvement in the Indian Students Association (ISA). Because there were no formal support infrastructures for APIDA students when I was in school, ISA became my home. I turned to ISA leaders for guidance on how to navigate poor academic advising; to understand how to get involved on campus; for counseling when I was ready to quit school because I could not handle the pressure of college. ISA was where I felt whole, normal, and connected. Because of the profound impact of ISA on my life, I eventually became president of the organization and found myself in the student leader milieu. Before that, I had not considered my involvement with campus diversity committees, program planning groups, or pan-Asian student meetings as leadership, or even significant developmental experiences.

By the time I entered a master's program in student affairs, I was very clear about who I wanted to be and the role I wanted to play in our profession: I wanted to be the person who understood APIDA student issues and helped students dream beyond their self-imposed, identity-attributed limitations. I wanted to be the administrator who encouraged APIDA students to think beyond being the "cultural entertainment" and to build on the "food, dance, and festival" roles Asian American students and groups were narrowly pigeon-holed into fulfilling for the campus at the expense of their own growth. Even though my mentors were outstanding, particularly the women of color, there was a significant gap in their understanding of Asian American issues through a critical lens. I wanted to be the advisor I didn't have when I was an undergraduate.

Reflecting on my career in student affairs over the past 15 years, while I hold optimism in my heart, I am dissatisfied with the progress we have made in authentically serving APIDA students in higher education. I maintain that one does not need to be of Asian descent to understand and serve APIDA communities; however, I believe we need to start by authentically understanding Asian American identity. The literature on APIDAs in higher education is limited (Museus & Kiang, 2009). A comparison of special issue research monographs on Asian Americans shows that we continue to have the same conversations, raise the same concerns, dispel the same myths, and offer very similar recommendations about how best to serve APIDAs in higher education (McEwen, Kodama, Alvarez, Lee, & Liang, 2002; Museus, 2009b). We need to serve APIDA students in higher education with a deeper, more critical understanding of their identities and identity-relevant needs. It is my hope that we can cultivate such an understanding so student affairs professionals can build more authentic relationships with the APIDA students they serve.

As the landscape of higher education diversifies, it is increasingly necessary to understand the topography if we are to meet the needs of today's college students. Many universities have made commitments to serve a diversifying student body through inclusion initiatives, yet APIDA voices are often overlooked or marginally considered in the Black-White paradigm that still operates on our campuses and in our communities (Bonner, Jennings, Chen, & Singh, 2006; Chen et al., 2006; Chew-Ogi & Ogi, 2002; Green & Kim, 2005; Inkelas, 2006; Lee, 2006; Okihiro, 1994; Teranishi, 2002). As we develop an inclusion-centered approach to higher education, we need a deeper dialogue on the identity exploration process of Asian American students.

My goal in this chapter is to provide a polycultural perspective for APIDA identity. The first section describes a framework for discussing Asian America through the exploration of terms such as *racial identity*, *ethnic identity*, and *Asian American*, which provide us with a common lexicon. I also discuss the complications associated with the term Asian American. In the second section, I take a deeper look at various approaches to Asian American identity development—particularly the operating stage models that examine racial or ethnic identity—and offer insight into the limitations of stage models as a framework for understanding Asian American identity. The third section presents an alternative, polycultural model for Asian American identity consciousness grounded in Critical Race Theory. The chapter concludes with implications for student affairs practitioners.

Who Gets To Be Asian American?

History of the Term

The term Asian American has been widely used to describe a diverse group of communities that have differing political histories, immigration histories, religious practices, linguistic roots, physical features, and cultural norms. Because of this diversity, it is critical that we understand the complexities behind the ownership of the term. The idea of Asian America was born out of a denunciation of the term *Oriental*, which was perceived during the civil rights movement as loaded with oppression and racism (Kibria, 1998; Shankar & Srikanth, 1998), and was used as a pejorative term to describe people of Asian descent, primarily Chinese and Japanese Americans, who made up the largest ethnic communities of Asian America before the 1965 Immigration Reform Act. In this context, Asian American emerged as a term of positive self-recognition and empowerment, representing the coalescence of communities on whom the term Oriental historically had been placed (Shankar & Srikanth, 1998).

Asian America Today

Today, Asian America is ethnically diverse, representing multiple national identities. According to the U.S. Census (2010), there are more than 14.7 million Asians in the United States. Asians comprise only 5% of the U.S. population, but they are one of the fastest increasing racial groups. In 2010, an additional 2.6 million (0.9%) identified as Asian in combination with another race. Within Asian America, the largest and fastest growing ethnic communities are Indian, Chinese, Korean, and Vietnamese. Because of its vast diversity, Asian America is commonly disaggregated, for dialogue purposes, into four major categories: (1) East Asian, which includes people of Chinese, Korean, Japanese, and Taiwanese descent; (2) Southeast Asian, which includes people of Vietnamese, Filipino, Thai, Cambodian, and Laotian descent; (3) South Asian, which includes people of Bangladeshi, Bhutanese, Sri Lankan, Pakistani, and Indian descent; and (4) Pacific Islander, which includes people of Native Hawaiian, Samoan, Tongan, Guamanian, and Fijian descent (Lai & Arguelles, 2003). (However, Spickard and Fong (1995) argued that Pacific Islander is an artificial collection of groups rather than a single ethnic group.) Although these categories do not encompass all Asian American communities, they offer insight into the complexity of Asian America (Lai & Arguelles, 2003).

Complexities of Nomenclature

Given the vast growth of these communities since the inception of the term Asian American, numerous complications are associated with the politics of identity nomenclature. In the United States, "Asian American" conjures a vision of a person with a particular phenotype, largely attributed to people of East Asian descent. Song (1998) explained,

> It should be axiomatic that the identity of Asian America has evolved historically from a set of structural relationships with no preconceived notion of who belongs and who does not. There is no one group that fits naturally into such a category for there is nothing natural, meaning essential or transhistorical, about the category Asian America. (p. 80)

Shankar and Srikanth (1998) proposed the notion of a *felt identity* to describe and define Asian America; that is, because of the history surrounding the formation of Asian America as a descriptive category, certain communities feel Asian American and others do not (p. 3). The notion of Asian American felt identity as one of consciousness rather than ethnic affiliation provides insight into why certain communities feel included in the dialogue on Asian America while other communities feel excluded.

Researching Asian America

Current research on Asian American identity exploration mimics and perpetuates the complexities associated with discussing Asian America. Most research studies on Asian American communities have privileged specific ethnic groups, notably East Asian American communities, and offered blanket recommendations assumed to be appropriate for all Asian Americans. For example, Yeh and Huang's (1996) study of ethnic identity development among Asian American college students was based on findings from a respondent pool in which 85% of the participants were of East Asian descent, 5% of Southeast Asian descent, and 1% of Indian descent. Similarly, in Tse's (1999) study of ethnic identity exploration of Asian Americans, of the 39 participants, only 1 was of Indian descent and 4 were of Filipino descent. In their study on Asian American academic persistence, Gloria and Ho (2003) surveyed 160 undergraduate students, of whom 83% were of East Asian descent, with no South Asian participants. Multiple studies have been conducted with specific Asian American ethnic communities or with a skewed sampling of such communities (Lew, Chang, & Wang, 2005; Pyke & Dang, 2003; Tuan, 2002).

Of utmost importance in considering and producing research about Asian American identity exploration is a clear recognition and intention of pan-ethnicity. While no participant sample pool can (or should be expected to) fully capture the essence of Asian America, skewed samples— those that exclude or marginalize Southeast Asian, South Asian, Pacific Islander, and multiracial experiences and voices—misrepresent Asian America and oversimplify the heterogeneity of the communities under the pan-Asian American umbrella. While these research studies on Asian American communities inspire a dialogue that gives voice to a historically overlooked racial category, they also (1) perpetuate the notion of who gets to be Asian American; (2) silence the experiences of marginalized communities within Asian America; and (3) impose recommendations for practice that might not be broadly applicable to multiple Asian American communities. As an alternative, researchers need to offer more specificity, clarity, and discussion about the implications of their participants' ethnicities and how they inform the outcomes of the studies. Naming studies is particularly important—as researchers, we must "call it what it is," intentionally disaggregating communities in our research.

Community-specific studies highlight the complexities of the Asian America category. These studies are critical, because they expand the idea of what is commonly understood by the term Asian American. One example is Ibrahim, Ohnishi, and Sandhu's (1997) study on Asian American identity, with specific attention to South Asian Americans. The specificity of this study allowed for deeper examination of identity formation in relation to shared cultural norms, geography, and immigrant histories. Similarly, Nadal's (2004) Filipino American Identity Development Model considered the uniqueness of Filipino identity formation, which is rooted in Spanish colonial influence, aboriginal roots, and sociocultural differences from other Asian American communities. Again, this study offered a detailed perspective on a community whose needs are often overlooked within Asian America. Community-specific studies provide the data we need to recognize and serve a diverse Asian America that includes multigenerational communities, multiracial/multiethnic communities, and communities with different socioeconomic conditions (Bemak & Chung, 1997; Das & Kemp, 1997; Fujiwara, 2008; Mathews 2000; Mitra, 2008; Teranishi, 2002). These studies allow us to tailor interventions and create specific systems to support and honor the diverse mosaic of Asian America, while underscoring the importance of disaggregating APIDA communities.

Just as it would be misleading to assume that a large-scale study of South Asians, Southeast Asians, or Pacific Islanders would reflect universal trends in the pan-Asian American community, it is misleading to think that large-scale studies that focus on East Asian communities reflect universal trends in Asian America. "When dominant narratives are presented as objective or neutral, they customarily become the presumptively natural and correct frame of reference" (Uba, 2002, p. 94). Although Uba made this statement to articulate the importance of unexamined narratives in dominant spaces, a similar dynamic is created when we present an East Asian-centered narrative as the pan-Asian American, objective, and natural frame of reference for Asian America. To truly respect the diversity of the communities that make up Asian America, we must honor the complexities of the contexts that inform identity formation, while incorporating those complexities into the dialogue.

Asian American Identity Development

The exploration of ethnic and racial identity plays a significant role in the holistic identity formation process for people of color (Phinney, 1990). Ethnic identity has been defined as the relationship with one's cultural identity; it relies on history, cultural traditions, rituals, language, and other attributes that a group of people share (Alvarez & Helms, 2001). Racial identity, on the other hand, has an expanded purview; it incorporates the acknowledgement, recognition, and impact of oppression based on race as the means by which one comes to formulate one's identity (Alvarez & Helms, 2001). In Asian American communities, the heavy intersection between racial identity and ethnic identity must be taken into account. According to Sodowsky, Kwan, and Pannu (1995),

> Racial identity is (a) based on a sociopolitical model of oppression, (b) based on a socially constructed definition of race, and (c) concerned with how individuals abandon the disenfranchisement and develop respectful attitudes toward their racial group. On the other hand, ethnic identity (a) concerns one's attachment to, sense of belonging to, and identification with one's ethnic group members (e.g., Japanese, Vietnamese, Indian) and with one's ethnic culture; (b) does not have a theoretical emphasis on oppression and racism; but (c) may include the

prejudices and cultural pressures that ethnic individuals experience when their ways of life come into conflict with those of the White dominant group. (p. 133)

Being able to understand how people of color negotiate their ethnic and racial identities, and how those identities inform and influence one another, is critical for higher education professionals. Although identity development models appear to be linear and positivistic in nature, it is essential to remember that these models merely serve as tools for inquiry and understanding, not diagnosis. The following sections offer an overview of Asian American identity development literature.

Identity Development Theory

The models described so far offer a point of entry for the exploration of Asian American identity, but they were not created with Asian Americans as the focal community. Particularly for Asian Americans, the ownership and impact of ethnic and racial identity is intertwined—meaning that a discussion of ethnic identity development without the consideration of the impact of racism or a discussion of racial identity development without the consideration of the sacrifice of one's ethnic affiliations is incomplete. This section explores different frameworks that have been developed with Asian American ethnic/racial identity as the focal point.

Acculturation Theory

Sue & Sue's (1971) model of acculturation proposed that Asian Americans fell into one of three categories: (1) *traditionalist* describes a person who values traditional ethnic values and practices, typically characterized by first generation immigrants; (2) *marginal* refers to those who reject Asian cultural norms and strive to fit into White society; and (3) *Asian American* refers to those who negotiate a balance between their Asian values and traditions and western community norms (Sue & Sue, 1971). Although it focused on people of Chinese descent, this model opened a powerful dialogue about the identity struggles Asian Americans might experience. The model's acknowledgment of the tension that emerges as a person tries to navigate, negotiate, and honor family values is a significant factor in Asian American identity development. However, the model oversimplified the identity development process and assumed that these characteristics are separate from one another. Under this model, a person is forced to choose between the values associated with ethnic identity and the values of the dominant culture—there is no category for integrating ethnic identity with mainstream norms. And this model contributes to existing stereotypes of Asian Americans (Yeh & Huang, 1996): The labeling assumes White identity as the norm and tracks Asian American identity development in relation to White norms.

Identity Development Model

Jean Kim (2001) offered a 5-stage model of Asian American identity development. This model was originally developed as the outcome of Kim's dissertation, which looked at the identity development of Japanese American women in 1981. As with any stage model, Kim's model is not without flaws; however, it used the experiences of Asian Americans as its foundation and is widely applied as a tool for understanding Asian American identity. Each stage represents a "social consciousness" about being Asian American. The first stage, *ethnic awareness*, is the recognition of one's ethnic identity, which comes from being around one's social communities, exposure to cultural activities, and ethnic group involvement. The second stage, *White identification*, manifests itself with the individual's realization of being different from his or her peers, which may lead APIDA students to "whitewash" their identity with the goal of fitting in and being accepted. During this stage, Asian Americans typically adopt White norms as their own and may be inclined to suggest that racism and racial differences do not exist.

The third stage, *awakening to social and political consciousness*, marks a dramatic shift of consciousness when APIDAs become conscious of their political and social identity beyond the "White lens." Before this stage, Asian Americans who deny the existence of racism tend to develop a sense of self-hatred and blame themselves for negative experiences they have encountered in school or society. This stage marks the awareness of racial dynamics and, more important, awareness of institutionalized White racism. In this stage, White norms are rejected in favor of building coalitions with other oppressed racial groups. The fourth stage, *redirection to an Asian American consciousness*, takes the racial identity exploration a step further; it is marked by a search for histories not taught and immersion in the Asian American experience (not to be confused with the cultural heritage experience of stage 1). In this stage, students usually become angry as they learn more about the historic oppression of Asian Americans and seek a peer group of others who are asking the same questions and experiencing similar emotions. The fifth stage, *incorporation*, is the result of a sense of resolution with one's Asian American identity. In this stage, the person reaches a comfort level with his or her racial identity and is able to integrate this identity with other social identities.

A major strength of Kim's Asian American Identity Development Model (AAID) is the coupling of ethnic and racial identities in one model, which illustrates how intertwined and yet dramatically different these two identities can be. Kim noted that all Asian ethnic groups experience racism based on their ethnic stereotypes; this is an important and necessary observation in considering Asian American identity development. Ironically, the AAID can be criticized in the same area. Kim claimed that "all Asian ethnic groups are perceived and treated from a common set of racial prejudices and stereotypes. For the most part, we do not accord different status or treat an Asian person differently depending on the ethnic group (Chinese, Japanese, Korean, Vietnamese, and the like) he or she represents" (Kim, 2001, p. 82). I disagree. I believe that different Asian ethnic groups are, in fact, treated differently, as illustrated in the differing media stereotypes of South Asians, Pacific Islanders, and multiracial Asian Americans compared with those of East Asian Americans. For example, it is highly unlikely that a person of Pakistani descent would be called a "Chink" or that a person of Tongan descent would be mistaken for Chinese. Kim's statement reflects a narrow interpretation and conceptualization of Asian America, which inaccurately assumes that a common set of racial prejudices binds Asian Americans.

Critique of Stage Models

Stage models such as Kim's AAID model have contributed to the understanding of ethnic and racial identity formation in Asian Americans. These models have expanded the identity exploration paradigm to include historically excluded and often marginalized experiences of people of color. Kim's model is useful because it considers ethnic and racial identities in one framework. Although stage models have transformed the way we examine identity exploration, they have some limitations.

First, by design and description, these models suggest a linear progression of consciousness—one cannot progress to a higher stage in a model without passing through the earlier stages. The inherent structure of stage models does not allow for flexibility in the human experience. If we were to consider how a multiracial or multiethnic Asian American (of mixed Asian ethnic background) might enter a stage model, it is unfair to assume that the point of entry to identity exploration would be at the stage of ethnic awareness. Multiracial or multiethnic Asian Americans might consider their racial identities before considering their ethnic identities, especially if their home environments contain no ethnic markers. A multiethnic Asian American might have a powerful Asian American consciousness without any connection to a sense of ethnic awareness, yet the stage model implies a sequential progression. This is unrealistic when we are dealing with the infinite possibilities of consciousness formation.

The configuration of stage models suggests that each stage functions as an independent and isolated descriptor of consciousness that does not overlap, or even occur simultaneously, with others. Thus, the model assumes that a person cannot be in multiple stages at one time. Yet, in Kim's 5-stage AAID model, individuals could be completely content with their Asian American identity in the ethnic awareness stage, and also be in the stage of incorporation by integrating that contentment with the rest of their social identities. As the model is structured, however, this multiple consciousness and dual-stage existence is not a viable option, as it is presented as a sequential process.

Second, racial and ethnic identity development stage models assume that individuals enter the identity exploration process through the lens of ethnic or racial identity first, or that they strive to see themselves only in the context of their racialized identity. In fact, the final stages of many models have names that suggest that once people have explored their racial or ethnic identity, they can incorporate it with their other social identities; for example, Integrative Awareness (Helms) and Incorporation (Kim). The inherent problem with this assumption is that it ignores the possibility of someone being a member of multiple oppressed groups and overlooks the likelihood that one is simultaneously negotiating multiple identity development processes.

The stage model infrastructure assumes an evolutionary trajectory of self-awareness; that is, that someone who is in a "higher" stage is more keenly self-aware and evolved than someone who is in stage 1 of a racial identity development experience. The idea of a vertical continuum of consciousness, with a clear top and bottom, is perpetuated in stage models.

Despite the shortcomings of stage models, they may still apply in theoretical spaces with acknowledgment of their limitations. If the models were not intended to be linear, could the stages be presented in a different order? Could the stage models be presented in random sequence and achieve similar insights into the racial identity development processes of Asian Americans? Even when we discuss stage models, we typically offer examples that take us through these models in a linear, age-progression fashion, associating certain stages with early childhood and others with school-age experiences. Although we remind ourselves that the paradigm is not intended to be linear, its impact assumes and presumes linearity while oversimplifying the identity development process.

Asian American Identity Consciousness: Refocusing Our Lens

Understanding the development of identity among Asian Americans is a central factor in supporting APIDA students on college campuses. To gain a clearer insight into the identity exploration journey, it is important to acknowledge multiple Asian Americas. I offer a point of entry approach to Asian American identity consciousness that is built on two foundations: Critical Race Theory and polyculturalism.

Critical Race Theory

Critical Race Theory (CRT) allows us to recenter the Asian American identity journey, with Asian Americans as the primary negotiators of their identities. As we strive to understand the factors that shape Asian American identity, it is helpful to draw from CRT to challenge the dominant story. CRT challenges dominant "claims of neutrality, objectivity, color blindness, and meritocracy" (Matsuda, Lawrence, Delgado, & Crenshaw, 1993, p.6) and allows us to resituate Asian American identity by drawing on narrative voices from the communities that actually make up Asian America. Legal scholar Robert Chang provided an expanded application of CRT and offered the following guiding principles (Chang, 1999):

- The Asian American experience is unique and situated differently than that of other oppressed groups. By excluding the Asian American perspective from the greater narrative of groups that have experienced oppression, we deepen the oppression of Asian Americans.
- Asian American narratives and lived experiences are critical in challenging the dominant paradigm.
- The narrative of race must extend beyond the Black-White binary.
- These principles offer a general infrastructure on which we can construct a frame to discuss Asian American identity. Additionally, the broad tenets of CRT allow us to examine how systemic racism has resulted in the oppression of people of color, how racism intersects with our other identities, and how we can move toward a socially just society by dismantling systems of oppression (Delgado, 1995; Matsuda et al., 1993; Teranishi, Behringer, Grey, & Parker, 2009; Yosso, 2006).

Polyculturalism

First described by historian Robin Kelley (1999), polyculturalism is a principle that identifies anti-racism rather than diversity as its core value. Vijay Prashad (2001) noted,

> Polyculturalism, unlike multiculturalism, assumes that people live coherent lives that are made up of a host of lineages—the task of the historian is not to carve out the lineages but to make sense of how people live culturally dynamic lives. Polyculturalism is a ferocious engagement with the political world of culture, a painful embrace of the skin and all of its contradictions. (xii)

Polyculturalism is distinct from multiculturalism in that it requires us to understand the ways in which our cultural histories intersect, draw parallels in the experiences and social location of communities, and sustain an emancipatory, anti-racist educational effort. Whereas multiculturalism stops at cultural representation and diversity awareness, polyculturalism challenges us to examine how the intersections of our identities perpetuate the oppression of certain groups and the dominance of other groups. Prashad emphasized that "culture cannot be bounded and people cannot be asked to respect 'culture' as if it were an artifact, without life or complexity. Social interaction and struggle produces cultural worlds, and these are in constant, fraught formation" (2001, p. 148). Polycultural theory complements CRT by emphasizing the dismantling of a dominant narrative and the need for more stories to be told from subordinated communities.

Point of Entry Model

Many scholars have noted that identity formation is multidimensional, complex, and contextual (Dhingra, 2007; hooks, 1990; Okazaki, Lee, & Sue, 2007; Root, 2002). To date, the models for understanding Asian American identity force us to examine identity formation through a narrow ethnic/cultural lens, as a Black-White racial binary, or on a continuum that assumes Asian Americans aspire to or negotiate Whiteness and White racism (Asher, 2001; Kim, 2001; Koshy, 2001; Mitra, 2008; Sandhu, 1997). We need to move to a conceptual identity model that is dynamic, is informed by interdisciplinary scholarship, acknowledges multiple heterogeneous Asian Americas, and honors the intersection of racial identity with other social identities—we need an "Asian Americanist" approach (Okazaki et al., 2007).

Departing from the stage model paradigm used to explain racial identity exploration and drawing from factor-based approaches to identity exploration, such as Horse's American Indian Identity (2001) and Wijeyesinghe's Factor Model of Multiracial Identity (2001), I propose a model for Asian American identity consciousness. This model allows for the possibility of multiple points of entry (or exit) on one's racial identity journey, which is fluid, continuous, and dynamic. Like Horse's and Wijeyesinghe's models, this one offers factors that inform one's racial identity consciousness, with the understanding that the racial identity consciousness is also informing one's relationship with one's other identities. This model can be presented in any order; it is nonlinear and nonhierarchical by design. It is grounded in the idea that individuals can begin the journey of racial identity exploration by engaging in their other identities. For example, a person could stumble onto his or her racial identity process while exploring gender identity and expression. By using this framework for racial identity exploration, we can consider multiple factors that influence this identity while acknowledging that some people may not consider racial identity to be a primary, salient identity.

Figure 1

Point of Entry Model for Asian American Identity Consciousness

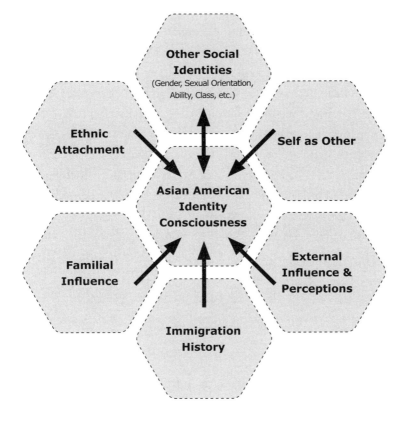

The Point of Entry Model of Asian American Identity Consciousness (POE Model) offers multiple factors that might have an effect on Asian American identity formation, such as the following.

Ethnic Attachment

A person's relationship to ethnic identity plays an integral role in the formation of Asian American identity. Ethnic markers—including religious practice, cultural norms, and language—influence attachment to one's ethnic (and subsequently racial) identity (Dhingra, 2010; Kim, 2001; Shankar & Balgopal, 2001). Referring to the notion of a felt Asian

American identity, one's ethnic attachment might encourage affiliation with a pan-Asian American identity or it could deter one from identifying as Asian American. For example, Filipinos' attachment to ethnic identity might draw them closer to the indigenous and Spanish roots of their culture and traditions (Nadal, 2004). In his study of Filipino students' experiences, Teranishi noted that some Filipino students might not relate to the term Asian American because "they don't have characteristics of regular Asians" (2002, p. 15). For a person of Filipino descent to feel Asian American, the Filipino experience has to be embraced through some process as authentically Asian American. Similarly, a person of Asian descent might affiliate strongly with his or her religious identity as a Muslim, which has a strong influence on identity construction but is not part of the dominant Asian American narrative (Mohammad-Arif, 2000; Patel, 2007). Alternatively, Asian Americans who are adopted by non-Asian American parents may have varying levels of exposure to an Asian ethnic experience (Bergquist, 2006; Louie, 2009). Thus, one's immersion (or lack of immersion) in ethnic identity, and how that identity is positioned in Asian America, shapes how likely one might be to explore an Asian American identity.

Self as Other

Physical appearance can be a strong point of entry into the Asian American identity journey. For many Asian Americans, phenotypic features (and how they are treated owing to the stereotypes that come with those features) define their race consciousness. Multiple studies have been done on how Asian American women have internalized White standards of beauty as universal standards (Kaw, 1993; Mok, 1998; Ting & Hwang, 2007). Internalized racism also forces people to engage with their racial identity. In a different context, many South Asians do not "look Asian" and are often not included in pan-Asian settings because of the idea that "Asian" implies a certain physical appearance that does not include brown skin (Kibria, 1998; Song, 1998). The repeated questioning of the authenticity of South Asians as Asians eventually influences how they choose their own identities as Asian Americans. Similarly, multiracial Asian Americans who think they do not look "Asian enough" or look "too Asian" might also grapple with their Asian American identity.

Familial Influence

Family plays a fundamental role as a POE into Asian American identity exploration, because of the deep personal influence that naturally emerges from a family structure (Aguilar-San Juan, 1997; Chou & Feagin, 2008; Espiritu, 2001; Kim, 2001; Sue & Sue, 1971). People receive messages about their identities and sense of self through their family members (nuclear and extended), and they internalize those messages; this, in turn, affects how they choose to identify as Asian Americans. An Asian American adoptee with White parents has a completely different context of familial influence than a third generation Asian American who lives in an extended family household. The messages people receive about their Asian American identity can be positive, negative, or ambivalent—they all shape the nature of a person's identity exploration process.

Immigration History

The circumstances through which people are labeled Asian American are tied to their immigration history and how far removed they are from that experience. Common in first generation immigrants who arrived in the late 1960s and early 1970s, the attachment to the possibility of "going back home" precipitated a natural detachment from fully participating in the American experience. Even when faced with racism, they likely absorbed the shock and internalized the perpetual foreigner stereotype. Conversely, second, third, and future generation Asian Americans live as people-of-color-Americans-of-Asian-descent, reacting to the perpetual foreigner stereotype, "passing" for another racial identity to avoid dealing with Asian-specific racism, or choosing other alternatives that result in a completely different perspective on Asian American identity (Ibrahim et al., 1997; Sandhu, 1997).

When we consider the circumstances of a person's immigration history, we must take into account a broad spectrum: sugar plantation laborers, picture brides, indentured laborers from other colonial settlements, political refugees, academic professionals, information technology workers, sweatshop workers, and others (Espiritu, 2008; Fujiwara, 2008; Okihiro, 1994). Through a polycultural lens, we can better articulate the circumstances and lived experiences of Asian Americans in the context of their immigration history and better critique the systems of dominance that disadvantage certain Asian American communities.

External Influences and Perceptions

External factors that affect racial identity exploration include experiences of racism, White perceptions and treatment of Asian Americans, other people of color's perceptions and treatment of Asian Americans, and political climate (Chou & Feagin, 2008; Dhingra, 2007; Lee, 2006; Leong & Schneller, 1997; Min & Kim, 1999; Sandhu, 1997). Asian Americans have been the targets of increased race-related violence, which forces them to confront their racialized identities (Alvarez, Juang, & Liang, 2006). Incidents such as the 9/11 attacks and the shootings at Virginia Tech in 2007 have heightened acts of racial profiling, violence, and discrimination toward Asian Americans (Chong, 2008; Prashad, 2005).

External influences often play a pivotal role in racial identity exploration, because they catalyze a loss of innocence and dissolve one's belief in a color-blind society. How one reacts to this loss of innocence is not necessarily predictable. One could use this realization to internalize racist beliefs and perspectives about Asian Americans or reject White norms (or both), and to associate with other communities of color. For example, in Asher's (2001) study of Indian American high school students, one of her participants preferred to associate with other students of color because he was trying to distance himself from being perceived as the model minority. This scenario shows how an Asian American student might be influenced by external perceptions of his identity. In this case, the student did not choose Whiteness as his norm; he chose to associate with other students of color, reflecting that he did recognize his non-Whiteness yet did not want to be discriminated against because of the stereotype associated with

Asian Americans. The most important consideration in this point of entry is that it is not necessary to identify with White norms to have a shift in consciousness. Consider an Asian American person who has been exposed to communities of color by living in predominantly Black or Latino neighborhoods. This person might have exposure to many empowered people of color, to the point that there is no need to experience White identification in order to achieve an awakening of consciousness.

Other Social Identities

Our existence is defined by the interactions and intersections of our social identities. Since our identities do not exist independently of each other, it is important to consider and incorporate those identities as major points of entry into Asian American identity exploration, and vice versa, with Asian American identity also informing the exploration processes of our other social identities. The complexities truly arise in the intersections of these social identities. In Kaw's (1993) study on Asian American women and cosmetic surgery, she noticed the irony in the pursuit of internalized White beauty norms by Asian American women—the same women asserted their independence and personal freedom to pursue these norms. This shows how racism and sexism inform and interact with one another.

Kumashiro's study of queer Asian American identity in men revealed that "heterosexuality was racialized as Asian, while queer sexuality was racialized as White" (1999, p. 502). The intersection of racial identity and sexual orientation leaves gay, lesbian, bisexual, and transgender Asian Americans dually marginalized and—depending on other factors, such as ethnic attachment and familial influence—forces them to choose between identities (Kumashiro, 1999; Li & Orleans, 2001). Similarly, Asian American women are often positioned to choose between feminism and femininity—to be good (or authentic) Asian women, they must abide by certain gender norms that are diluted by the values espoused by feminism (Aguilar-San Juan, 1997; Chow, 1987; Nandi & Fernandez, 1994). Likewise, the intersection between social class and race might influence how one engages racial identity to overcome subordination by class (Dhingra, 2007; Mitra, 2008). As reflected in these examples, it is at the intersections of identities that we see the greatest need for a multidimensional approach to Asian American identity exploration.

Theory to Practice: Serving APIDA Students

Early in my career, because of my own lack of preparation in how best to meet the identity-relevant needs of APIDA students, I approached these students solely through an ethnicity/culture lens, assuming that they all needed to examine and develop an attachment to their ethnic/racial identities. I assumed that most of them identified with the term Asian American and that those who did not were somehow lacking in self-awareness. My assumptions could not have been more wrong. Through reflections on my own experiences as a multicultural affairs professional, I hope to connect theory to practice in a way that liberates us to serve APIDA students more authentically.

Rethinking Nomenclature and Definitions

Nomenclature is much more powerful than we realize. When I began working in multicultural affairs, and specifically with APIDA students, I noticed three phenomena. First, when topics of diversity or inclusion were discussed on campus, Asian Americans were rarely included in the conversation. Diversity initiatives regarding campus climate, retention, and representation tended to focus on Blacks and Latinos. I believe those issues are very important, but I regret the historic practice of excluding APIDA communities from the discussion. An interesting byproduct of this exclusion is that APIDA students may not view themselves as people of color, because they interpret that to mean Black or Latino. I noticed this phenomenon when I first began working in a multicultural center: APIDA student groups rarely used the center or felt a connection to the space.

The second issue I noticed was that when Asian Americans were included in the conversation, it was in exotified ways. For example, Asian Americans had significant representation when it came to offering cultural performances, festival-type programs, and other experiences that commodify APIDA communities. Although there is nothing wrong with celebrating culture, this "food-dance-festival" diversity by itself perpetuates the forever foreign myth, overshadowing the historic legacies of generations of APIDA communities in the United States. APIDA communities are reduced to being the entertainment rather than members of the community. The combination of this kind of diversity and the exclusion of APIDA students from conversations about campus climate may lead educators to assume that APIDA students do not have any issues. Most significantly to student affairs professionals, in this scenario APIDA students are not challenged to reflect critically on the broader construction of their own identities.

The third phenomenon I noticed was that when APIDA communities did come together, the group was often East Asian-centered. Pan-Asian events were often dominated by Chinese, Japanese, Korean, and sometimes Vietnamese students. Students of South Asian, Pacific Islander, and other communities, who are usually lumped into the Asian American category, did not feel Asian American, so they often did not connect with this community. As discussed earlier, felt identity is an important component of a person's affiliation with the APIDA category, even though the category has its own problems and complexities.

For several years I served on the planning committee for a graduation event for students of color. Historically, Asian American students did not attend, because they did not see themselves as people of color. One year, with meaningful partnerships across offices, the planning committee included racial categories in the invitation, even naming specific categories such as South Asian and others to maximize inclusion. Some South Asian students raised the concern that they (or their families) did not identify with the term *South Asian* and recommended that we use the term *Desi*, which more broadly encompassed South Asian diasporas. Administrators resisted this recommendation because of their unfamiliarity with the term. As I reflect on that experience, I think about the missed opportunities for learning, student engagement, and authentic inclusion. The APIDA students made it clear that they wanted to be connected to a student of color experience, and they told us what it would take to get APIDA communities into the room. The challenge for administrators is to imagine that kind of inclusion and self-definition with them.

When we discuss diversity and inclusion, who is being included and excluded? When we say "Asian American," of whom are we speaking? As student affairs professionals, we must be broad in our approach to inclusion initiatives. We must redefine our perception of Asian America beyond our stereotypical imagination of that term. By recognizing that students are at different points in their identity exploration process and that Asian American is a felt identity, we should develop intentional programming, educational opportunities, and conversations that maximize a student's point of entry to Asian American identity consciousness.

Creating Community and Leadership:
APIDA Student Organizations

During my career in multicultural affairs, I advised more than 30 APIDA student organizations. I know firsthand the impact APIDA student organizations can have on their members: I attribute my own academic persistence and professional success to my involvement in the ISA. As I reflect on my interactions with and service to APIDA groups, I also recognize my shortcomings as a student affairs professional.

As I said earlier, I approached all APIDA student groups with the assumption that the "Asian" part of the group name carried the most salience for the members. This assumption was challenged in my first (and most humbling) experience serving APIDA sororities and fraternities. My institution was very progressive in its service of culturally based Greek organizations. As the result of a student-led initiative, our campus was one of the first in the nation to have an Asian American Pan-Hellenic Council composed of APIDA sororities, and I was the first advisor to this council. Because of my preconceived notions, I was determined to find a way to show these student leaders that Greek life was a waste of their time and an inauthentic way to be involved. But during my first year as advisor, I was extremely impressed by the amount of service, philanthropy, leadership, and identity consciousness I saw in the sororities that made up the council. The women leaders explained to me that owing to male dominance in APIDA cultural groups, it was often hard for them to find opportunities to lead; and owing to White dominance of general service groups, combined with the stereotypes APIDA women had to navigate, they could not find a home in those groups either. What I had dismissed as an emulation of power and privilege was really a thoughtful navigation at the intersections of these women's identities and a social critique of how we underserve our students. APIDA women understood how the intersections of their gender identities and racial identities impacted their lives as students, and they developed a solution to the problem. This experience radically changed the way I worked with APIDA student groups.

The leaders of APIDA sororities and fraternities were engaging in a race-consciousness journey through their gendered organizations; this realization challenged me to consider how I worked with other groups. I worked with several faith-based APIDA groups—including the Muslim Students Association, the Hindu Students Council, a Chinese Bible study group, and the Sikh Students Association—and I began to see parallel patterns. Students who joined these organizations shared the identity of their faiths, but some of these students were also keenly aware of the intersections of their religious and racial/ethnic identities in the current/ emergent political climate. Historically, the Muslim Students Association and the Sikh Students Association did not affiliate with APIDA groups, but after 9/11 and the profiling of these communities, both groups found a home in the multicultural center.

I realized that I did not fully appreciate the fact that APIDA groups that shared an intersection with another identity—such as religion, gender, or sexual orientation—had to navigate an institutional infrastructure that did not consider intersections of identities. I did not consider that APIDA religious groups felt excluded among other faith-based groups, or that the sororities and fraternities felt marginalized in a predominantly White Greek system. APIDA sororities did not feel embraced by student activities, fraternal life, or multicultural affairs. Ultimately, groups with intersecting identities had no true place of belonging in the student affairs infrastructure.

Higher education institutions should develop and support diverse programmatic initiatives that allow Asian American students to explore and nurture their identities through different points of entry. In student affairs, we should pay special attention to groups that are formed to support intersecting identities, such as Asian American fraternities and sororities, gay/lesbian/bisexual/transgender organizations, ethnicity-specific organizations, and religious organizations—these groups can offer a safe space for students, a peer group, and experiences that strengthen their persistence in college. As student affairs practitioners, we should engage in intentional dialogue about the role of APIDA student organizations in the identity development process and how our current infrastructures suppress or support this process. Stage models of student development have opened the door for us to understand various facets of student identity in specialized ways. We must take the opportunity to build on this research and explore how our students' identities intersect and how those intersections shape their experiences on college campuses. We must support our students as holistic beings.

In my experience serving APIDA students and groups, I encountered very few identity-relevant leadership pipeline programs that encourage APIDA students and professionals to contextualize their leadership styles within their own racial/ethnic identities or even consider that there may be a connection between identity and leadership. In general, I noticed that APIDA student leaders who had a positive connection with their racial/ethnic identities tended to affiliate only with APIDA groups or other groups that served students of color broadly. Conversely, I noticed that APIDA student leaders who did not have a connection (or had a negative connection) with their racial/ethnic identities avoided APIDA groups and criticized them.

In my later years in multicultural affairs, with the guidance of APIDA student leaders, I organized the Asian American Leadership Institute

(AALI). AALI was designed to create a space where students could engage in identity exploration in the context of leadership development and vice versa; we hoped to create many opportunities to develop a positive sense of self as it related to Asian American identity consciousness. Every part of AALI was deliberate by design. From the creation of the recruitment materials, to the organization of the curriculum, to the faculty, to the selection of the student co-chairs, each component was intended to strengthen our partnerships with other student affairs offices and Asian American studies, and to increase the leadership pipeline of APIDA students. What I did not anticipate was the ripple effect AALI would have on APIDA leadership and mainstream campus involvement, and the significant opportunity it would give me to reflect on my own biases as an educator.

Conclusion

In higher education, we must be prepared to serve a rapidly diversifying student body. Asian American students are one of the fastest growing communities in education overall, and we must make affirmative efforts to fully understand Asian America.

Honoring multiple Asian Americas means recognizing that we must create an identity exploration paradigm that is as flexible and diverse as the category of Asian America—a paradigm without hierarchies of consciousness. We must develop academic frameworks that do not force people to choose among their identities but encourage them to embrace all of them. The Point of Entry Model for Asian American Identity Exploration offers this flexibility, without a hierarchy of awareness or a litmus test of Asian American authenticity.

There is political solidarity in the category Asian American, but we must not assume that all Asian Americans share similar or even parallel journeys of identity exploration. "Watching a river flow by, one notices the confluence of different tributaries flowing into the river, with some parts hitting rocks or taking wider turns, and others taking different paths. Similarly, there is diversity among Asian Americans, who come from different places, have different appearances, and encounter different obstacles, though appearing on the surface to have a common identity" (Uba, 1994, p. vii). If Asian American identity exploration is the river, we must consider the inherent nature of the river, as well as the elements that affect its flow, as we formulate ways of understanding the river without defining it entirely.

References

Aguilar-San Juan, K. (1997). Foreword: Breathing fire, confronting power, and other necessary acts of resistance. In S. Shah (Ed.), *Dragon ladies: Asian American feminists breathe fire* (pp. ix–xi). Boston, MA: South End.

Alvarez, A. N., & Helms, J. E. (2001). Racial identity and reflected appraisals as influences on Asian Americans' racial adjustment. *Cultural Diversity and Ethnic Minority Psychology, 7*(3), 217–231.

Alvarez, A. N., Juang, L., & Liang, C. T. (2006). Asian Americans and racism: When bad things happen to "model minorities." *Cultural Diversity and Ethnic Minority Psychology, 12*(3), 477–492.

Alvarez, A. N., & Kimura, E. F. (2001). Asian Americans and racial identity: Dealing with racism and snowballs. *Journal of Mental Health Counseling, 23*(3), 192–206.

Asher, N. (2001). Rethinking multiculturalism: Attending to Indian American high school students' stories of negotiating self-representations. In C. C. Park, A. L. Goodwin, & S. J. Lee (Eds.), *Research on the education of Asian and Pacific Americans* (pp. 55–73). Greenwich, CT: Information Age Publishing, Inc.

Baxter Magolda, M. B. (2003). Identity and learning: Student affairs' role in transforming higher education. *Journal of College Student Development, 44*(1), 231–247.

Bemak, F., & Chung, R. (1997). Vietnamese Amerasians: Psychosocial adjustment and psychotherapy. *Journal of Multicultural Counseling and Development, 25*(1), 79-88.

Bergquist, K. J. S. (2006). From kim chee to moon cakes: Feeding Asian adoptees' imaginings of culture and self. *Food, Culture and Society: An International Journal of Multidisciplinary Research, 9*(2), 141–153.

Bonner, F. A., II., Jennings, M. E., Chen, Y., & Singh, S. M. (2006). Asian American students. In L. A. Gohn & G. R. Albin (Eds.), *Understanding college student subpopulations: A guide for student affairs professionals* (pp. 387–410). Washington, DC: National Association of Student Personnel Administrators.

Chang, R. S. (1999). *Disoriented: Asian Americans, law and the nation-state.* New York, NY: NYU Press.

Chen, G. A., LePhuoc, P., Guzman, M. R., Rude, S. S., & Dodd, B. G. (2006). Exploring Asian American identity. *Cultural Diversity and Ethnic Minority Psychology, 12*(3), 461–476.

Chew-Ogi, C., & Ogi, A. Y. (2002). Epilogue. In M. K. McEwen, C. M. Kodama, A. N. Alvarez, C. T. H. Liang, & S. Lee (Eds.), *Working with Asian American college students* (New directions for student services, no. 97, pp. 91–96). San Francisco, CA: Jossey-Bass.

Chong, S. S. H. (2008). "LOOK, AN ASIAN!": The politics of racial interpellation in the wake of the Virginia Tech shootings. *Journal of Asian American Studies, 11*(1), 27.

Chou, R., and Feagin, J. (2008). *The myth of the model minority: Asian Americans facing racism.* Boulder, CO: Paradigm.

Chow, E. N. L. (1987). The development of feminist consciousness among Asian American women. *Gender and Society, 1*(3), 284–299.

Das, A., & Kemp, S. (1997). Between two worlds: Counseling South Asian Americans. *Journal of Multicultural Counseling and Development, 25*(1), 23–33.

Delgado, R. (1995). *Critical race theory: The cutting edge.* Philadelphia, PA: Temple University Press.

Dhingra, P. (2007). *Managing multicultural lives: Asian American professionals and the challenge of multiple identities.* Stanford, CA: Stanford University Press.

Dhingra, P. (2010). Hospitable to others: Indian American motel owners create boundaries and belonging in the heartland. *Ethnic and Racial Studies, 33*(6), 1088–1107.

Espiritu, Y. L. (2001). "We don't sleep around like White girls do": Family, culture, and gender in Filipina American lives. *Signs, 26*(2), 415–440.

Espiritu, Y. L. (2008). *Asian American women and men: Labor, laws and love.* New York, NY: Rowman & Littlefield.

Fujiwara, L. (2008). *Mothers without citizenship: Asian immigrant families and the consequences of welfare reform.* Minneapolis, MN: University of Minnesota Press.

Gloria, A. M., & Ho, T. A. (2003). Environmental, social, and psychological experiences of Asian American undergraduates: Examining issues of academic persistence. *Journal of Counseling and Development, 81,* 93–105.

Green, D., and Kim, E. (2005). Experiences of Korean female doctoral students in academe: Raising voice against gender and racial stereotypes. *Journal of College Student Development, 46*(5), 487–500.

hooks, b. (1990). *Yearning: Race, gender, and cultural politics.* Boston, MA: South End Press.

Horse, P. G. (2001). Reflections on American Indian identity. In C. Wijeyesinghe & B. W. Jackson (Eds.), *New perspectives on racial identity development: A theoretical and practical anthology* (pp. 91–107). New York, NY: NYU Press.

Ibrahim, F., Ohnishi, H., & Sandhu, D. S.(1997). Asian American identity development: A culture-specific model for South Asian Americans. *Journal of Multicultural Counseling and Development, 25*(1), 34–51.

Inkelas, K. K. (2006). Racial attitudes and Asian Pacific Americans: Demystifying the Model Minority. In F. Ng (Ed.), *Studies in Asian*

Americans: Reconceptualizing culture, history, and politics. New York, NY: Routledge.

Kaw, E. (1993). Medicalization of racial features: Asian American women and cosmetic surgery. *Medical Anthropology Quarterly, 7*(1), 74–89.

Kelley, R. (1999, September/October). Polycultural me. *Utne Reader.* Retrieved from http://www.utne.com/1999-09-01/the-people-in-me.aspx

Kibria, N. (1998). The contested meanings of "Asian American": Racial dilemmas in the contemporary U.S. *Ethnic and Racial Studies, 21*(5), 939–956.

Kim, J. (2001). Asian American identity development theory. In C. Wijeyesinghe & B. W. Jackson (Eds.), *New perspectives on racial identity development: A theoretical and practical anthology* (pp. 67–90). New York, NY: NYU Press.

Koshy, S. (2001). Morphing race into ethnicity: Asian Americans and critical transformations of Whiteness. *boundary 2, 28*(1), 153–194.

Kumashiro, K. K. (1999). Supplementing normalcy and otherness: Queer Asian American men reflect on stereotypes, identity, and oppression. *Qualitative Studies in Education, 12*(5), 491–508.

Lai, E., & Arguelles, D. (Eds.). (2003). *The new face of Asian America: Numbers, diversity, and change in the 21ˢᵗ century.* Berkeley, CA: AsianWeek.

Lee, S. S. (2006). Over-represented and de-minoritized: The racialization of Asian Americans in higher education. *InterActions: UCLA Journal of Education and Information Studies, 2*(2). Retrieved from http://repositories.cdlib.org/gseis/interactions/vol2/iss2/art4

Leong, F., & Schneller, G. (1997). White Americans' attitudes toward Asian Americans in social situations: An empirical examination of potential stereotypes, bias, and prejudice. *Journal of Multicultural Counseling and Development, 25*(1), 68–78.

Lew, J., Chang, J., & Wang, W. (2005). UCLA community college review: The overlooked minority: Asian Pacific American students at community colleges. *Community College Review, 33*(2), 64–84.

Li, L., & Orleans, M. (2001). Coming out: Discourses of Asian American lesbians. *Sexuality and Culture, 5*(2), 57–78.

Louie, A. (2009). "Pandas, lions, and dragons, oh my!": How White adoptive parents construct Chineseness. *Journal of Asian American Studies, 12*(3), 285–320.

Mathews, R. (2000). Cultural patterns of South Asian and Southeast Asian Americans. *Intervention in School and Clinic, 36*(2), 101–104.

Matsuda, M. J., Lawrence III, C. R., Delgado, R., & Crenshaw, K. W. (1993). *Words that wound: Critical race theory, assaultive speech, and the First Amendment.* Boulder, CO: Westview Press.

McEwen, M. K., Kodama, C. M., Alvarez, A. N., Liang, C. T. H., & Lee, S. (Eds.). (2002). *Working with Asian American college students* (New directions for student services, no. 97). San Francisco, CA: Jossey-Bass.

Min, P. G., & Kim, R. (Eds.). (1999). *Struggle for ethnic identity: Narratives by Asian American professionals.* Walnut Creek, CA: AltaMira Press.

Mitra, D. (2008). Punjabi American taxi drivers: The new White working class? *Journal of Asian American Studies, 11*(3), 303–336.

Mohammad-Arif, A. (2000). A Masala identity: Young South Asian Muslims in the US. *Comparative Studies of South Asia, Africa, and the Middle East, XX*(1 & 2), 67–87.

Mok, T. A. (1998). Asian Americans and standards of attractiveness: What's in the eye of the beholder? *Cultural Diversity and Mental Health, 4*(1), 185–202.

Museus, S. D. (Ed.). (2009a). *Conducting research on Asian Americans in higher education. New directions for Institutional Research* (no. 142). San Francisco, CA: Jossey-Bass.

Museus, S. D. (2009b). A critical analysis of the exclusion of Asian Americans from higher education research and discourse." In L. Zhan (Ed.), *Asian American voices: Engaging, empowering, enabling* (pp. 59–76). New York, NY: NLN Press.

Museus, S. D., & Kiang, P. N. (2009). Deconstructing the model minority myth and how it contributes to the invisible minority reality in higher education research. In S. D. Museus (Ed.), *Conducting research on Asian Americans in higher education* (New directions for institutional research, no. 142, pp. 5–15). San Francisco, CA: Jossey-Bass.

Nadal, K. (2004). Filipino identity development model. *Journal of Multicultural Counseling and Development, 32,* 45–62.

Nandi, P. K., & Fernandez, M. (1994). Liberation of Asian American women: An uncertain quest. *International Journal of Sociology of the Family, 24,* 1–22.

Okazaki, S., Lee, R. M., & Sue, S. (2007). Theoretical and conceptual models: Toward Asian Americanist psychology. In F. T. L. Leong, A. Inman, A. Ebreo, L. Yang, L. Kinoshita, & M. Fu (Eds.), *Handbook of Asian American psychology* (pp. 29–46). Thousand Oaks, CA: Sage.

Okihiro, G. Y. (1994). *Margins and mainstreams: Asians in American history and culture.* Seattle, WA: University of Washington Press.

Patel, E. (2007). *Acts of faith: The story of an American Muslim, the struggle for the soul of a generation.* Boston, MA: Beacon Press.

Patton, L., McEwen, M. K., Rendón, L., and Howard-Hamilton, M. (2007). Critical race perspectives on theory in student affairs. In S. R. Harper and L. D. Patton (Eds.), *The realities of race on campus* (New directions for student services, no. 120, pp. 39–54). San Francisco, CA: Jossey-Bass.

Phinney, J. S. (1990). Ethnic identity in adolescents and adults: Review of research. *Psychological Bulletin, 108*(3), 499–514.

Prashad, V. (2001). *Everybody was Kung Fu fighting: Afro-Asian connections and the myth of cultural purity*. Boston, MA: Beacon Press.

Prashad, V. (2005). How the Hindus became Jews: American racism after 9/11. *South Atlantic Quarterly, 104*(3), 583–606.

Pyke, K., & Dang, T. (2003). "FOB" and "whitewashed": Identity and internalized racism among second generation Asian Americans. *Qualitative Sociology, 26*(2), 147–172.

Root, M. P. P. (2002). Methodological issues in multiracial research. In G. C. Nagayama Hall & S. Okazaki (Eds.), *Asian American psychology: The science of lives in context* (pp. 171–193). Washington, DC: American Psychological Association.

Sandhu, D. S. (1997). Psychocultural profiles of Asian and Pacific Islander Americans: Implications for counseling and psychotherapy. *Journal of Multicultural Counseling and Development, 25*(1), 7–22.

Shankar, L. D., & Balgopal, P. R. (2001). South Asian immigrants before 1950: The formation of ethnic, symbolic, and group identity. *Amerasia Journal, 27*(1), 55–85.

Shankar, L. D., & Srikanth, R. (1998). Introduction: Closing the gap? South Asians challenge Asian American studies. In L. D. Shankar & R. Srikanth (Eds.), *A part, yet apart: South Asians in Asian America* (pp. 1–24). Philadelphia, PA: Temple University Press.

Sodowsky, G. R., Kwan, K. K., & Pannu, R. (1995). Ethnic identity of Asians in the United States. In J. G. Ponterotto, J. M. Casas, L. A. Suzuki, & C. M. Alexander (Eds.), *Handbook of multicultural counseling* (pp. 123–154). Thousand Oaks, CA: Sage.

Song, M. (1998). Pakhar Singh's argument with Asian America: Color and the structure of race formation. In L. D. Shankar & R. Srikanth

(Eds.), *A part, yet apart: South Asians in Asian America* (pp. 79–102). Philadelphia, PA: Temple University Press.

Spickard, P. R., & Fong, R. (1995). Pacific Islander Americans and multiethnicity: A vision of America's future? *Social Forces, 73*(4), 1365–1383.

Sue, S., & Sue, D. W. (1971). Chinese-American personality and mental health. *Amerasia Journal, 1*, 36–49.

Teranishi, R. T. (2002). Asian Pacific Americans and critical race theory: An examination of school racial climate. *Equity and Excellence in Education, 35*(2), 144–154.

Teranishi, R. T., Behringer, L. B., Grey, E. A., and Parker, T. L. (2009). Critical race theory and research on Asian Americans and Pacific Islanders in higher education. In S. D. Museus (Ed.), *Conducting Research on Asian Americans in Higher Education* (New directions for institutional research, no. 142, pp. 57–68). San Francisco, CA: Jossey-Bass.

Ting, J. Y., & Hwang, W. (2007). Eating disorders in Asian American women: Integrating multiculturalism and feminism. *Women and Therapy, 30*, 145–160.

Tse, L. (1999). Finding a place to be: Ethnic identity exploration of Asian Americans. *Adolescence, 34*(133), 121–138.

Tuan, M. (2002). Second-generation Asian American identity: Clues from the Asian ethnic experience. In P. G. Min (Ed.), *The second generation: Ethnic identity among Asian Americans* (pp. 209–237). New York, NY: AltaMira Press.

Uba, L. (1994). *Asian Americans: Personality, patterns, identity, and mental health.* New York, NY: Guilford Press.

Uba, L. (2002). *A postmodern psychology of Asian Americans: Creating knowledge of a racial minority.* Albany, NY: State University of New York Press.

U.S. Census Bureau. (2010). *Overview of race and Hispanic origin:2010.* Washington, DC: U.S. Department of Commerce.

Wijeyesinghe, C. (2001). Racial identity in multiracial people: An alternative paradigm. In C. Wijeyesinghe & B. W. Jackson (Eds.), *New perspectives on racial identity development: A theoretical and practical anthology* (pp. 129–152). New York, NY: NYU Press.

Yeh, C. J., & Huang, K. (1996). The collectivistic nature of ethnic identity development among Asian-American college students. *Adolescence, 31*(123), 645–662.

Yosso, T. J. (2006). *Critical race counterstories along the Chicana/Chicano educational pipeline.* New York, NY: Routledge.

CHAPTER FOUR

Creating a Legacy

Multiracial and Multiethnic Asian
Pacific Islander American Professionals
in Higher Education

Sara Furr, Bernard Liang, and Stephanie Nixon

In 2010, the multiracial population (those who selected two or more races in the national census) was 9 million, or 3% of the population. In comparison, as of 2010, 15% of Asian Americans and 56% of Native Hawaiian and Pacific Islanders are multiracial. The multiracial population was the third fastest growing group over the decade, following Asian and Native Hawaiian or other Pacific Islander (U.S. Census Bureau, 2011). The population of students who identify as multiracial continues to grow on our college and university campuses, and among those entering the field of student affairs through graduate preparation programs. Research is limited on the experiences and needs of people who identify as Asian Pacific Islander American

(APIA) or Asian Pacific Islander Desi American (APIDA), or on the factors that affect identity development in multiracial and multiethnic persons. Research on identity development has typically focused on one aspect of identity, and studies often focus on the differences between members of dominant and subordinate identity groups.

This study was designed to explore the experiences of multiracial (defined as those with backgrounds from various races) and multiethnic (those with backgrounds from different ethnicities, perhaps within the same race) professionals who identify with one or more Asian or Pacific Islander race or ethnicity. Several themes emerged in respondents' narratives related to situational variables that affected identity development and the relative importance of aspects of their identities. Implications for graduate preparation programs and institutions of higher education are also discussed.

Asian American Identity Development Theory

Jean Kim (1981) described a stage model of identity development for Asian Americans based on a study of the experiences of second-generation Japanese American women. According to Kim, Asian Americans progress through five stages of identity development. *Stage 1, Ethnic Awareness* typically occurs before the person enters the school system and comes from interactions with family members and other relatives. *Stage 2, White Identification* is marked by Asian Americans' strong sense of being different from their peers. Depending on the extent to which a person identifies with White people, he or she may experience active or passive White identification. During *Stage 3, Awakening to Social Political Consciousness*, individuals often shift from a world view focused on individual responsibility to understanding the social context associated with race and racism. This shift is critical to enable people to change their self-concept from negative to positive. The critical aspect of *Stage 4, Redirection to an Asian American Consciousness* is immersion in the Asian American experience. Individuals in this stage acquire racial pride and a positive self-concept through connection with their racial heritage. *Stage 5, Incorporation* is marked by confidence in one's self-identity, which enables a person to relate to others or groups that are different without losing a sense of individual identity.

Attempting to apply this model through the lens of multiracial/multiethnic Asian Americans is highly problematic. Even though the model provides some basic understanding, the stages are much more complicated for multiracial/multiethnic persons. This lack of information emphasizes even more strongly the need to have a better understanding of Asian American professionals who identify as multiracial or multiethnic.

Although not specifically focused on multiracial identity, Jones and McEwen's Model of Multiple Dimensions of Identity (2000) recognizes the complexity of intersecting social identities and acknowledges that different dimensions of identity will be more or less important for each person, given a range of contextual influences. The complexity of identity development in a group that spans such a wide range of ethnic, language, and cultural backgrounds is addressed in Mamta Accapadi's chapter on Asian American Identity Consciousness: A Polycultural Model, which employs a point of entry framework for APIDA identity consciousness. This nonlinear, nonstage model introduces multiple dimensions that affect relationship to identity, including external perceptions, ethnic attachment, and immigration status. The model also addresses the impact of stereotypes about Asian American communities on individuals' relationships with their identities.

Models of Multiracial Identity Development

Research focused on multiracial identity development, while increasing, remains limited. Root (1990) offered a model of positive resolution of biracial identity that differed from earlier studies focused on minority identity development. Root's research suggested the existence of fluidity of identity in the experiences of some biracial and multiracial persons, depending on the context and the impact of racism in their experiences. Renn (2000) identified additional factors that influence multiracial students' identities, including cultural knowledge of their heritage groups, phenotype, and the context of campus and peer culture.

Renn's study included qualitative interviews with 24 students representing three New England institutions. Two major themes emerged from the study: (1) students' relationship to public and physical spaces, and (2) the impact of peer culture on their sense of identity. Renn proposed a framework that would reflect the patterns of how students chose to identify themselves in their institutional and peer cultures. The patterns are neither hierarchical nor sequential; rather, they illustrate different relationships to a sense of racial identity for biracial and multiracial students.

The first pattern, *monoracial identity*, included students who chose to identify with one category of their racial heritage; in the second pattern, *multiple monoracial identities*, students chose to identify monoracially with more than one group at a time, depending on context. These students exhibited a fluidity of movement among different monoracial affinity groups but sought out or claimed membership in more than one monoracial community at different times. Students who exhibited the second pattern had racial heritages that included having two parents of color as well as one parent who identified primarily as White. In the third pattern, *multiracial identity*, students chose to construct a category separate from monoracial communities. Students in this group attended both institutions with defined mixed-race heritage student groups and spaces, and institutions that lacked a critical mass of students from multiracial backgrounds. In the fourth pattern, *extraracial identity*, students totally rejected the racial categories included in the U.S. racial and social construct. According to Renn, some students in the fourth group focused on culture rather than race, while others focused on the deconstruction of race and the fluidity of identity. The first four patterns of identity sometimes depended on situational factors, but in the fifth pattern, *situational identity*, students exhibited some or all of the other four patterns at different times. How they chose to identify in particular situations usually was connected to a sense of belonging and feeling accepted in student groups and communities, and whether institutional policies or processes forced them to select a specific monoracial or multiracial identity regardless of their internal construction of a racial identity.

Students' racial identity was affected by the presence or absence of a critical mass of individuals with mixed-race heritage; access to multiple communities that affirmed the range of choices people made about monoracial, mixed-race, and other ways of identifying themselves; and institutional and peer cultures. Although Renn's research looked only at the experiences of traditionally aged undergraduate students, the recognition of the salience of situational factors on one's construction of identity and the inherent limitations of monoracial identity models for multiracial individuals are relevant in the identity development of Asian American multiracial and multiethnic professionals.

Methodology

The study was conducted using a series of 17 qualitative questions to collect open-ended narrative data. Participants self-selected into completing the survey, identifying themselves as multiracial or multiethnic (defined as having biological parents of more than one race or ethnicity, one of which was Asian American). Participants were identified through snowball sampling, with invitations to participate sent to e-mail lists of professionals, including the Asian Pacific American Network and Multiracial Network of the American College Personnel Association (ACPA) and the Asian Pacific Islanders Concerns Knowledge Community of NASPA–Student Affairs Administrators in Higher Education. Invitations to participate and to distribute the survey link also were sent through the e-mail list for the Social Justice Training Institute and the APIs in Higher Education mail group. A total of 550 people were invited to participate.

Of the 16 respondents, 13 identified themselves as multiracial or biracial, and 15 identified as multiethnic. The respondents' experience in higher education ranged from current graduate students to a person with 18 years in the field. Participants represented a wide variety of functional area experience; the majority had worked in multicultural affairs, residence life, and academic support.

Research Findings

A variety of themes emerged in the participants' narratives. The responses were coded into theme categories, and the themes were compared for overlap and relationships among the categories. The following discussion focuses on the variables that affected identity development as multiracial and multiethnic Asian Pacific Islander Americans over time, as well as key factors that influenced participants' relationship to their identities in particular periods.

Participants reported several variables that affected their personal identity. These variables fell into three areas: environment, physical appearance, and navigating multiple identities. Each area has several components.

Environmental variables that affect multiracial/multiethnic identity include the racial makeup of one's geographic home, access to supportive communities, and familial/interpersonal relationships. Participants reported that the relationship to their family members affected their own multiracial/multiethnic experience; particularly whether one had siblings and how they self-identified. Additionally, participants who reported a strong relationship with their parents also reported stronger ties to all elements of their racial/ethnic identity and were more likely to identify as multiracial or multiethnic.

Participants reported that physical appearance affected their multiracial/multiethnic identity in several ways. We make assumptions about people's identity when we meet them. If we verbalize these assumptions, they can have an effect on the other person. For multiracial/multiethnic Asian Pacific Americans, the first distinction is whether they are assumed to be White or a person of color. A respondent described the challenge this way: "It was more that other people chose for me—put me in the 'White' box—and I had to assert my right to be in another box or, eventually, in both." Assumptions by others had a direct impact on how participants saw themselves.

Finally, navigating multiple identities was an important variable in each of the life stages explored in this study; specifically, the availability of terminology to describe oneself as biracial, multiracial, or multiethnic. Participants reported that a lack of terminology affected their direct experience. Without terms to identify them as multiracial or multiethnic, participants felt forced to choose between identities instead of fully embracing all aspects of their identities.

Importance of Identities

The relationship of a person to his or her identities is unique, which made a "shared experience" difficult to identify in the survey. However, the importance of each participant's multiracial and multiethnic identities was a clear factor. For some, their comfort level and acceptance in communities differed along various lines, including appearance, skin tone, individual experience, background, and which community they were present in.

> "I remember growing up being thought of as being less than any other person who was of some Asian descent who was full-blooded. People talked about some ranking of Asian Americans, and as someone who was mixed Asian, I was 'ranked' lower than everyone, even biracial Asian Americans. Also, I had a difficult time finding someone who related to my experience until I was a professional, [although I] met mentors who could relate more generally."

Most participants reported explicit consideration of their identity, frequent self-examination, and exploration of self-worth. Identity influenced everything from academic and career choices, to connections to their cultural heritage, to relationships with family members. One person spoke of the experience of looking more multiracial than a sibling who presented a more Asian appearance, and the differences they experienced in their acceptance by various communities.

In particular, participants spoke about their connection to their APIA identities. They spoke of their APIA identity as something they valued (perhaps making them more likely to participate in the study). Physical appearance was often mentioned in connection with their experience, but there were also anecdotes about positive and negative relationships with family members; connections to Asian or Pacific Islander language, culture, and traditions; and lack of access to communities and colleagues with similar backgrounds or experiences. The issue of stereotypes elicited an interesting mix of responses. Some spoke of their acceptance of their APIA identity, while others described how their experiences shaped negative stereotypes of APIA groups, including those communities to which they belonged.

Family Life

In describing their family life, respondents tended to focus on five variables: general environment, family composition, geographic location, assumption of identity, and presence of role models. A quarter of the respondents reported a positive experience growing up biracial, multiracial, or multiethnic; this was directly related to where they lived. Those who grew up in what they perceived to be diverse environments reported more positive experiences than those who grew up in small towns, predominantly White environments, or areas with few Asian Americans or Pacific Islanders. Respondents reported being misunderstood, assumed to be White, or assumed to be "full" API.

Over half of the respondents reported having no role model, which created challenges in understanding their own identity as biracial, multiracial, or multiethnic. Most of those who did identify role models named family figures, such as parents or grandparents. While family members can serve as role models, being limited to them can diminish one's ability to identify as biracial, multiracial or multiethnic.

> "In college I chose to firmly define myself as Asian American—biracial was not really a term that was common. I did not start using the term biracial until about 10 years ago, as the multi-

racial population started gaining attention because of census issues and occasional remarks in the media."

Geographic location was the variable that most affected participants' experience growing up biracial, multiracial, or multiethnic. Living in a generally diverse area, with other mixed families or people of mixed identity, helped participants find their own identity. By contrast, growing up in predominantly White communities or areas with a single predominant race identity hindered participants' personal development.

Undergraduate Years

Among the participants, the undergraduate experience was marked by changes in identity development, cultural exploration, and identifying areas of support. All but one respondent reported such changes in their undergraduate years. They reported changes in cultural saliency, becoming connected to API and other communities of color, and becoming more connected to one's multiracial identity.

Participants reported an increase in exploration of their cultural identity during their undergraduate years. Much of this exploration occurred through academics, either in their chosen major or minor or through additional coursework. Many used involvement in cultural organizations or their own personal reading and research to gain a better understanding of self. However, limited availability of such organizations and communities seemed to inhibit connections to their multiracial/multiethnic identity.

Although the undergraduate experience generated an increased understanding of self, respondents experienced challenges. Finding a mentor or role model was not easy. The most frequently cited challenges were not feeling completely accepted in various communities, having to choose one identity over the other, and feeling like a "forever foreigner." Participants managed these challenges by finding support from academic classes, student organizations, and personal relationships with partners, family, or faculty.

One of the most unfortunate findings was that many of these respondents have not felt supported by their institutions, either as students or now, as professionals. Those who did feel supported cited specific faculty and staff members. Still, one respondent felt support by faculty only while acting in ways that reinforced and perpetuated negative APIA stereotypes. This lack of support is significant, considering that these are students who have gone on to be student affairs professionals. Would we have more multiracial or multiethnic Asian Pacific Islanders in the field if they felt more supported by their institutions?

> "I often felt like the 'token' person talking about an experience and I often felt like there were people who really didn't understand any perspective but their own."

Graduate School

In describing their graduate experience, participants said they were influenced primarily by the curriculum, faculty, and peers. Seeing themselves reflected in the curriculum as multiracial or multiethnic APIAs had a positive effect on their satisfaction in their graduate program. Some said that to feel more connected they would search for ways to include their experience in the curriculum, regardless of whether or not it was a requirement of the program.

Peers also had an influence on satisfaction. Generally, increased awareness of racial issues by peers increased the level of satisfaction. Participants said that having peers who were able to talk about multiracial/multiethnic issues increased their comfort level and satisfaction. Most participants reported feeling a general acknowledgment and acceptance of their identity.

Faculty influence also played an important role in the experiences of these participants. They reported that while faculty were generally supportive, some issues arose. For example, one participant described being asked to speak on behalf of her racial group in a graduate-level class. In this person's opinion, faculty should develop a better understanding of race, especially of multiracial and multiethnic issues and experiences.

The common denominator among participants is a feeling that professionals, including themselves, lack sufficient preparation for working with multiracial/multiethnic APIA students. Some spoke in generalities about professional development in graduate school, but most participants said that graduate school only enhanced abilities they already had rather than preparing them to work with these students. In fact, a number of study participants remarked that they are often called upon to serve as the unofficial expert on multiracial/multiethnic APIA issues on their campuses.

Professional Experience

The APIA professionals in this study generally felt unprepared and only mildly supported on their campuses. Some said that university administrative support was in the form of words but not action. One person noted that although she was encouraged to participate in the faculty and staff group of color, she generally did not feel welcome because of her multiracial (APIA and White) identity.

In response to the question "How prepared is your institution to support multiracial/multiethnic students, faculty, and staff?" one respondent wrote,

> "I do not think they want to or are prepared to support multiracial/ethnic or any staff and faculty of color. Support for students falls mostly in typical racial/ethnic categories, and nothing exists for multiracial/ethnic students that I know of."

In searching for professional positions, these participants expressed a need to have a level of comfort with their prospective college employer, and they looked for communities of support both on and off campus. Many did not find any multiracial or multiethnic groups in which to participate; however, those in larger cities found more opportunities to connect, even if the groups were not specifically communities of color or multiracial/ multiethnic communities.

Implications

The majority of participants included in this brief study reported positive changes in and development of their sense of identity over time, although they identified factors that would have helped. Future research should continue to explore the complexity of identity development for multiracial and multiethnic individuals, and their place in Asian Pacific American communities and communities of color. This study was limited by the sample size and the challenge of identifying potential participants, given the low representation of this population in higher education professional roles. There is still much to learn as increasing numbers of professionals who identify as both APIA and multiracial or multiethnic enter the higher education field.

Research should seek to understand the impact of environment on identity development and identity choices for this population. How one is perceived and treated by others in dominant (White) racial identity groups and in communities of color may influence the relevance of physical appearance for those who identify as both multiracial and APIA. The salience of physical appearance might also be affected by access to communities beyond monoracial affinity groups. Preliminary studies of multiracial students have shown the fluidity of multiracial identity construction and the search for a sense of belonging to a community; however, these issues have not been fully explored in a professional context or in relationship to APIA identity and the particulars of one's upbringing or educational and work experiences. This situation reinforces the importance of access to communities that validate the intersections of these and other components of social identities and allow for self-exploration.

Our research questions focused on the intersection of multiracial and multiethnic identity and APIA identity. Our study did not overlay other identities, such as gender identity and expression, socioeconomic status, sexual identity, family and ethnic immigration history, and other social identities that might influence racial identity construction. We believe that higher education professionals, students, and campuses would benefit from studies that seek to include and affirm a wholeness of identities and backgrounds.

Another area of study might be the exploration of a common curriculum in higher education graduate preparation programs for student affairs professionals. Participants in our study reported an overall lack of coverage of APIA and multiracial identity development theories and models in their coursework. Beyond preparing professionals to meet the developmental needs of increasing numbers of multiracial and multiethnic students, college student development literature and programs might be strengthened on a broader scale with the inclusion of more complex models of identity development.

The 2010 U.S. Census data show a large increase in Asian, Native Hawaiian, and other Pacific Islanders, and people who identify as being of two or more races. This has implications for higher education and U.S. society at large. Additional research into the influx of multiracial and multiethnic students, perhaps as a longitudinal study, can create more inclusive environments for these citizens.

References

Jones, S. R., & McEwen, M. E. (2000). A conceptual model of multiple dimensions of identity. *Journal of College Student Development, 41,* 405–414.

Kim, J. (2001). Asian American identity development theory. In C. Wiejeyesinghe & B. Jackson, *New perspectives on racial identity development: A theoretical and practical anthology.* New York, NY: NYU Press.

Renn, K. A. (2000). Patterns of situational identity among biracial and multiracial college students. *Review of Higher Education, 23*(4) 399–420.

Root, M. P. P. (1990). Resolving "other" status: Identity development of biracial individuals. *Women and Therapy, 9,* 185–205.

U.S. Census Bureau. (2011, March). Overview of race and Hispanic origin: 2010. (2010 Census Briefs.) Retrieved July 9, 2011, from http://www.census.gov/prod/cen2010/briefs/c2010br-02.pdf

CHAPTER FIVE

Honoring the Intersections

The Experiences of a Desi Queer Professional in Student Affairs

Raja G. Bhattar

Simply being me, all of me, is a revolution. (Anonymous)

Every day that I choose to get up and go to work and embrace my authentic self, I am creating change. "We all fight, every day, for the right to live in this body we're given without being questioned, judged, discriminated against, or attacked. That message should ring true to nearly every social justice movement. This simple concept can be a powerful way to connect all these issues" (Remick, 2009). I carry many identities, some visible and others invisible, yet each identity plays a key role in my understanding of myself and the world around me.

I am Desi and queer. For many years, I saw these two identities as mutually exclusive, but I have come to a more holistic integration as I have grown in my personal and professional journey. As a Desi, I associate myself with the Asian Pacific Islander Desi American (APIDA) community; as a queer person, I identify with the lesbian, gay, bisexual, transgender, and queer (LGBTQ) community. Though I do not represent the experiences of the many people in these categories, my story is part of this greater cultural fabric. As a member of both groups, understanding how these two aspects of myself intersect has been critical to how I choose to live my life. Embracing these identities, I bring a unique set of perspectives, politics, and privileges to my work as a student affairs professional. Though our profession and society continue to become increasingly diverse, there have been very few opportunities to understand the complexity of experiences of professionals with multiple intersectional identities.

As I live these complex intersections daily, my journey is part of a broader community history that is worth communicating. Even more important, sharing my stories and being a professional on campus, I provide students with a role model that was never available to me at that age.

Though I do not fully represent the immensely diverse and complex experiences of APIDA LGBTQs, I attempt to broaden the awareness of these experiences in our field as I engage myself and allies in finding strategies to support one another. Living and speaking my authenticity, I make space for others to do the same. Every day I show up to work, I engage in a conversation, demanding visibility and acknowledgment. In embracing the need for creative and more complex forums for understanding my experiences, I employ the scholarly personal narrative form of academic study that places one's experience at the core, with supporting information and broader contexts of interpretation. "Scholarly personal narrative is a research methodology that blends the rigor of traditional scholarship with the writer's personal experience" (McManus, 2011). By fusing personal accounts and informal interviews with colleagues, I provide implications, ideas, and suggestions on how our profession can support people with similar experiences.

What's In a Name?

I exist at the crossroads of my many selves, constantly negotiating spaces and communities. "I know I do not clearly fit within many 'boxes,' and I have grown comfortable with that (most of the time). I recognize what it feels like to identify with a community, but not necessarily feel included within it" (J. M. Johnson, personal communication, June 5, 2011). As a Desi queer man, I often find myself outside people's notions of what it means to be a particular identity. Even using these terms has been a long process in my self-awareness and acceptance, yet I choose to use them because I feel they best fit my self-understanding at this moment.

APIDA and LGBTQ are broad umbrella categories that encompass an incredible diversity of identities. It is difficult to fully understand the complex nature of our identities. One of the earliest known uses of APIDA was by Dr. Mamta Accapadi (2006) at the University of Texas Multicultural Information Center; it was a pan-Asian term that felt inclusive to the student communities that represented Asian America. Similarly, LGBTQ is a broad and ever-changing umbrella term for people on all points of the sexuality and gender spectrum. The beauty of social justice work is that by acknowledging these differences, I can be an ally even to those who share my identity, as we examine the similarities and further our solidarity and support.

Bridging Two Continents: Understanding the "D" in APIDA

Born in India and raised in the United States since the age of 7, I was very aware of my ethnic identity from an early age. From being "volunteered" by my parents to participate in community celebrations of *Diwali* to spending hours after school learning *Kannada* alphabets, I was constantly encouraged to be proud of being Indian. And yet, my parents told me that I was "not Indian enough" when I did not take Advanced Placement (AP) science courses or score high marks on the SAT. I internalized these messages and distanced myself from the kids I was supposed to be like; instead,

I became a member of the Alianza Latina, the Latino student organization in high school. For the first time, I found a group of people who were also the "others" on campus and who welcomed me without any judgment. In my senior year, I was elected president of the organization.

After high school, I attended a large private university in Boston, beginning in fall 2001. As I became more politically active, I started identifying as South Asian; I wanted a term that represented the shared experience of those of us from South Asia living in the United States, especially after the events of 9/11. I enrolled in graduate school in a state where opportunities to connect with people who looked like me or shared the same identities were very limited. There was an Indian Student Association on campus, but my internalized experiences from high school kept me from even attending a meeting. I began identifying as Asian so I could find a community with which I could connect. Even at professional conferences, I attended Asian networking events and celebrations, but I still could not find any other people who looked like me or who considered South Asians as part of the community. Surrounded by professionals of many Asian communities, I felt alone and invisible. As I became more involved in our professional organizations, the first South Asian professional I met was Dr. Mamta Accapadi, who introduced me to the term *Desi*. Literally translated, it means "from the homeland"; using the term is a way for those of us from South Asia to identify ourselves in our own language. Though not fluent in Hindi, I understood the word and liked the fact that it provided a culturally specific term to define myself. It was my way of representing the uniqueness of my experience while acknowledging the shared struggles as a member of the APIDA community. Like Pacific Islanders, I believe Desis have a unique experience under the APIDA umbrella, and I think this term will become more widely used.

Queering the Rainbow: Understanding the "Q" in LGBTQ

Like my racial identity, my sexual identity has changed over time. I came out as bisexual to a few close friends in high school. Though I knew I was mainly attracted to other men, I believed that bisexuality would be easier to explain to my friends, especially those who identified as APIDA. I lost several APIDA and other friends soon after coming out. In a traditional Desi community, sex and intimacy are neither discussed nor displayed, and I did not know where to turn. I felt shame and fear as I began to accept and explore my sexuality. Over time, I became more comfortable defining myself as gay. I am descended from a long line of religious leaders, and my fear of losing my family kept me closeted from them until just a year ago, though I have been active in LGBT and intersectional work since high school.

In graduate school, a friend introduced me to the term *queer* as way to define my nonheterosexuality without feeling constricted by labels such as *gay* and *bisexual*. Although the word has many negative connotations for older LGBT people, it has been reclaimed as an umbrella term encompassing a wide spectrum of sexual and gender identities. As I started developing a campus support network of queer people of color, this term allowed our small community to gather and acknowledge the complexity of our sexualities and racial identities. In my professional career, I find that identifying as queer is important as a political statement: In reclaiming this word, I take back the power to define myself. I find that more and more students are self-identifying as queer as a way to challenge traditional definitions.

I share these stories to illustrate the complexity of our journeys to understanding our self-identities. Beverly Tatum (2000) suggested that "the concept of identity is a complex one, shaped by individual characteristics, family dynamics, historical factors, and social and political contexts" (p. 9). Though these identities may at times seem inconsistent and even contradictory, the experiences they provide shape our understanding of our communities and ourselves (Merchant & Willis, 2001). Each of us has a unique journey; just because a colleague and I identify with a particular group does not mean we understand that identity in the same light. My intricate layers make me who I am.

Filling the Void: Why I Pursued a Career in Student Affairs

As a college student, I felt out of place and isolated. There was no LGBTQ resource center on campus, and the multicultural center did not address issues of sexuality or other diversity issues. I had no APIDA mentors; the mentors who identified as LGBTQ were White. For the longest time, I thought I was the only Desi who was queer; I believed that these two identities were mutually exclusive and that I was an anomaly. A colleague at Syracuse University had the same experience:

> I really felt a strong lack of role models for me as a queer Desi during my undergrad years. It was shocking to me that all the Desis were straight and all the visible queers were White. I especially had no queer people of color as role models or mentors, and I felt that it was really important for queer Desis to be present in higher education. (A. Taneja, personal communication, June 12, 2011)

This visibility is critical if we are to engage our communities in transformational conversations. The internal struggle to balance and come to terms with my multiple identities would have been greatly aided by having an APIDA LGBTQ professional role model. When I first met another APIDA LGBTQ person at a national conference in graduate school, I hugged her. It was like finding a long-lost family member. I wondered what my journey would have been like if I had met her in college. A person does not have to be Desi and queer for me to identify with him or her, or have a mentoring relationship. As a colleague said, "Be open, be on the lookout for kindred spirits—your strongest allies may be people who seem to have little in common with you at first glance" (M. Boodram, personal communication, June 12, 2011). Mentors can be peers and friends, and can play critical roles in supporting my personal and professional work. "I have met several friends from my involvement [in professional organizations] whom I rely on to call and seek professional advice, moral support, and comfort as a person and a professional. There is a different level of understanding with these people . . . I know they understand me and my identity much more than others do" (J. M. Johnson, personal communication, June 5, 2011).

Being the Change: Seeking Authenticity in All Spaces

After graduate school, I worked at a small private liberal arts university with LGBTQ, women, and multicultural communities on campus. In this position, I finally felt able to bring all of myself to my work with students and to address issues of privilege and oppression. I could finally be queer and Desi simultaneously, while acknowledging the privilege of being a male in both cultures. As I explored these intersections, I engaged students in similar reflections and challenged them to think about how they identify and why. I was able to bring my connections and resources—organizations doing intersectional work—onto campus to challenge our notions of gender, sexuality, race, and more. I was being the role model I had always wanted when I was in college.

But even in this space, I had to constantly prove my authenticity. A colleague would say, "I don't see race or color, I only see you," or "Really? You're from South Asia? You don't *look* Asian. I would never have guessed." It is hard to avoid these kinds of comments and questions from colleagues and students, many of whom are White. How do I respond? Sometimes I wish I could pull out my family tree to show my lineage going back hundreds of years in India, a country on the Asian continent.

Recently, a queer faculty member asked, "Why do you wear those gay shirts all the time?" I was surprised at his reaction to my many shirts with messages about LGBTQ rights, such as "Legalize Gay." Should I be wearing heterosexual shirts? Sexuality is often an invisible identity—wearing these shirts is a strategy to bring awareness to my queer identity and to encourage conversations about LGBTQ rights. When I walk into a room, my brown skin and my male gender are apparent, but my queerness is not. I believe visibility is key to our movement. Too often, our community is stereotyped with images of gay White men. I choose to live my life in a way that encourages a broader understanding of queerness by LGBTQ, APIDA, and other communities.

It is incredible to me that I am now the director of the LGBT campus resource center at a large public university. As I begin this journey, I hope to be the visible role model that I did not have as a student. On a campus with more than 60% students of color, I am excited to be a queer person of color directing this center and leading communitywide conversations on the intersection of sexuality with our many other identities. As Audre Lorde said, "My fullest concentration of energy is available to me only when I integrate all the parts of who I am, openly, allowing power from particular sources of my living to flow back and forth freely through all my different selves, without the restrictions of externally imposed definition" (2004, p. 69).

Reflections

Cicero wrote, "We don't see things as they are, we see things as we are." Looking back on my experiences, I know that the person I am today came from the experiences I have lived. From talking with older APIDA LGBTQ professionals, I know how lucky I am to be able to engage in these conversations openly, sharing stories and finding support from other APIDA LGBTQ colleagues and allies across the country. As our community becomes more visible and better understood, we will be able to appreciate the complexity of ourselves and those around us. "The intersection of all my identities has made me a more powerful, resilient advocate" (L. MadhavaRau, personal communication, June 11, 2011). If our profession is committed to enhancing experiences of APIDA LGBTQ people on campus, we need to acknowledge the complex intersections of multiple identities, support APIDA LGBTQ role models, and learn how to develop alliances.

> Ensure there is adequate representation, do not tokenize people, and understand that APIDA LGBTQ professionals are more than their identities and do have skills outside of being 'brown/

brownish' and 'queer/queerish.' Do not assume you know their experiences and actually ask and listen to their concerns as a professional. If you do not support them, they will leave to a place they feel valued and welcomed. (J. M. Johnson, personal communication, June 5, 2011)

This chapter is intended to begin the conversation on this topic. By sharing our stories, we affirm our struggle and achievements. Sharing my story has been a powerful tool for me to reflect on my experiences; it reaffirms my passion and the reason for my work. I have tried to be true to my voice and experience as I continue to navigate my intersecting identities and communities. I urge other APIDA LGBTQ professionals and allies to share their experiences and continue this conversation.

References

Accapadi, M. (2006, June). We are Asian Americans too! South Asian Americans in the context of Asian America. Presented at the 19th National Conference on Race and Ethnicity, Chicago, IL.

Lorde, A. (2004). Age, race, class, and sex: Women redefining difference. In M. L. Andersen & P. H. Collins (Eds.), *Race, class, and gender: An anthology* (pp. 64–71). Belmont, CA: Thomson and Wardsworth.

McManus, S. (2011). Making room for the "I" voice in scholarship. Retrieved from http://www.wihe.com

Merchant, B. M., & Willis, A. I. (Eds.). (2000). *Multiple and intersecting identities in qualitative research.* Mahwah, NJ: Lawrence Erlbaum Associates.

Remick, E. (2009, October 30). Obesity time bomb: Rad fatty: Erin Remick. [Web log comment]. Retrieved from http://obesitytime-bomb.blogspot.com

Tatum, B. D. (2000). The complexity of identity: "Who am I?" In M. Adams, W. Blumenfeld, C. R. Castaneda, H. W. Hackman, M. L. Peters, & X. Zuniga, *Readings for diversity and social justice* (pp. 9–14). New York, NY: Routledge.

PART III

Strengthening AAPIs through
Organizations and Leadership

CHAPTER SIX

Transformative Leadership

The Influence of AAPI College Student Organizations on the Development of Leadership for Social Change

Cynya Michelle Ko

On the 26th anniversary of the bombing of Pearl Harbor, a Japanese American Yale University freshman studying in his room was confronted by a loud group of fair-haired fellow students, who pelted him with water balloons while shouting, "Bomb Pearl Harbor! Bomb Pearl Harbor!" One of them, a member of the Yale Debate Association, recited Franklin Roosevelt's "a date which will live in infamy" speech. Journalist-author Nicholas Lemann, in his 1999 book *The Big Test: The Secret History of the American Meritocracy* (1999), tells how the experience changed Japanese American student Don Nakanishi from a "meek little pre-med" to a leader. Nakanishi dropped his biology major and ultimately settled on political science. There was no Asian student association at Yale but, having grown up in East Los Angeles, he considered himself an honorary member of the Mexican American community, so he joined Movimiento Estudiantil Chicano de Aztlan (MEChA). He spent the next couple of years educating himself about the experiences of Japanese people in the United States. In 1969, more than a century after the first Chinese American enrolled at Yale in 1850, Nakanishi recruited a small group of Asian American students and founded the Asian American Students Association of Yale.

Asian American student organizations have a long history, but it is a story that has been excluded from the canon on the history of American higher education, books such as *The American College and University: A History* (Rudolph, 1990), *American Higher Education: A History* (Lucas, 1994), and *A History of American Higher Education* (Thelin, 2004). Meanwhile, virtually all U.S. institutions of higher education have an explicit commitment to the development of leaders; however, not enough students emerge as leaders. Susan Komives (1996), co-founder of the National Clearinghouse for Leadership Programs, noted that few colleges achieve this goal and those that achieve some level of success do so with a mere handful of students. Recognizing this failure, educators have called on leaders from all levels of higher education institutions to rise to the challenge of developing the next generation of leaders who will strive for positive social change. One example of how higher education fulfills its critical role in shaping the quality of leadership in modern American society can be found in the successes of Asian and Pacific Islander American college student organizations.

From Isolation to Empowerment: Chinese Students' Alliance

At the turn of the 20th century, Asian American college student organizations began appearing across the country, reflecting the influx of an Asian and Pacific Islander student body. Beginning in 1872, the first 100 government-sponsored mission students from China arrived to study in America, coming in annual detachments of about 30 boys each. They were brought to the Connecticut Valley to study for 15 years. However, in 1881, in the shadow of rising racial discrimination, mob violence, and race riots against the Chinese in the United States, the program was aborted. The Chinese students who arrived in America in the early 20th century differed from their predecessors in that the first wave of students were a tight-knit group with heavy government supervision, whereas this second wave came as individuals to attend institutions of higher education throughout the country. Historians Judy Yung (1995), Weili Ye (2001), and Stacey Bieler (2004) captured the elaborately organized and influential Chinese student organizations of this second wave in detailed accounts of early Chinese student life in America.

Chinese students felt isolated in America and were intrigued by the student governments and societies. The desire to learn about American democracy and the reality of isolation led students in Berkeley, Oakland, and San Francisco to create the Chinese Students' Alliance of America in 1902. As some of these college students transferred to other schools and new students arrived from China, the East Coast became the center of Chinese student associational life. In 1905, the Chinese Students' Alliance of the Eastern States was established at a meeting in Amherst, Massachusetts. That same year, the organization published the first issue of the national *Chinese Students Monthly* to unite Chinese students and inform the Chinese and American public about their opinions on events in China. By the fall of 1911, two-thirds of the Chinese students in America were members of the Chinese Students' Alliance of the United States, which incorporated its eastern, midwestern, and western regional organizations. By 1917, membership in the national organization reached 15,000. At prestigious eastern universities such as Cornell, Princeton, Harvard, and Yale, 100% of Chinese students were members. This was dramatic growth from the 23 students who had formed the original alliance in the Bay Area in 1902.

Members of the Chinese Students' Alliance of the United States described it as a "laboratory of self-government" that encouraged students to train for a lifelong career, to value each other, to cultivate a sportsmanlike spirit, to cooperate, and to practice self-sacrificing service. The alliance was seen "as both a natural product of the democratic spirit of the United States and as a nonscholastic activity that would help students develop into the American ideal: an independent, well-rounded person" (Bieler, 2004, p. 171). In the *Monthly*, Sieu Tsung Lok, the first Chinese student at Randolph Macon Woman's College in Lynchburg, Virginia, and a leader of the Eastern Alliance, wrote, "Every student will be called upon to be the leader [when they return to China] either in town self-government or in national constitutional government." She called on her fellow students "to seek every practical means to increase our knowledge and experience" in America and to be prepared for political responsibility awaiting them in China (Ye, 2001, p. 27).

At the heart of the organization were the local clubs, which provided opportunities for companionship, service, breaking down linguistic and cultural divisions, working together toward a common goal, influencing local communities, and developing leadership skills. Each year, the three regional organizations sponsored summer conferences at which students held elections, debates, mock parliaments, oratory competitions, talks by prominent speakers, and stunt competitions in English and Chinese. Each fall, the *Monthly* opened the school year with editorials welcoming new students, inviting them to get involved, and describing the benefits of membership, as well as reports and pictures from the summer conferences. It was at regional and national conferences that other Chinese American student organizations—such as the Chinese Students Christian Association, the Flip Flap Fraternity, and the Chinese Foresters Club—were formed. These organizations became the first Chinese American religious, fraternity, and professional clubs in the United States.

These early organizations played a prominent role in the lives of Asian American students. They helped alleviate the isolation Chinese students felt, and many of the leaders eventually became prominent political leaders. Wellington Koo, an alumnus of Columbia College who had majored in political science with a focus on international diplomacy, was a student leader at the local, regional, and national level for the Chinese Students' Alliance. As editor-in-chief of the sporadically published *Chinese Students' Bulletin*, he renamed it *Chinese Students' Monthly* and began publishing during the academic year. He was the first Chinese student to serve as editor-in-chief of an American university newspaper, the *Columbia Daily Spectator.* As a graduate student, Koo was the creative impetus behind the unification of Chinese student groups across the country. As an American-trained Chinese diplomat, his many endeavors altered the perception of China in the world.

Embracing Ethnic Identity Development: Filipino American Student Organizations

When *pensionados*, government-sponsored Filipino students, first arrived in America in 1903, they created the Filipino Students Club at the State Normal School (now San Diego State University). By 1905, the *Filipino Students Magazine* was being published in Berkeley. By 1912, more than 200 Filipino students had received an American education through the program. The original *pensionados* returned home to well-paying positions in agriculture, business, education, engineering, and government.

The second wave of Filipino students arrived between 1910 and 1940 as nonsponsored students who came to the United States with their own resources. Many struggled to stay in school and ended up in the labor market. But in 1924, campus enrollment was becoming affected by changes in immigration laws and policies that virtually suspended immigration from the Philippines for 40 years until 1965. While the census count of Filipino Americans doubled between 1970 and 1980, the number of degrees earned by Filipinos at the University of California (UC) between 1980 and 1990 quadrupled (Gonzalves, 2010). The political awakening of college students in the late 1960s and early 1970s coincided with the formation of Filipino college student organizations such as Pilipino American Collegiate Endeavor (PACE) at San Francisco State University in 1967, Pilipino American Alliance (PAA) at UC Berkeley in 1969, Samahang Pilipino at UCLA in 1972, and Kababayan at UC Irvine in 1974. Pilipino Cultural Night (PCN) was established in the early 1980s; it has become a central organizational activity for thousands of Filipino American college students across the United States. During a year-long exploration of what it means to be Filipino American, students take on various tasks connected to PCN, including script writing, casting, set design, costume making, catering, choreography, dancing, fundraising, music, outreach, publicity, and securing venues. They spend countless hours in preparation to produce each culture night. Artist-scholar Theo Gonzalves' analysis of the phenomenon highlights how PCNs play a central role in the ethnic identity development of Filipino American college students by addressing their questions about Philippine and Filipino American culture. Through their student organizations and PCNs, Filipino American students have created a living laboratory for the development of social change leadership through sustained engagement and education about their Filipino and Filipino American issues, history and culture.

Responding to Racial Exclusion: The Creation of Early Japanese American Student Organizations

In college, as in K–12 public schools, early Asian American students experienced social exclusion and isolation. Japanese American student organizations tell the story of why and how Asian American student organizations were created in the United States. The establishment of early Japanese American student organizations was a response to racial exclusion in the 1920s and 1930s, filling the void for college students who faced institutional racism and a lack of support networks. Organizations such as the Nisei Bruin Club at UCLA, the Nisei Trojan Club at the University of Southern California (USC), and the Japanese Men's Student Club and Japanese Women's Student Club at UC Berkeley afforded Japanese Americans resources and opportunities from which they were excluded in mainstream campus clubs.

Nisei writer Yoshiko Uchida's autobiography, *Desert Exile*, is a testament to the vital opportunities Nisei organizations provided for Japanese American students, as well as the long-term effect of involvement in Asian and Pacific Islander American (APIA) student organizations on heightening racial/ethnic awareness and commitment to one's community. Uchida graduated from high school early to remove herself from "the alienation of the Nisei from the world of White students in high school only to find the situation worse in college" (Uchida, 1982, p. 42). She tells of "retreating quite thoroughly into the support and comfort afforded by the Japanese American campus community" and says that "if we hadn't had these ethnic organizations to join, I think few Nisei would have had the opportunity to hold positions of leadership or responsibility" (p. 44). As a senior at UC Berkeley in 1942, Uchida, along with approximately 700 other University of California students, had her college education cut short when President Franklin D. Roosevelt ordered the evacuation of Japanese Americans from the West Coast and their imprisonment in internment camps. But her involvement as a leader in these college clubs gave her the strength to tell the story. She eventually became known as the first Nisei writer to commit her career to the stories of her community and has been credited with almost single-handedly creating a Japanese American fiction genre for youth. Over the course of her career, she published more than 40 works, including nonfiction for adults and fiction for children and teenagers addressing Japanese American issues of citizenship, ethnicity, identity, and intercultural relationships.

Creating a Safe Space: Asian American Greeks

Discrimination in the form of segregation, antimiscegenation laws, immigration quotas, and exclusion was the norm for Asian Americans until the 1970s. (However, a small number of Asian American students were welcomed into traditional Greek organizations, particularly on the East Coast at institutions such as Beloit, Columbia, Colgate, Cornell, Rutgers, and Yale.) Although fraternities were always exclusionist in both racial and socioeconomic terms, explicit discriminatory entrance requirements did not become widespread until the beginning of the 20th century when the student population on college campuses diversified. Many Greek organizations responded by implementing exclusionary clauses to ensure that their members would be of like mind, religion, and race. By 1928, more than half of the national fraternities and sororities had written policies or constitutions that plainly excluded applicants on the basis of religious affiliation and race.

At a time when Greek life dominated extracurricular activities, legal barriers to obtaining jobs and housing, pursuing fields of study, and joining mainstream college student organizations spurred the creation of the first Asian American fraternity and sorority. In 1926, six Chinese American men at UC Berkeley banded together to establish Pi Alpha Pi fraternity with the purpose of fostering brotherhood, academic excellence, Asian American experience, leadership, and philanthropy—and partly as a coping mechanism against racism. In 1928, two Japanese American women at the University of California, Southern Branch (now UCLA), established Chi Alpha Delta as a haven against racism. From the late 1930s to the 1960s, Chi Alpha Delta tried unsuccessfully to secure a house on Greek row. Even though the organizations provided opportunities, they continued to operate in a climate of economic disenfranchisement, exclusion, discrimination, legal segregation, and isolation.

Thirty years after the founding of the first Asian American sorority in the United States, Margaret Ohara, a third-generation Japanese American and an entering UCLA freshman, was awarded a $200 Panhellenic scholarship for being the most well-rounded student from her high school senior class. When she arrived at the Panhellenic Sunday Tea, the mistake was apparent: Ohara, a Japanese surname, had been mistaken for O'Hara, an Irish name. Ultimately, the Panhellenic Council denied her admission into any sorority and, hence, the scholarship. In 1959, Ohara and eight other charter members founded Theta Kappa Phi to create a sorority that would give Asian American women the opportunity to belong to a Greek letter organization. Technicalities related to racial segregation excluded Chi Alpha Delta and Theta Kappa Phi from participation and membership in mainstream rush recruitment and from the Panhellenic Council. Along with Omega Sigma Tau and Lambda Phi Epsilon (Asian American fraternities founded in 1966 and 1981, respectively), the two sororities formed the UCLA Asian Greek Council, which remains the governing body for the four historically Asian American fraternities and sororities at UCLA.

Developing a Collective Voice for Advocacy: The Third World Liberation Front

By the late 1960s, the activism of Asian American students extended to coalition building for access to higher education and ethnic studies. For more than a century, APIA college students have used the collective voice of student organizations to address campus and community concerns, rallying for Asian American studies programs, resource centers, and increased faculty and staff representation. In December 1968, students at San Francisco State College (now San Francisco State University) called for ethnic studies and open admissions under the slogan of self-determination. It was the first campus uprising involving Asian Americans as a collective force, and it marked the beginning of the Asian American movement. Organized by members of the Third World Liberation Front—a coalition of student organizations including the Asian American Political Alliance (AAPA), Black Student Union (BSU), Intercollegiate Chinese for Social Action (ICSA), Latin American Student Organization (LASO), Mexican American Student Confederation (MASC), Native American Student Organization (NASO), and Pilipino American Collegiate Endeavor (PACE)—the strike focused on a redefinition of education, one that was more relevant and accessible, and that served the needs of these communities in America. It was the longest student strike in American history; it ended in March 1969 with a compromise that included the establishment of the nation's first School of Ethnic Studies. The experience changed the lives of the Asian American student activists in many ways; however, all participants voiced a common theme: a deep-rooted commitment to social change for the benefit of their communities. The experience produced a community of leaders who would continue to pursue their ideals.

Impact of the Immigration and Nationality Act of 1965 on American Higher Education

During the era following the civil rights movement, changes in immigration unintentionally opened the doors of higher education to large numbers of APIA students. The Immigration and Nationality Act of 1965 (also known as the Hart-Celler Act) turned the immigration tide, but it was not intended to be a means for significantly altering the immigration flow; rather, it was a symbolic act, an extension of civil rights beyond the United States (Center for Immigration Studies, 1995). It unwittingly resulted in one of the greatest waves of immigration in the history of the United States. The Act reversed decades of systematic exclusion and restrictive immigration policies by abolishing the national origins quota system that had regulated the ethnic composition of immigration for more than 40 years. Under the new law, the three major qualifications for immigration were family reunification, occupational immigration, and political refuge. Policymakers intended to favor European countries by assigning 80% of the quota immigrants to family reunification preferences and allowing an unlimited number of nonquota immigrants for spouses, unmarried children under 21, and parents of U.S. citizens (Hing, 1993; and Min, 2005). However, the vast majority of post-1965 immigration originated from Asian, Latin American, and Caribbean countries, which radically altered the American racial and ethnic makeup (Min, 2005). More than 8 million Asian immigrants were admitted to the United States during the 38-year period between 1965 and 2002, accounting for 34% of total U.S. immigrants (Min, 2005).

The United States is a nation of immigrants; however, the country's ambivalent posture—proud of our immigrant heritage yet wary of new arrivals—is one of the most powerful dynamics in the politics of American immigration (Meilaender, 2001). "How a nation treats the immigrants speaks volumes about the nation" (R. S. Chang, 1999, p. 27); consider this when examining the climate and environment in the United States for Asian and Pacific Americans. Since colonial times, waves of immigration have been followed by lulls—periods of restricted immigration (Meilaender, 2001). This understanding helps contextualize the environment in which APIAs have entered American institutions of higher education. The doors (Getman, 1992) and gates (Kerr, 1991) of access to colleges and universities did not simply swing open.

Building a Support Network for Refugees: Southeast Asian American Student Organizations

A look at some Southeast Asian ethnic groups sheds light on student organization formation following the largest refugee migration to the United States since World War I. The first recorded Vietnamese student to attend Harvard College arrived from Vietnam in 1964. Four years later, there were enough Vietnamese students at San Diego State University to form the Vietnamese Student Association. In 1975, fearing communist persecution in the former Indochina after the collapse of the governments of Laos and Cambodia, 1.25 million refugees fled to America. Between 1976 and 1979, Vietnamese American student organizations were founded at a variety of institutions, including USC (1976); George Mason University in Virginia, UC San Diego, and UCLA (1977); the University of Maryland College Park (1978); and UC Irvine and Virginia Tech (1979).

Similar trends can be seen among Cambodian students. Many Cambodian refugees settled in Long Beach, which became the largest Cambodian community in the United States. In 1981, students at Cal State Long Beach formed the Cambodian Student Society. Hmong (an Asian ethnic group from the mountainous regions of China, Vietnam, Laos, and Thailand) student associations were established in the 1980s at institutions such as UC Santa Cruz, Cal State Fresno, and the University of Wisconsin Eau Claire with the goals of social and mutual support, educating the campus community about Hmong culture, providing opportunities for leadership and self-government, and giving the Hmong student community a voice on campus. The first Laotian refugees arrived in 1979; they had no knowledge of a written language and little formal education, and over the intervening years have had the highest rate of youth going to prison among all Southeast Asian Americans. Many Laotian refugees and their children credit their success to the growing network of Laotian student associations in colleges and universities, which provide academic support, a strong network of students with similar cultural experiences, and direct service to the Laotian community (Papphaybou, 2003).

The Misunderstood Racial Minority: Learning to Stand Up and Speak Out as Asian Americans

In the early 1980s, UC Irvine was shocked by the suicides of two Vietnamese American students and the known attempts of several more during one academic year. In response, the school formed the Asian/Pacific Student and Staff Association and the Asian Pacific Awareness Conference to explore issues facing Asian American students. A common theme that emerged was the pressure of being the model minority. The term *model minority* refers to Asian Americans as the success story—a minority group that has overcome hardship to achieve the American Dream. Fundamental to the myth is the idea that all Asian American college students are successful. This myth has led educators to dismiss Asian Americans as a no-need population and the general public to be unsympathetic toward the concerns of Asian Americans. The notion of Asian Americans as a model minority may seem like a compliment; however, it has been consistently criticized for four decades by Asian American community leaders, institutions, researchers, and educators, with growing concern over the negative consequences. Efforts to make Asian American issues known, complaints of discrimination, and calls for remedial action are seen as unwarranted and inappropriate, and may spark resentment—all of which renders the oppression of Asian Americans invisible (R. S. Chang, 1999) and places Asians among the most misunderstood racial minorities in higher education (Chang, 2008).

The model minority myth played a key role in establishing a racial hierarchy that denied the oppression of Asian Americans while simultaneously legitimizing the oppression of other ethnic racial minorities and poor Whites (Chang, 1999). In the 1970s, articles that spoke of Asian Americans "outwhiting Whites" ("Success Story," 1971) spurred resentment and hostility toward Asian Americans. By the 1980s, the myth rationalized a backlash on both the educational and economic fronts. Asian Americans were criticized for being overrepresented at elite colleges and universities (Takagi, 1992). In the 1980s, admissions applications by Asian American students to elite institutions increased dramatically, yet acceptance rates remained static or declined, leading to an investigation of admissions policies and admissions officers. Between 1983 and 1986, organizations including the Asian American Student Association at Brown University, the Asian American Association at Harvard, and the East Coast Asian Student Union developed and sustained claims of discrimination against some of the most elite colleges in the nation—including Brown, Harvard, Princeton, Stanford, Yale, UC Berkeley, and UCLA. The investigations found that the model minority myth translated into numerous misconceptions among admissions officers that may have affected their decisions and admissions policies, which had been adjusted so that standards for admittance of Asian American students were more strenuous. Brown University and UC Berkeley admitted that their admissions practices were biased and revised their procedures. "According to the *Chronicle of Higher Education*, the evidence for discrimination against Asian Americans was ambiguous . . . but the fact that the evidence was not plainly incontrovertible was disturbing. . . . Officials from Harvard to Berkeley emphatically denied willful intent to discriminate against Asian applicants" (Takagi, 1992, p. 50). This controversy over Asian American admissions endures as Asian American postsecondary enrollments continue to increase.

American institutions of higher education continue to experience an epidemic of disturbing racial incidents that alarm educators and threaten the safety of the learning environment for all students. The stories reveal the precarious position of APIA students when they are not sufficiently supported by their institutions and the struggle these students endure as they seek positive learning environments. Sometimes APIA students are forced to act. Journalist David Morse (1998) chronicled an incident at the University of Connecticut (UConn) in 1987 that involved eight Asian international and Asian American students riding a bus to an off-campus, residence-hall-sponsored Christmas dance. Sitting at the back of the bus was a group of intoxicated White students, including football players, who began spitting chewing tobacco at them and yelling, "Chinks!" and "Oriental faggots!" Despite angry protests from the victims, the spitting continued until the bus pulled up to the club 45 minutes later. For 3 hours, two of the football players continued to harass the Asian students inside the dance—trying to pick fights, elbowing the victims, making animal sounds, screaming insults, mooning them, and even spitting beer in one of their faces—without any intervention. When the victims complained to the resident assistants, they were threatened with write-ups and told to "shut up" and not spoil the party. The students contacted campus public safety and the dean of students, but the university did not acknowledge that the harassment constituted racism or a hate crime; in fact, the institution did not address the incident seriously until the victims threatened to go to the media.

Organizing for Inclusion

This response sparked campus protests, including Professor Paul Bock's hunger strike for justice. Until this incident, Bock, a Chinese American mathematics professor, had had little interest in or knowledge of the plight of Asian American students. At the time, UConn had cultural centers for African American, Latino, and female students but no special services for Asian students. In fact, Asian students were denied funding from its Minority Advancement Program. With nowhere to go for support, the victims established the Asian American Students Association (AASA) as a political voice for the Asian American community and, with the support of Professor Bock, advocated for an investigation of institutionalized racism at UConn, establishment of a cultural center, and courses in Asian American studies. Professor Bock also initiated what has become the Asian American Faculty and Staff Association. Both the Asian American Cultural Center and the Asian American Studies Institute were established at UConn in 1993.

After college, Marta Ho, one of the victims and primary student leaders behind the creation of the AASA at UConn, spent 3 years doing community work with the InterRelations Collaborative, a nonprofit research and education organization dedicated to building intergroup relations among rapidly diversifying student populations in New York

City and the Tri-State area. She said, "UConn gave me that incident . . . to do something really different than I would have done if I had just gone through school without really thinking about these things" (p. 7). Another of the victims, Tina Chin, went on to become a lawyer for the Enforcement Division of the Commission of Human Rights and Opportunities in Hartford. Historically, Asian American students have responded to discrimination and lack of resources in one of two ways: they have become active in their communities and on campus, or they have persisted through the feelings of both isolation and alienation (Liang, Lee, & Ting, 2002).

The environment of a college or university—the campus climate—can have a significant effect on student access, retention, and academic success. Campus climate influences the adjustment and persistence of various racial groups; it is important to understand the impact of this climate, especially racism, on APIA involvement in student organizations (Liang et al., 2002). The challenges faced by APIA students are a national problem that has become more apparent with the growth of the APIA population in higher education (Rhoads, Lee, & Yamada, 2002) and their assertion that universities are not meeting their needs (Chew & Ogi, 1987).

Advocates for Positive Social Change: Asian Pacific American Student Organizations

Many students involved in APIA student organizations have become leaders of their campuses and communities in addressing institutional inequity. APIA college students work synergistically, purposefully, and productively through their student organizations to establish, maintain, and advance APIA studies and student services in American higher education. In the spring of 1991, student organizations in the Cross-Cultural Center at UC Irvine established the Ethnic Students Coalition Against Prejudicial Education, advocating for the implementation of ethnic studies programs. The student umbrella organizations—African American Student Union, Asian Pacific Student Association (APSA), and MEChA—unified and coordinated major rallies to generate campus support. Two years later, despite numerous meetings and promises from administrators, the university offered programs in African American and Chicano-Latino studies but continued to offer only two courses in Asian American studies. In spring 1993, APSA—the umbrella and advocacy organization for APIA student organizations at UC Irvine—led a 35-day rotational fast and educational vigil protesting the lack of administrative action in establishing Asian American studies. APSA bookended the strike with educational sit-ins advocating Asian American student services in the form of an academic advisor and an additional staff position in the Cross-Cultural Center. The protest received considerable media attention and galvanized the Asian American community on and off campus. UC Irvine was one of only two UC campuses without an Asian American studies program, even though 43% of its undergraduate population were Asian/Pacific Islander students—the highest percentage in the continental United States. UC Irvine students believed this was unacceptable and demonstrated their commitment to the establishment of Asian American studies and student services. The hunger strike and an educational sit-in at the chancellor's office resulted in the administration's commitment to expedite hiring of an academic counselor, a program coordinator for the Cross-Cultural Center, and four professors to teach Asian American studies.

Two thousand miles away, students at Chicago's Northwestern University embarked on a three-and-a-half-year struggle under the leadership of the Asian American Advisory Board (AAAB), a student organization. Following the rejection of proposals in fall 1991 and winter 1993 to hire an Asian American advisor, the AAAB submitted a new proposal in February 1995, asking for an Asian American studies program; it was rejected 2 weeks later by the new university president. In April, the AAAB gathered more than 200 students at "The Rock" at the center of campus and embarked on a hunger strike. With 17 students committed to the full hunger strike and 60 others pledging a day of fasting, the students set up camp in two large tents. After 23 days of hunger strikes and three rallies, the AAAB agreed to the university's offer of "short-term solutions" during "long-term deliberations." In the months and years that followed, Asian American student organizations led similar protests for ethnic and Asian American studies at Princeton, Columbia, and the University of Maryland College Park.

APIA students have also become visible catalysts in the fight against the invisible racism Asians and Asian Americans encounter off-campus in the larger society. In 1996, under the leadership of APSA and the Vietnamese American Coalition, UC Irvine led a multipronged year-long Nike Awareness Campaign protesting the company's abusive labor practices in Indonesia, Vietnam, and other countries. UC Irvine became the first major American university to call for a boycott of Nike's university-licensed apparel and to pass a resolution prohibiting the sale and distribution of Nike products on campus. APIA student leaders have a history of effecting extraordinary social change (Louie & Omatsu, 2001).

Emergent Ethnicity and Religiosity: Korean American Christian Fellowships

Sociologist Rebecca Y. Kim highlighted the visibility of Korean American Christian fellowships on both East and West Coast campuses (which have the largest concentrations of Korean American students) in her 2006 book *God's New Whiz Kids? Korean American Evangelicals on Campus*. UCLA alone offers more than 10 Korean Christian fellowships, and every top-ranked university and college in the country has at least one. Pastors and staff leaders point out that these organizations address feelings of marginalization and mattering as well as provide Korean American students with leadership opportunities they would not have in a diverse or White majority campus ministry. Korean American fellowships, as peer groups and student organizations, influence the development of leaders.

The Desi Voice: South Asian A Cappella Groups

In 1996, as an extension of the elaborate offerings of South Asian college student organizations, students at the University of Pennsylvania who wanted to express their subcontinental culture through music established Penn Masala, the world's first Hindi a cappella group. Fusing various musical traditions—including Hindi film music, hip-hop, pop, R&B,

rock, and Indian classical styles—they sing primarily in English or Hindi but also in Arabic, Kannada, Punjabi, and Tamil. Tapping into the growth of collegiate South Asian a cappella groups, the Indian Student Alliance at the University of Iowa hosts one of the nation's largest annual South Asian a cappella competitions, Gathe Raho, bringing together groups from Boston University, Carnegie Mellon, UC Berkeley, the University of Illinois, the University of Michigan, Northwestern, St. Louis University, Stanford, Vanderbilt, and Case Western Reserve. These a cappella groups are sustained activities that give students the opportunity to apply leadership principles and develop leadership skills.

Hawai`i Clubs

From Boston to Washington, Hawai`i clubs help college students make the transition from Hawai`i to life on the mainland. They produce luaus and other programs and events, developing leaders while they educate and engage the campus community in Hawaiian culture. Even before Hawai`i attained statehood, students from Hawai`i at the University of Oregon formed a student organization in 1941 called *Hui-o-Kamaaina* (the Club of Old Times) to encourage cooperation and unity among students from Hawai`i and to develop knowledge and appreciation of Hawaiian culture. These organizations play a key leadership role in providing social support for Hawaiian students on the mainland, which aids in the students' adjustment and acclimation, and ultimately helps institutions with retention. The organizations educate the campus community about traditional and contemporary Hawaiian culture beyond coconuts, palm trees, and grass skirts. With hundreds in attendance, Yale University's Hawai`i Club hosted a weekend symposium in 1995 on sovereignty for native Hawaiians and launched the annual East Coast Hawai`i Symposium, which has brought hundreds of students together to address issues such as Hawai`i's brain drain (at Princeton in 1996) and the state's effort to create a global niche (at MIT in 1999). These symposiums empower students to consider leadership in the future of Hawai`i by engaging them in reflection and dialogue.

Conclusion

For Don Nakanishi—the Yale student who decided to form the Asian American Students Association in 1969 and created his own place to stand—and for many Asian American students before and after him, marginalization was not an option. Awakened by injustice, Nakanishi was empowered to transform his environment at Yale. Ever since then, these student organizations have served as an antidote to isolation, empowering their members to contribute to the campus and to the wider community. Without these organizations, Asian and Pacific Islander American students have limited options and risk ending up on the margins of the mainstream. For many APIAs, their experiences in student organizations have enabled them to become leaders. Nakanishi himself went on to become a writer, educator-scholar, and community leader who is recognized for developing the fields of Asian American political and educational research. He continues to write articles, books, and reports after spending 35 years as a professor and two decades as the director of UCLA's Asian American Studies Center, leading it to its place as the nation's largest, most comprehensive and renowned research, teaching, publications, library and archival collecting, and public educational institute focusing on Asian Pacific Americans.

References

Bieler, S. (2004). *Patriots or traitors: A history of American-educated Chinese students.* Armonk, NY: M. E. Sharpe, Inc.

Center for Immigration Studies. (1995, September). *Three decades of mass immigration: The legacy of the 1965 Immigration Act.* Retrieved from http://www.cis.org/articles/1995/back395.html

Chang, M. J. (1999). Expansion and its discontents: The formation of Asian American studies programs in the 1990s. *Journal of Asian American Studies, 2*(2), 181–206.

Chang, M. J. (2000). Improving campus racial dynamics: A balancing act among competing interests. *The Review of Higher Education, 23*(2), 153–175.

Chang, M. J. (2008). Asian evasion: A recipe for flawed solutions. *Diverse Issues in Higher Education, 25*(7), 26.

Chang, R. S. (1999). *Disoriented: Asian Americans, law and the nation-state.* New York: New York University Press.

Chew, C. A., & Ogi, Y. A. (1987). Asian American college student perspectives. In D. J. Wright (Ed.), *Responding to the needs of today's minority students* (pp. 33–48). San Francisco: Jossey-Bass.

Getman, J. (1992). *In the company of scholars: The struggle for the soul of higher education.* Austin, TX: University of Texas Press.

Gonzalves, T. (2010). *The day the dancers stayed: Performing in the Filipino/American diaspora.* Philadelphia, PA: Temple University Press.

Hing, B. (1993). *Making and remaking Asian America through immigration policy, 1850–1990.* Stanford, CA: Stanford University Press.

Kerr, C. (1991). *The great transformation in higher education, 1960–1980.* Albany, NY: SUNY Press.

Komives, S. R. (1996, July/August). A call for collaborative leadership. *About Campus, 1*(3), 2–3.

Lemann, N. (1999). *The big test: The secret history of American meritocracy.* New York, NY: Farrar, Straus and Giroux.

Liang, C. T. H., Lee, S., & Ting, M. P. (2002). Developing Asian American leaders. In M. K. McEwen, C. M. Kodama, A. N. Alvarez, S. Lee, & C. T. H. Liang (Eds.), *Working with Asian American college students* (New Directions for Student Services, no. 97, pp. 81–90). San Francisco, CA: Jossey-Bass.

Louie, S., & Omatsu, G. (2001). *Asian Americans: The movement and the moment.* Los Angeles, CA: UCLA Asian American Studies Center Press.

Meilaender, P. C. (2001). *Toward a theory of immigration.* New York, NY: Palgrave.

Min, P. G. (2005) Asian immigration: History and contemporary trends. In P. G. Min (Ed.), *Asian Americans: Contemporary trends and issues* (pp. 7–31). Thousand Oaks, CA: Pine Forge Press.

Morse, D. (1998, May 17). *After the incident.* Retrieved from http://articles.courant.com/1998-05-17/news/9807220652_1_white-students-second-student-eight-students

Phapphaybou, T. (2003). Laotian Americans: You're from where? In E. Lai & D. Arguelles (Eds.), *The new face of Asian Pacific America: Numbers, diversity, and change in the 21st century* (pp. 99–102). Los Angeles, CA: UCLA Asian American Studies Center Press.

Rhoads, R. A., Lee, J. J., & Yamada, M. (2002). Panethnicity and collective action among Asian American college students. *Journal of College Student Development, 43*(6), 876–891.

Success story: Outwhiting the Whites. (1971, June 21). *Newsweek,* pp. 24–25.

Takagi, D. (1992). *The retreat from race: Asian American admissions and racial politics.* New Brunswick, NJ: Rutgers University Press.

Uchida, Y. (1982). *Desert Exile.* Seattle: University of Washington Press.

Ye, W. (2001). *Seeking modernity in China's name: Chinese students in the United States.* Stanford, CA: Stanford University Press.

Yung, J. (1995). *Unbound feet: A social history of Chinese women in San Francisco.* Berkeley, CA: University of California Press.

CHAPTER SEVEN

APIA Professional Development through the Asian Pacific American Network

The Past Four Decades

Glenn DeGuzman, Monica Nixon, and Sunny Park Suh

For decades, Asian and Pacific Islander American (APIA) student affairs professionals and graduate students worked in isolation on college campuses. Early pioneers recognized the critical nature of supporting one another in student affairs work and laid the groundwork for developing the professional connections to sustain themselves. The Asian Pacific American Network (APAN) of the American College Personnel Association (ACPA) was the first national organization for APIAs in student affairs, and it has continued to serve as a model and catalyst for similar organizations. It is important to recall these historical foundations as we continue recruiting, developing, and retaining APIA professionals in the field.

When Patricia Takemoto attended her first ACPA convention in Chicago in 1976, she did not see any other APIAs. The former assistant director of student activities at Northern Illinois University remembers that not many ethnic minorities were in the student affairs profession back then. "When I entered student affairs at Northern Illinois University, it was very White" (personal communication, January 2011). The 1976 convention was also Charlene Chew's first. Chew, who was then assistant director of residential life at the University of California, Irvine, recalls, "I saw one other APIA . . . but that was it" (personal communication, December 2010).

Both Takemoto and Chew would continue to attend ACPA conferences, and both were singled out for their contributions to the student affairs field. Takemoto was the first APIA to receive ACPA's Annuit Coeptis Emerging Professional award in 1979, and Chew received the same honor 2 years later. Takemoto ultimately became assistant vice chancellor at the University of Wisconsin before leaving the field. Chew, with her partner Alan Ogi, wrote a groundbreaking chapter entitled "Asian American Student Perspectives in Colleges" that was published in the summer 1987 *New Directions for Student Services*. In addition, she has mentored many APIAs in the student affairs field. She is currently director of residential life at the University of California, Santa Barbara.

These two influential women did not cross paths in their careers; however, they shared similar experiences as APIAs in student affairs. Their presence in ACPA in the 1970s reflected the emergence of the Asian American perspective in the field of student affairs. Takemoto and Chew, along with others, were part of the "prologue" of organized efforts to provide a more structured support network for APIA student affairs professionals.

This chapter describes the groundbreaking history of the Asian Pacific American Network (APAN) and how it has adapted to meet the evolving needs of APIA student affairs professionals. Using personal narratives and archival data, we celebrate the history of APIA student affairs administrators in the field of higher education and document the themes that emerged in the community. For more than 30 years, APAN has evolved to meet the needs of APIA student affairs staff and graduate students, who now comprise 1.8% and 0.4%, respectively, of ACPA's membership (Stephanie Gatson, personal communication, June 8, 2011). We underscore APAN's importance as a model and catalyst for other organizations and discuss the network's time line, strategic plan, and emerging initiatives, as well as the impact of APIA professionals on students, institutions, and the profession.

Historical Time Line

ACPA and NASPA–Student Affairs Administrators in Higher Education have grown into two of the largest and most comprehensive student affairs organizations, supporting and fostering college student learning through the generation and dissemination of knowledge to inform policies, practices, and programs for student affairs professionals and the higher education community. NASPA, which was founded in 1919, has more than 12,000 members; ACPA, which was founded in 1924, has nearly 7,500 members in the United States and around the world (ACPA, 2011; NASPA, 2011).

APAN was one of the first groups of its kind to form within student affairs. Over the past several decades, APAN has supported generations of APIA professionals, nurturing leadership on campuses and in the field, and generating knowledge about supporting APIA students. Unfortunately, little has been documented about the people and the organizational challenges involved with APAN's development. Using data collected through interviews, archives, and other sources, we present key developments and findings for each decade, beginning with the 1970s.

Foundation (1970s): Establishment of the Committee on Multicultural Affairs

APAN arose from a larger force that was emerging across fields, including counseling. In the early 1970s, brothers and psychologists Derald Wing Sue and Stanley Sue wrote about the need to train counselors to serve the unique needs of Asian Americans in the context of counseling

(Leong & Gupta, 2008). Their work brought attention to the needs of APIAs in general and served as a focal point for student affairs educators.

Around 1970, ACPA members created the Black Task Force. This group evolved into the Minority Task Force in 1974, in response to a push to bring more attention to minority issues within the profession. The group was formalized at the 1977 APAN convention in Denver. In 1979, the Committee on Multicultural Affairs (CMA) was established, with Chris Campbell as its first elected chair (Campbell, 1985). In a survey administered that year, ethnic minorities comprised roughly 10% of ACPA's 8,200 members (Campbell, 1985, p. 2). In 1980, CMA formed an advisory council to increase minority representation, to which Charlene Chew was appointed. She became CMA's Far West Region representative in 1981 (Campbell, 1985). Other early activists in CMA included Nancy Asai and Paul Shang, who served on the CMA board in the 1980s.

Seeds (1980s): Establishment of the Asian American Network

As minority affairs gained prominence in the field, APIA organizations began to emerge and organize in the 1980s. As early as 1982, conversations percolated in California, with the development of Leadership Education for Asian Pacifics (LEAP), an organization that provided leadership training for APIAs (LEAP, 2011). Asian Pacific Americans in Higher Education (APAHE) was founded in 1987, in part to uncover the truth behind allegations of admissions quotas in the University of California system (Banerjee, 2001). ACPA continued its commitment to APIA leadership and organization. As CMA continued to grow in the mid-1980s, pioneers such as Chris Campbell, Harold Cheatham, and Mary Howard created multicultural subcommittees called Information Groups. These groups were originally called the Issues for African Americans Network, Issues for Asians Network, Issues for Latinos Network, and Issues for Native Americans Network. By 1987, these subcommittees were formalized and renamed as CMA networks. In 1987, Paul Shang was appointed the first chair of the new Asian American Network (AAN) (Shang, personal communication, June 2003). These informal gatherings drew a handful of attendees, among them Charlene Chew-Ogi and Alan Ogi, Rich Shintaku, Linda Ahuna, Nancy Asai, and Jeanie Takeda. The number of APIA student affairs professionals remained low during the 1980s, but the next decade brought significant increases in the field and in ACPA.

Roots and Shoots (1990s): Emerging Leaders

With AAN firmly established as a CMA network, the 1990s saw unprecedented growth in the number of APIAs in the field, not only within AAN but also in CMA. At the beginning of the decade, though, with only a handful of APIAs involved in the organization and communication limited to telephone and the annual convention, it was challenging to create sustainable impacts.

Fary Koh, who attended her first ACPA convention in 1991, recruited Belinda Huang to help her organize an AAN meeting and social at the 1992 convention, which drew roughly 10 people (Koh, personal communication, February 2011; M. Wong, personal communication, January 2011). In 1993, Belinda Huang and Rey Guerrero were appointed AAN co-chairs for a 2-year term. At their first meeting, about six people showed up (Huang, personal communication, December 2010). Their initial goal for AAN was to bring people together and create a community.

Beginning with the 1994 convention, attendance at AAN meetings began to grow, increasing to 20 to 40 members. The network received a tremendously positive response to its 1994 CMA Culture Fest performance of the poem "Asian Is Not Oriental." Michael Paul Wong said, "It was very emotional, and it underscored our shared racism and political awareness" (personal communication, January 2011). Huang and Guerrero encouraged members to make presentations on issues that affected APIA students, and they began organizing regional meetings and socials once or twice a year. Huang said, "People needed to meet other APIAs in the profession and get the support. People sought a way to survive in the academy when they were the only one" (personal communication, December 2010). To make the group more inclusive, the name was changed to the Asian Pacific American Network.

Betty Chung and Michael Paul Wong served as APAN co-chairs from 1995 to 1997. Their goals of creating a stronger presence for APIAs and a stronger coalition between APAN and the other CMA networks were pursued by a number of rising young and energetic APAN professionals and graduate students (Chung, personal communication, January 2011). This new wave of APIA professionals established an APAN listserv, a website, and an online directory, which had a tremendous effect on group communication and solidarity. APAN also created a library of resources, an annual newsletter, regular conference socials, a mentoring program, and additional board positions, including regional coordinators. These initiatives took the network to the next level at the 1997 ACPA/NASPA Joint Conference in Chicago: APAN co-chairs Tim Chang and Sunny Park Suh launched the first APAN preconference leadership program, which included a full day of workshops focused on professional development and a panel of senior APIA professionals (Chang, personal communication, December 2010). The program brought APIAs from the two national organizations together for the first time. Also notable that year, Chung was elected chair of CMA, the first APIA to hold the position. She was also the first chair to host annual CMA meetings with network chairs. In 1998, Amiko Matsumoto and Peter Wu became APAN co-chairs. They focused on strengthening outreach and mentorship, and hosted a second preconference program in St. Louis (Matsumoto, personal communication, December 2010).

Blossoms (2000s): Strategic Planning and Emerging Initiatives

The 21st century brought many new opportunities for APAN. In addition to the regular work of managing and connecting with a growing membership base of professionals and graduate students, this decade saw new relationships, technological challenges, and a new organizational structure. APAN created its first strategic plan, developing a long-term vision and an organizational structure.

Glenn DeGuzman and Donna Lee-Oda served as APAN co-chairs from 2001 through 2003, working with approximately 250 members. The increasing membership led to an increase in the number of APAN leaders. The new leaders introduced the APAN Research Award and Mentoring Award, revived the APAN newsletter, and introduced choreographed cultural dance performances by APAN members at the CMA Culture Fest. In 2001, Paul Shang became the ACPA president-elect—the first Asian American to hold an elected office in the association. He received the Annuit Coeptis Senior Professional Award in 2005.

To maintain strong leadership during officer transitions, APAN leaders instituted overlapping co-chair terms. APAN co-chairs during the early part of the decade included Amnat Chittaphong, Cherry Mae Aromas, Monica Nixon, Daisy Rodriguez-Patel, Irene Kao, and Windi Sasaki. As new members joined, this generation of leaders continued to articulate the need for ongoing community, professional development, and support.

Changes in technology provided a significant boost for APAN's work. In 1995, APAN had created a listserv that was hosted by the University of Maryland and managed by an APAN member. The listserv was the first of its kind for any of the CMA networks, and it included many non-ACPA members. The unmonitored mailing list was popular among student affairs professionals nationwide, who posted announcements, job openings, conference events, and APIA-related discussion topics. With the wealth of technological developments in the first decade of the 21st century, APAN expanded its use of the ACPA-sponsored listserv, blogs, Facebook, online webinars, and a new membership database to help APIA professionals (both in and outside of APAN) maintain contact throughout the year.

Relationships with other APA groups developed rapidly in the mid-2000s. NASPA's APIKC (Asian Pacific Islanders Concerns Knowledge Community) was formalized in the early part of the decade. Collaboration between the two groups grew as the 2007 ACPA/NASPA Joint Conference in Orlando approached, with a year-long planning effort of a 2-day preconference, called "Asian Pacific Islanders Promoting Educational eXcellence (APPEX)." This collaboration was the first for the two groups, and 40 people attended the session. ACPA and NASPA both recognized the networks for their collaboration. Building on this foundation, APAN and APIKC worked together again later that year in an unexpected way. After the tragic shootings at Virginia Tech by an Asian American student in April 2007, APAN and APIKC issued a joint statement mourning the extensive loss of life and cautioning against profiling APIA students.

Stepping into conversations about visibility and collaboration, Irene Kao and Windi Sasaki, whose co-chair terms began in 2007, created a strategic planning task force to collect feedback from APIA professionals and chart goals for the next 5 years. The strategic plan included three goals: (1) personal and professional development, (2) community development, and (3) leadership development. Priorities were online networking through blogs and Facebook, connecting with faculty on research projects, understanding membership trends, and refining APAN's mentoring model.

In 2009, APAN launched free quarterly webinars under the leadership of Windi Sasaki (2007–09 co-chair), Bernie Liang (2008–10), and David Pe (2009–11). The webinars provided professional development opportunities beyond national conventions and addressed topics such as guidance from those serving in director positions, advice about pursuing doctoral studies, and state and federal priorities and legislation. The webinars have become one of APAN's most successful initiatives, drawing 25 to 45 participants per session (Pe, personal communication, December 2010).

The current leaders—David Pe, Stephanie Nixon, and Sara Furr—are focusing on reconnecting with former APAN members and senior APIA leaders in the field. They also continue defining the role of APAN in CMA. Nixon said, "I value the openness of APAN as an organization to constantly question itself. This is not something I experience in most other organizations" (personal communication, January 2011).

Reflections: Common Themes

Interviews with new and seasoned professionals provided a rich collection of stories and experiences filled with struggles and successes. Many of the same concerns and topics emerged among our respondents, providing a framework to identify common themes and steps for APIA professionals to take in coming years. Quotes from the interviews are included to illustrate the themes.

Safe Space

As the number of APIA professionals grew in the 1990s, their need to connect and bond with one another was palpable. Creating supportive networks was essential to provide a safe place for APIAs to talk about their work experiences and struggles and be able to let down their guard: "I probably wouldn't have lasted so long in the field without the help of the APA community." "Not only was it a safe place, but APAN and CMA provided a tremendous amount of support with racial or gender challenges we faced at work." "I found [APAN] to be the first professional space I'd entered where I felt that there was a desire from the group for me to be able to be myself."

Supportive Community

People were hungry to be a part of a community, which resulted in lasting friendships and bonds. Professionals who had previously been in diverse undergraduate and graduate settings may have found themselves the only one or one of few APIAs in their new work environments. In the pre-Facebook era, the APAN listserv offered a way to stay in touch with understanding colleagues throughout the year, and it gave people a place to share their frustrations and celebrations: "When I first got involved, it surpassed my expectations. It was like digging in the sand and finding this incredible tunnel." "Many of my former APAN network colleagues remain my closest professional contacts after almost 20 years!"

Knowledge Base

Being a part of APAN enhanced exposure to current research and literature. APAN was especially helpful in disseminating information about emerging research and resources on APIAs, which aided those with responsibility for serving APIA students: "Being a part of this community shaped my research agenda. I went on to spend years researching Asian Americans in higher education." "APAN keeps multiculturalism and race-based stuff central to my work."

Personal Identity Development

Being a part of APAN gave people a place not only to learn more about themselves professionally but also to solidify their voice, personal identity, and ultimately their confidence: "I learned how my personal experiences as a multiracial person not only influenced how I respond in the professional work life, but also helped me find my own path. My level of confidence was possible only because of my experiences at APAN." "Knowing myself and my cultural values/style/skills gave me strength."

Leadership and Professional Development Opportunities

Participating in APAN also gave members a valuable opportunity to serve in formal and informal leadership roles. One respondent said that being tapped to be the APAN chair was her first leadership role, which increased her confidence, desire to give back, and motivation to improve her skill sets beyond APAN and CMA. Others agreed that APAN primed many people to develop and refine presentation, research, and networking skills to fulfill other leadership roles: "I was so grateful for that opportunity; it led me to develop even more leadership skills and opportunities." "We started to run workshops on APA issues, diversity issues, and ethnic identity. It was wonderful to develop those skills as well as educate others about these topics." "My professional development as co-chair expanded my repertoire of skills."

Mentoring

Participating in APAN often meant finding a role model or mentoring younger professionals, or training and educating others about APIA and diversity issues. One co-chair highlighted the connection she felt with all the chairs who had preceded her. Feeling good about supporting and helping others was a common theme. "At the joint conference. I met all these dynamic people. People I looked up to, people I wanted to be with professionally. It was so nice to have the mentorship." "We work to pass on the torch."

Impact of APIA Student Affairs Professionals

Enrollment of APIA students at postsecondary education institutions grew fivefold between 1979 and 2009, and the APIA population in the United States is projected to reach nearly 40 million by 2050 (Grasgreen, 2011). Despite this demographic growth, the absence of APIAs within university administrative ranks has been overlooked. Research on APIA student affairs administrators is almost non-existent; however, studies from other disciplines indicate that APIAs struggle with issues of access and equity in the work place. In a national study of ACPA, NASPA, and APAHE members, APIAs were found, compared with other administrators of color, to have lower educational levels and shorter job tenure, and they faced more hostile work factors, such as tokenism and glass ceiling, that hindered their entry into and advancement within the profession (Suh, 2005). According to Neil Horikoshi, president and executive director of the Asian and Pacific Islander American Scholarship Fund, continued underrepresentation of Asian administrators in higher education further exacerbates low institutional support for APIA students (Grasgreen, 2011). Studies show that APIA student affairs professionals play an important role in students' lives (Grasgreen, 2011), and our respondents illustrate how their impact as role models, pioneers, and leaders extends to non-APIA students, their institutions, professional organizations, and the profession itself.

Institutional Impact

Respondents in the study shared many ways in which they have affected their institutions. Every person functioned as a strong advocate for APIA students and the complex issues tied to their identity and cultural values. One respondent said, "Asian American students were seeking us out because they were more comfortable talking to us (some even bringing in their parents)." Even when they were not specifically charged to work with APIA students, respondents frequently found themselves serving APIA students directly and indirectly, helping students discover their voices, representing students in institutional settings, and pushing schools to be more inclusive. One APIA professional said, "I advised the APA student group, helping them find a voice both within their group and among other ethnic groups. My background also made me more aware of certain APA concerns and trends."

Respondents also talked about working in solidarity with other underrepresented groups, providing sustainable models of cross-cultural organizing and coalition building, and serving as role models to a broad range of students of color. Many of the people we interviewed cited the particular challenge of being one of very few APIA administrators on campus—sometimes the only one and often the first—even on campuses with significant APIA student populations. One practitioner said, "I have found that I am usually only one of, at most, two APIA administrators wherever I have worked, so I've tried to advocate for others from the APIA community. It has been challenging, because often services and offices do not exist to support Asians from either a student or professional standpoint."

Despite the pressure and marginalization they faced, these professionals created networks of support, established APIA services, and paved the way for other APIA staff to follow. They also raised campus awareness about identity and social justice, resulting in the reexamination of racial stereotypes, what it meant to support a multicultural campus, and whom campus cultural centers should serve. One practitioner said, "The multicultural center had always served the African American and Latino student populations, so I was able to reach out to the [APIA] students in meeting their academic, social, and developmental needs. And, on a broader scale, I also affected other student affairs professionals and departments."

In some cases, our respondents indicated that APIA student affairs staff played key roles in creating Asian American studies programs and student services on campuses: "Having all the students of color demand APA studies was amazing, a real testimony to their development. That our Latino, Black, and Asian American students were able to work together in a cohesive fashion to advocate to create a more inclusive education was beautiful."

Professional Impact

In addition to their leadership on campus, the APIA professionals we interviewed have had a positive impact on professional organizations and the student affairs profession. One respondent said, "I do believe I have been able, in partnership with others in APAN and other networks, to continue challenging the visibility of AAPI professionals in leadership roles within our larger organizations and maintaining voice from our community—whether speaking to an AAPI-related issue or not." Those we interviewed have challenged existing organizations and created new ones to provide a safe space, a healthy community, and pathways for new APIA professionals. Sometimes this has meant pushing against a racial paradigm in the profession that continues to narrowly represent the needs and experiences of APIA students, staff, and faculty. Through organizations such as APAN and APIKC, our respondents have offered professional mentoring, skills development, career networking, and legitimized best practices to take back to campuses. Within larger organizations such as ACPA and NASPA, those we interviewed have served as elected leaders, championed issues and research that affect APIA communities, and opened countless doors for emerging APIA professionals.

Conclusion

The current and future challenges facing APIA student affairs educators can be traced back in history to the voices of experience, those who, over the last four decades, developed networks and strategies not only to survive, but also to thrive. Understanding the past allows current and future practitioners to reflect and devise progressive initiatives, programs, and services that will continue to enhance APIA professional development and student services, as well as effect positive change in professional organizations and the academy. This history should be celebrated and cherished as we enter our fifth decade, so future generations continue this legacy.

References

American College Personnel Association (ACPA). (2011). *About ACPA*. Retrieved from http://www2.myacpa.org/about-acpa

Banerjee, N. (2001, April 13–19). APAHE goes national. *AsianWeek*. Retrieved from www.asianweek.com/2001_04_13/news3_apahe.html

Campbell, R. E. (1985). *ACPA committee on multicultural affairs. History (MS-319)*. Available from the National Student Affairs Archives, Center for Archival Collections, Jerome Library, Bowling Green State University, Bowling Green, OH.

Chew, C. A., & Ogi, A. Y. (1987). Asian American college student perspectives. In D. J. Wright (Ed.) *Responding to the needs to today's minority students* (New directions for student services, no. 38, pp. 39–48). San Francisco, CA: Jossey-Bass.

Grasgreen, A. (2011, June 28). New voice for Asian students. *Inside Higher Ed*. Retrieved from http://www.insidehighered.com/news/2011/06/28/new_group_formed_to_represent_asian_pacific_islander_colleges

Leadership Education for Asian Pacifics (LEAP). (2011). About LEAP. Retrieved June 8, 2011, from http://www.leap.org/index.html

Leong, F. T. L., & Gupta, A. (2008). History and evolution of Asian American psychology. In N. Tewari & A. Alvarez (Eds.), *Asian American psychology: Current perspectives*. New York, NY: Psychology Press.

National Association of Student Personnel Administrators (NASPA). (2011). *About us*. Retrieved November 23, 2011 from http://naspa.org/about/default.cfm

Suh, S. P. (2005). *Characteristics of Asian Pacific American student affairs administrators: Implications for practice in higher education* (Doctoral dissertation). Retrieved from Columbia University Teachers College Dissertations & Theses: The Humanities and Social Sciences Collection. (Publication No. AAT3175732).

CHAPTER EIGHT

Connecting Generations Through Legacy

The History and Development
of the Asian Pacific Islanders Concerns
Knowledge Community

Hikaru Kozuma and Karlen N. Suga

In *Narrative Leadership: Using the Power of Stories*, David Fleming said that "organizations and individuals must construct and reconstruct meaning" as a tool to understand an organization's current situation (Fleming, 2001, p. 37). He also wrote,

> As individuals, we all relate to stories because our lives are stories. Every individual life contains characters, plots, scripts and a host of other ingredients found in a good story. When we forget this truth, we lose an important interpretive tool for discerning

direction and creating meaning both personally and organiza-
tionally. (p. 35)

As we present the history and development of the Asian Pacific
Islanders Concerns Knowledge Community, we relate its significance
and impact as an organization on the careers and personal growth of
Asian American and Pacific Islander (AAPI) student affairs professionals and students in higher education.

In 2009, a valuable opportunity arose for the NASPA–Student Affairs
Administrators in Higher Education Asian Pacific Islanders Concerns
Knowledge Community (APIKC) to engage in storytelling of this
nature. NASPA comprises more than 12,000 student affairs professionals
representing a wide variety of functional areas, years of experience, institutions, and levels of organizational responsibility. APIKC is an affinity-
based group within NASPA. Among its goals, APIKC seeks to educate
and inform NASPA members about current issues, trends, and research
related to AAPIs in higher education. As one of the ethnicity-based
knowledge communities, APIKC is committed to honoring and respect-
ing the multiple and diverse communities that exist within the greater
Asian and Pacific Islander category and strives to increase knowledge and
understanding of the student affairs profession.

APIKC facilitates key networking opportunities that assist members
with professional development and ultimately helps build a sense of
belonging within APIKC and NASPA. In their chapter on background
and statistics, Wang and Teranishi report that AAPI members account for
4% of the total NASPA membership, compared with African American
members at 16% and Latino members at 8%. Native Americans (3%) and
those who identify as multiracial (1%) are the two smallest ethnic groups
in the association. Through NASPA and APIKC, Asian Pacific Islander
Desi American (APIDA) members have been given new opportunities to
engage in regional and national leadership positions and to build skills that
have led to professional advancement at their colleges and universities.

At the 2009 NASPA Annual Conference in Seattle, a founding
member of APIKC proposed that the community participate in the 2010

Annual Conference theme, "Live the Legacy, Be the Movement," by documenting the community's history. As APIKC co-chairs, we recognized an opportunity to learn about the group's history and help maintain a solid foundation for the future. It also served as a chance for participating members to learn about leadership and become involved with a national organization. The storytelling through the Legacy Project honored the work of those who helped establish the organization and showed members how they could shape the future direction of APIKC. A group of APIDA-identified new professionals conducted interviews and wrote the story of the development of APIKC, which was then posted online for members and others to read.

John Dewey and Jurgen Habermas, whose teachings serve as the backbone philosophies on reflection, agreed that exploring history is critical to generate knowledge (Moon, 1999). It is important for professionals and students to have a sense of the history and development of an organization or institution to enrich their professional lives and personal growth. Storytelling enabled those interviewed in the Legacy Project to reflect on their experiences and involvement, which ultimately led to learning for everyone who participated. Through this process, those involved experienced firsthand one of the knowledge community's values—family connections—and created intergenerational connections among members.

The NASPA APIKC Story

The current version of the APIKC was established in 2001, after years of attempts to represent and lend a voice to students and professionals who identified as part of the ethnic and social minority within the greater NASPA organization. The first attempt to organize was in 1988, with the first meeting of the Minority Caucus at the NASPA Annual Conference in St. Louis, Missouri. The Minority Caucus morphed into a group called the Network for Educational Equity and Ethnic Diversity (NEEED) and became one of a dozen NASPA interest networks that enabled members to identify special interests and connect with other members who shared similar interests. NEEED consisted primarily of African American and Latino professionals. At that first meeting, Henry Gee (who later became a founding member of APIKC) was the only non-African American, non-Latino professional in attendance. Ten years later, after NEEED had established a presence within NASPA, Gee became the first non-African American, non-Latino chairperson of the group.

In 2001, NASPA moved forward with plans to transform NEEED and other interest networks into knowledge communities (KCs). The purpose of the KCs was to create connections among members of various affinity groups and to encourage and facilitate the dissemination of knowledge about specific populations of students and professionals. KCs are a forum through which NASPA members connect and collaborate on topics and issues related to identity, functional area, and student population. The dissemination of knowledge is a key function of KCs—they encourage and assist members with proposals and presentations of sessions at national and regional conferences. Although knowledge creation is considered to be one of the most important tasks of the communities, connecting professionals and students through affinity groups is the most celebrated. The field of student affairs thrives on relationship development and maintenance with students and colleagues alike. The connections made through APIKC and other KCs are invaluable, regardless of institutional affiliation, functional area, professional role, or geographic region. APIKC is led by national co-chairs, regional representatives, and national committee chairs for initiatives and programs (such as research and scholarship, and public relations). All of these leaders transcend functional area, years of experience, and geographic area.

APIKC has grown significantly over time. Former APIKC co-chair Sunny Lee recalled a time when APIKC's social and professional gatherings at NASPA national conferences attracted 15 to 20 members; by contrast, a networking event at the 2010 NASPA Annual Conference in Chicago attracted about 60 members. APIKC membership varies widely, from undergraduate students who are just entering the world of higher education to senior student affairs staff members with many years of service. Throughout the years, leadership team members have created and implemented programs and initiatives that contributed to the visibility of APIDAs in NASPA and in the greater higher education community. Among them are an APIKC-based distance mentoring program, collaborations with other higher education organizations, the development of annual awards and publications, and an increasing number of presentations on APIDA issues at the regional and national levels.

The Legacy Project

The Legacy Project provided an opportunity to capture APIKC's rich history and, for its current and future members, it also provided a chance to learn about the development of the organization. To execute the project, we enlisted the assistance of three new professionals who identified as APIDAs. Part of the impetus behind that choice was to facilitate connections between senior members of the KC who had established themselves in the profession and new professionals just beginning their journey. To create conditions for reflection and a good learning environment, we used information from *Reflection in Learning and Professional Development* by Jennifer A. Moon. Moon wrote about the roles that time, facilitators, and the right kinds of questions play in optimum reflection (Moon, 1999). We developed questions that elicited thoughts about the interviewees' involvement with APIKC, encouraging them to reflect on what they had gained. The fruits of the project are a timeline highlighting significant events in APIKC's history and a narrative centered on the themes of the interview responses, which included a sense of belonging to and engagement in NASPA and APIKC, mentoring, and advocacy. The Legacy Project can be found on the NASPA website at http://www.naspa.org/kc/api/legacy_project.cfm. We explore APIKC's contributions and the lessons learned from the Legacy Project in the next two sections.

APIKC's Contributions

Each year since its establishment in 2001, APIKC's efforts have built upon those of the previous year to sustain progress and move the community forward. Whether it is providing tips for job interviewing or continuing its strong mentorship efforts, the KC's accomplishments have provided a roadmap for the future. Our profession and association emphasize the development of the whole student (see NASPA, 1987), and APIKC has applied the same approach to its members. In various ways, APIKC has contributed to NASPA and the field of student affairs in general, and has helped to develop countless student affairs professionals.

APIKC has increased knowledge of issues that pertain to our community in several ways. By establishing the Research and Scholarship co-chairs as part of the leadership team, as well as a Research and Scholarship Committee, our knowledge community has promoted and supported new research for professional development opportunities. An example is the preconference workshops at the national conference. Beginning in 2007 and working with the American College Personnel Association (ACPA) Asian Pacific American Network (APAN), the KC established Asian Pacific Islanders Promoting Educational eXcellence (APPEX), an interactive summit designed to address the professional and leadership development of APIDA student affairs professionals in a multiculturally competent and holistic context. Through a series of workshop presentations in a preconference institute format, APPEX encourages APIDA professionals to rely on identity as a professional strength and source of empowerment. The APPEX workshops have become a fixture at the NASPA Annual Conference; each year, they address new topics that are relevant to student affairs and to our community. Over the years, the number of programs and workshops centered on APIDA issues has increased at regional and national conferences. APIKC has been a driving force behind this increase, encouraging its members to submit proposals and providing guidance when needed. Fifteen years ago, one might have found one or two sessions focused on APIDA issues at any regional or national conference; now there are always a number of sessions at NASPA conferences. In addition to increasing knowledge at conferences, the KC has used various other outlets, such as the Internet, to disseminate information. For example, APIKC has expanded its reach and connected members who are geographically far apart through webinars such as Voices from the Top, in which senior student affairs officers share their journeys, help members find co-presenters for annual and regional conferences, and facilitate online networking through websites such as Facebook.

APIKC has become a strong voice in NASPA and throughout the student affairs field. KC members have assumed national leadership roles—such as KC national director, NASPA regional vice president, and president—and have brought critical issues to the fore and proved the community's effectiveness in advocacy. A prime example occurred in 2006–07, when APIKC and the Latino/a Knowledge Community raised a controversial issue that ultimately led to a national discussion. One of NASPA's regions had selected for its regional conference a hotel that was in the middle of a labor dispute in which the workers—mostly Latino and Asian—were striking. Although a contract had already been signed and it was too late to change the venue, the APIKC leaders kept the issue alive, pushing for an examination of how such a conflict of interest might have been avoided and how similar complex situations could be navigated in the future. In recognition of the national co-chairs' tenacity in raising the level of discussion on issues of social responsibility as an association, APIKC received the Region VI Visibility Award. In March 2007, NASPA adopted a policy that requires planning committees for regional and national events to be diligent and informed on labor issues when they are choosing sites for major events.

APIKC has also challenged itself, wrestling with its own sense of inclusion and diversity. Issues pertaining to Pacific Islanders and South Asians have been brought up for discussion, which strengthens the organization and creates opportunities to change organizational culture. Shein (1992) defined culture as

> . . . a pattern of shared basic assumptions that the group learned as it solved its problems of external adaptation and internal integration, that has worked well enough to be considered valid and, therefore, to be taught to new members as the correct way to perceive, think, and feel in relation to those problems. (p. 12)

As NASPA members became part of the APIKC they learned about its strong history of advocacy. As one senior member said in his interview, the purpose of the KC was "to provide advocacy to the NASPA regional and national boards on critical issues affecting the API population." Through its members' actions, the KC performed and continues to perform its advocacy function.

APIKC's ongoing contributions would not have been possible if not for the intergenerational connections in the organization. Leaders such as Doris Ching, Henry Gee, Hal Gin, Evette Castillo Clark, Amy Agbayani, and several others paved the way for mid-level and entry-level student affairs practitioners to contribute and grow in the profession and in NASPA. Each generation of members used their experiences to provide advice on career choices, professional development, and personal growth. Many interviewees mentioned how an older member had influenced their growth and journey; older members also spoke about how their peers had helped them navigate challenges in their career. Without the work and guidance of previous members and leaders, the opportunities that many APIDA professionals have today would not exist, and the landscape of our community would be starkly different.

To recognize the work of its members and capture its history, the KC has instituted awards. At the 2002 NASPA Annual Conference in Boston, APIKC created its first award, the Shattering the Glass Ceiling Award, to honor senior student affairs officers who have had an outstanding impact on the APIDA community and the student affairs profession through their leadership, mentoring, service, scholarship, and involvement in NASPA. In 2005, APIKC established its second award, the Very Important Participant (V.I.P.) award; and in 2008, it created the Outstanding Mentoring Award, which recognizes individuals who have made significant contributions to the student affairs profession and the APIDA community through mentoring. In 2009, the Shattering the Glass Ceiling Award was renamed the Doris Michiko Ching Shattering the Glass Ceiling Award, and the Outstanding Mentoring Award was renamed the Henry Gee Outstanding Mentoring Award, in honor of the first recipients. Inherent in an organization's culture are artifacts, values, and fundamental assumptions regarding what is important within the culture (Lundberg, 1990). These awards are more than just a way to honor and acknowledge the contributions of their recipients; they also serve as embodiments and artifacts of the qualities APIKC strives to uphold.

In addition to the collective accomplishments of APIKC, it is important to acknowledge the individual leaders who shaped this movement. Until 2008, national co-chairs were selected by the previous set of co-chairs. Chairing such a dynamic group involves many functions and a great deal of responsibility, which was not taken lightly by any of the leaders who were selected to fill these roles. Goal setting, assessment, effective communication, accountability, and marketing are just some of the responsibilities of those in national and regional APIKC positions. A statement by a legacy member to a co-chair who was addressing a difficult situation expresses the level of responsibility and the potential for criticism: "I have learned that, as one is placed in a higher position, one also becomes more open to public criticism. The way one handles a controversial situation is a very important aspect of leadership." Lessons learned from difficult situations, as well as successes, contribute to each leader's professional development, professional mobility, and mobility within the national organization. As an example of the influence of NASPA membership on professional mobility, in the academic year 2010–11, 10 of APIKC's 20 leadership team members were offered new and better jobs. One of the 10 reported that the university specifically referred to NASPA involvement as justification for offering a salary that was significantly higher than the one initially posted.

When asked if she had words of advice for future members of APIKC, one member said, "We come from collectivist cultures, and at the heart of APIKC is social justice. Remember that our ancestors are watching." APIKC has fostered strong relationships and connections among its members. Through these strong bonds, the knowledge community has served as a gateway to NASPA and to the field of higher education.

Outcomes and Reflections on the Legacy Project

In addition to highlighting the many contributions of APIKC—

including generation of knowledge, advocacy, and community building—the Legacy Project proved to be a meaningful opportunity for learning and making connections through reflection, particularly for the interviewers, who were new to the student affairs profession and NASPA. Without reflection on their experience, learning could not occur (Burnard, 1991; Pearson and Smith, 1985). All interviews were conducted in 2009 and 2010. Asked to reflect on the interview process, one interviewer said that he had not been aware of the various perspectives that a KC leader had to balance:

> "There is so much involved in being a leader within a group like the APIKC that members never see. One of the biggest challenges leaders in these kinds of positions face is that you are 'on' all the time. While it is important and key in a role like this to lead with heart, there are times where you need to put your personal feelings aside in favor of what will benefit the group as a whole."

The interviewers agreed that gaining a realistic sense of these complexities and challenges helped them visualize and plan their future involvement. Another interviewer said, "This experience has motivated me to delve further into how to get involved on both the regional and national levels, so I can one day reflect the legacy in the field, like the people I interviewed." Observing the impact that NASPA and APIKC involvement had had on the interviewee heightened the interviewer's interest in expanding his professional development by getting more involved himself.

Another significant aspect of the interview process was the connections and stories shared. One interviewer commented that even though he knew both of his interviewees personally and interacted with them on a regular basis, he had not known the details of their journey in the organization. The concept of reflection includes a link to the past that allows those who reflect to go over their experiences to help shape learning and thinking for the future (Moon, 1999). The interviewees' insights prompted the interviewer to reflect on the differences and similarities between their experiences within the organization:

"This experience connected a lot of the stories, legacies, and knowledge that I always knew existed in the KC, but was never able to fully understand and comprehend. Interacting through interviews allowed me to gain further insight into where the KC has been and where it will go in the future. Comparing perspectives between legacies and myself gave me the opportunity to explore and reflect upon what my role is and how I can contribute to the rich history."

The information gathered through the sharing of stories informed the interviewers of possible pathways in front of them. The reflection "brought together past experiences and their meanings with imagination of the future situation" (Moon, 1999, p. 153).

Although the interviewers had a chance to learn from the stories of professionals who were established in NASPA and in the student affairs profession, the interviewees also gained from the experience. Two interviewees had personal and family relationships with their interviewers. Both were inspired to reflect on the journey that the young professionals were taking and expressed excitement and confidence in their future success. One interviewee said,

"I am deeply blessed to be able to work alongside [the interviewer] on a daily basis. I have watched him grow into an outstanding young professional and I am giddy with the thought of what the future holds for him. As a result, it was profound for me to sit with him and have him interview me. It was literally sitting and chatting with a family member. I was humbled to serve as a relative elder in that moment—what an honor."

The sentiment expressed by this particular interviewee articulates how APIKC has affected its members. The personal, emotional connections made in the knowledge community are comparable to those in a family unit and are represented by the Hawaiian word *'ohana*. Members often address each other as "brother" and "sister" in both formal and informal communication, and many seek to connect in person and via e-mail or phone outside of NASPA events. A former APIKC co-chair recalled members of the KC visiting her home state; she said, "I was as excited to see my APIKC family as I was my own family. I got the exact same feeling: I was surrounded by love, comfort, and acceptance. A piece of my heart came home again."

In Asian and Pacific Islander cultures, elders are an honored and important part of everyday life. Cultural values such as *nana ikekumu* (look to the source/look to your teachers) are at the center of members' personal and professional practice. The mentoring described in Legacy Project interviews motivated professionals to strive to achieve personal and professional goals. One member reflected on how her relationship with a mentor she met through APIKC has influenced her life:

> "[My mentor] has helped me reach great milestones, including leadership in my professional association, development as a student affairs practitioner, and pursuing my doctorate. At a 2007 conference in Orlando, she sat with me on a bench and discussed my future. She kept telling me, 'You can do it.' That year I applied [to the doctoral program]."

Four years later, in 2011, this member received her doctoral degree, thus accomplishing a major life and personal goal.

Another key theme in the interviews was appreciation for the value of the work done to develop APIKC. Student affairs professionals know how hectic the academic year can be, and they know there is no such thing as having real down time to relax before things become busy again. Because leadership roles in NASPA are on a volunteer basis, these people are even busier than most, and opportunities for reflection are rare. One interviewee said, "The content of the interview permitted me to reflect on our years of formal KC leadership. Again, it provided a profound opportunity to think about, and verbalize, the great work of the KC. What a joy that was."

Finally, the learning and reflecting engaged in by both interviewers and interviewees resulted in a strong sense of pride in the community. One interviewee noted,

"The interview required me to pause and think seriously about where AAPIs had been, as individuals, on their campuses and in the profession a decade ago, before they came together as an organized group that is providing fellowship and support for one another. It was heartening to imagine that, in a short 10 years, AAPIs had moved away from feeling isolated and prejudiced to now feeling strengthened, empowered, and confident. I was encouraged that the interviewer approached me with confidence and ease as he presented his questions. This was an entirely different picture from that of a decade earlier, when AAPIs had approached me in need and near-desperation for professional support. In this sense, I gained a sense of pride in AAPI student affairs professionals for their ability to develop a vigorous, viable organization that became a model for other NASPA Knowledge Communities. I was impressed that the AAPI professionals had developed a group that would ensure continuity in leadership, innovation, creativity, high quality, and endurance—all of the characteristics for which the APIKC had become known. It was gratifying to know that AAPIs were now being recognized and appreciated on their campuses, and that they were reaching out and working effectively and collaboratively with other diverse groups. I gained even greater pride in the significant contributions they were making to their campuses and profession."

Conclusion

APIKC has played an important role in the development of its members, and its impact reaches beyond those who are actively involved. Through its exploration and dedication to increasing knowledge, the KC has been a source of strength for NASPA and has increased the effectiveness of student affairs professionals as educators by addressing the needs and issues of today's students. Exploring APIKC's history provided numerous opportunities for learning and development. We draw inspiration from the stories—they will help give APIKC direction and purpose, and thus create a foundational pillar to shape its future. Hearing these stories is critical for the development of our community. As Donald Schön (1988) said,

> Storytelling is the mode of description best suited to transformation in new situations of action. . . . Stories are products of reflection, but we do not usually hold onto them long enough to make them objects of reflection in their own right. . . . When we get into the habit of recording our stories, we can look at them again, attending to the meanings we have built into them and attending, as well, to our strategies of narrative description. (p. 26)

The Legacy Project gave all of those involved—especially the new professionals who served as interviewers—an invaluable opportunity to learn and to gain a renewed sense of purpose from the history of APIKC. Those who were interviewed had an opportunity to reflect on the importance of mentorship and pass information on to the next set of leaders. They felt pride in the community and in how far it has come in the past decade. By using storytelling as a form of ongoing reflection, APIKC will continue to develop and grow as the times and the needs of its members change.

References

Burnard, P. (1991). *Experimental learning in action.* Aldershot, England: Avebury Press.

Fleming, D. (2001). Narrative leadership: Using the power of stories. *Strategy and Leadership, 29*(4), pp. 34–37.

Lundberg, C. C. (1990). Surfacing organizational culture. *Journal of Managerial Psychology, 5*(4), 19–26.

Moon, J. A. (1999). *Reflection in learning and professional development.* New York, NY: Routledge Falmer.

National Association of Student Personnel Administrators (NASPA). (1987). *A perspective on student affairs.* Washington, DC: Author.

Pearson, M., & Smith, D. (1985). Debriefing in experimentally-based learning. In D. Boud, R. Keogh, & D. Walker (Eds.), *Reflection: Turning experience into learning* (pp. 69–83). London, England: Kogan Page.

Schein, E. H. (1992). *Organizational culture and leadership.* San Francisco, CA: Jossey-Bass.

Schön, D. (1988). Coaching reflective teaching. In P. Grimmett & G. Erickson (Eds.), *Reflection in teacher education* (pp. 19–29). New York, NY: Teachers College Press.

CHAPTER NINE

Asian American and Pacific Islanders in Leadership

Pipeline or Pipe Dream?

Audrey Yamagata-Noji and Henry Gee

Asian American and Pacific Islanders (AAPI) are not only the fastest growing ethnic group in the United States, they are the most diverse and most complex. The U.S. Census Bureau recognizes more than 40 separate ethnic groups, and AAPIs span 10 generations of Americans, including the nation's most recent immigrants. AAPIs do not have a common language, religion, or culture. Despite myths and stereotypes that portray AAPIs as exceptional models of success, especially in education, they are largely underrepresented and underserved in higher education.

Generally, AAPIs attend colleges and universities at higher rates than African Americans and Latinos. But despite their participation rates, AAPIs are rarely found at the highest level: the presidency. Among more than 4,000 higher education institutions, AAPIs comprise less than 1% of presidents and chancellors. This meager representation is startling and unacceptable. At a time when our national population is diversifying at an unprecedented rate, such a paucity of AAPIs serving as college and university presidents is a call to action. This chapter focuses on training and development to increase the number of AAPI leaders commensurate with the AAPI student population in higher education. However, we realize that while a focus on leadership training may have a significant impact on individual success, it will have a limited impact on organizational change unless non-AAPI leaders, policymakers, institutions, and national associations help establish and promote inclusive policies and attitudes.

A 2006 survey by the American Council on Education (ACE) revealed that 49% of U.S. college presidents and chancellors were 61 years or older (ACE, 2007). The time to diversify leadership opportunities in higher education is now. "The leadership of American higher education is about to experience a dramatic changing of the guard. This coming turnover is unprecedented in its size and scope and requires all institutions to think intentionally about their next generation of leaders" (Bridges, Eckel, Cordova, & White, 2008).

Reporting on diversity at the presidential level over a 20-year period (1986–2006), ACE found that the proportion of people of color serving as college presidents grew from 8.1% to 13.5% (Bridges et al., 2008). Still, in 2006, 86% of college presidents were White. When disaggregated by ethnic group, the overall increase in presidents of color totaled a mere 3.9% over the 20-year period. Hispanic presidents increased by 2.3%, African Americans by 0.9%, Asian Americans by 0.5%, and American Indians by 0.2%. The proportion of female presidents increased from 10.5% to 23% during the same time frame, with women leaders concentrated at community colleges.

Minorities are most likely to hold diversity and student affairs positions. More than 80% of diversity officers and 20% of student affairs officers are people of color (King & Gomez, 2008). Thus, it appears that if people of color hold leadership roles in higher education, they will most likely be in positions designated to address diversity issues or in student affairs. Where do AAPIs fit into this picture? In their chapter in this book, Teranishi and Wang report that AAPI representation in student affairs senior administration is 2.5%, even though the NASPA–Student Affairs Administrators in Higher Education membership is 4% AAPI and student enrollment nationally is close to 15% AAPI. These alarming statistics show that the idea of Asian American and Pacific Islanders as college and university presidents, or even student affairs leaders, is still a pipe dream.

The Pipeline Problem

The dearth of AAPIs in visible positions of leadership on college campuses is dismaying and indefensible. Baseless excuses are often used to rationalize not hiring AAPI professionals for these positions:

We want to hire more AAPIs, but . . .

- They just don't interview well.
- They are all from STEM fields.
- We don't have that many AAPI students.

And besides . . .

- No Asian Pacific Islanders are applying for positions with us.
- All the Asian faculty we know are in the hard sciences and are not interested in leadership roles.
- There just aren't that many high-profile Asian Pacifics in student affairs leadership positions to be promoted.

In the 1980s and 1990s, there appeared to be significant progress with the noted appointments of several recognized AAPI leaders. In reality, the overall rate of AAPI appointments to higher education CEO positions is anything but impressive; rather, it indicates a serious flaw in higher education. However, the AAPI pipeline to presidencies is not a topic of scholarly research in higher education, and data are hard to find. AAPIs are often ignored in diversity efforts to increase the representation of women and men of color in presidential and senior-level management positions, including in student affairs. It is difficult to track presidential appointments at many schools, especially small private colleges. There is a growing network of AAPIs in community colleges, which is helping to support the appointments of AAPI community college presidents.

Many people mistakenly assume that AAPIs are either sufficiently represented or do not need representation. The issue of sufficient representation rests on whether issues of parity and equity should be applied to AAPIs. From an affirmative action viewpoint, some might argue that because AAPIs are overrepresented in college student enrollment, there is no need to recruit them for visible leadership positions. As a result of this incorrect assumption, many institutions have purposely not established diversity agendas that embrace and target the hiring and advancement of AAPIs.

When AAPI leaders began to make their presence felt on the higher education scene, there was a false reading that AAPIs had achieved some type of recognizable representation. In fact, over the past three decades, AAPIs have been losing ground, especially at baccalaureate institutions. The recent chief executive appointments of Gabriel Esteban at Seton Hall, Leroy Morishita at California State University East Bay, and Phyllis Wise at the University of Illinois Champagne-Urbana are highly celebrated because these people are deserving and well-qualified, and because AAPI presidential appointments are so rare.

Why do we need AAPIs in positions of leadership? Looking again at the notion of representation, if the national average of AAPI undergraduates is around 15% (with some public universities in California exceeding 50%), it stands to reason that there should be at least 15% AAPI college presidents and senior executives. The actual figures—less than 1% AAPI college presidents and only 2% AAPI chief academic officers (King & Gomez, 2008)—show the need for a major initiative to place AAPIs in executive positions commensurate with AAPI student enrollment.

Cultural Values and Profiling

AAPIs are the perfect team players; they are known to take direction well, work hard, work for the good of the cause, and practice loyalty and humility. More often than not, AAPIs listen and observe before speaking. They are humble, modest about their accomplishments, and work diligently until a job is done. They wait to be recognized and believe that hard work and dedicated efforts will be recognized; but this frequently does not happen, and AAPIs are once again overlooked and undervalued.

Many AAPIs have been raised with philosophies that do not support risk-taking behaviors, which are required if one is to advance in higher education. As a consequence of their reluctance to stand up and speak out, AAPIs are categorized as "not leadership material." Because of this reluctance, the needs of AAPIs are often overlooked or misunderstood, or do not even appear on the radar screen.

Why are attributes such as modesty and hard work not valued? Could it be because these traits are seen in persons with foreign-sounding names and features that distinguish them as non-White? Does the fact that some of these people are small in stature and speak with an accent trigger the perception that AAPIs are not leadership material? It may be that traditions in institutions of higher education are so deeply ingrained that only one leadership profile exists: the outgoing, articulate, charismatic, politically focused person who is comfortable in the board room, on the golf course, or at a high-stakes dinner with potential funders. Frequently, AAPIs are told, "We know your work, but we don't know you." Uncomfortable with sharing personal information in the workplace, AAPIs are often misperceived as not being leadership material.

Many AAPIs hit the glass ceiling when they attempt to advance. All too often, AAPIs are relegated to small promotional steps or completely passed over. In a choice among a group of equally qualified candidates, the AAPI is rarely selected. Why does this happen?

Perceptions of AAPIs can be very detrimental to career advancement:

- Quiet and nice, but not a leader.
- Does great work, but we do not know much else about him/her.

- Not very assertive; not very communicative.
- Does not stand out as leadership material, blends in with the group.
- Works hard, but not seen as a leader.
- At times, is so driven that others cannot keep up.

These stereotypes give a false read on the leadership capabilities of AAPIs. If these views are pervasive in an organization, the AAPI who might appear to reflect these characteristics is pigeonholed, while the AAPI who does not fit these expectations may be ostracized as being atypical: "not your usual Asian." This leads to a lose-lose situation in which AAPIs feel they should either blend in with the stereotypical expectations for "Asians" by not being too assertive, too outspoken, or too direct. The diversity within the AAPI ethnic groups is culturally, linguistically, and historically immense. In fact, some recent Asian immigrants have been labeled as pushy, demanding, and close-minded. All too often, others decide what AAPIs should be like.

Many senior officials hold on to a westernized view of leadership—one that values individual performance over group orientation. AAPIs who participate in leadership programs with Leadership Education for Asian Pacifics (LEAP) describe how they have been passed over for promotions, not mentored beyond their current assignment, and not invited to participate in opportunities outside of their assignment. In its survey, ACE (2006) found that only 15% of Asian American chief academic officers had participated in leadership programs, compared with 57% of African Americans and 30% of Hispanics. Is this low participation rate due to AAPIs choosing not to participate or to the fact that AAPIs tend to wait to be recognized and invited to participate—never wanting to assume their importance to the organization? In either case, the low participation rate is yet another concern related to the underdevelopment of leadership skills among AAPIs.

The Career GPS

Sunil Chand (president emeritus, College of Dupage) coined the phrase "career GPS" to emphasize that many AAPIs need assistance to find their way in the career development maze. But AAPIs usually have to go it alone, because there are so few AAPIs to emulate—mentors are few and far between. Thus, the pipeline cannot be opened because there is no roadmap. Many AAPI faculty become so engrossed in their research and faculty work that they are oblivious to the necessity of social networking for career advancement. As a general rule, AAPIs are very family oriented and might prefer not to attend social events where they will be expected to join in non-work-related conversation. And although they tend to be team oriented, some prefer to work alone.

How does one learn to be more outgoing, more extroverted, more assertive, and more social? Those AAPIs who lack a career GPS need a navigational system that shows the way; warns of potholes, detours, and roadblocks; and points out the shortcuts and straightaways. Many AAPIs, without a sufficient support and mentoring system, attempt to move into leadership roles without guidance and without direction—kind of like moving into the passing lane unaware of oncoming traffic.

When pressed to hire or to promote a person, do the institution and its leadership value what the AAPI professional can contribute as a leader? Or do stereotypes overpower the decision-making process? Are AAPIs valued for the unique leadership perspective they would bring to the institution? In addition to the work the AAPI professional undertakes to develop increased leadership skills, institutions of higher education must assume part of the responsibility for leadership development. Certainly, institutions that value and model diversity should have clear priorities that focus on explicit professional development opportunities.

With such low numbers of AAPIs in key leadership roles, who is available to mentor budding AAPI leaders? Clearly, non-AAPIs must commit to mentoring AAPIs, helping them gain leadership experience and career direction.

Talent Search and Talent Development

Headhunters are hired to find talented candidates for specific positions. What do they look for? How do they conduct their talent searches? Because of the minimal number of AAPIs in visible leadership positions in higher education, headhunters do not have a ready pool of AAPIs from which to recruit. Search firms have confirmed our observations that AAPIs are not on the recruitment radar screen for positions of leadership in higher education. Boards of trustees and other executive-level leaders must tell their human resource staff to cast a wider net when they are recruiting people for leadership roles.

In addition to the need for greater awareness of the talent search aspect, we are concerned about the talent development side. What is our responsibility, and what can we do to ensure that AAPIs have every opportunity, full preparation, and the support they need to succeed? With that question in mind, we focus on specific ways of identifying professionals who are motivated to develop their leadership experience, knowledge, and skills. We must work from both ends of the spectrum: on one end, to change incorrect perceptions of AAPIs as leaders and, on the other end, to support AAPIs in developing the skills and higher profiles that will enable them to be recognized as leaders.

Building the Pipeline: The Leadership Development Program in Higher Education

In spring 1995, President Bob Suzuki of California Polytechnic State University, Pomona (Cal Poly Pomona), organized a summit of key AAPI higher education and community leaders to address concerns about the AAPI leadership pipeline in higher education. It was apparent that an insufficient number of AAPIs were poised to take over college presidencies and vice presidencies when Suzuki and other AAPI leaders retired. With Suzuki's support, encouragement, and guidance, various individuals were tasked with developing a leadership pipeline model that would include recruiting AAPI vice presidents, deans, and faculty members for leadership training and mentoring, to help them advance into presidencies.

J. D. Hokoyama, president and CEO of Leadership Education for Asian Pacifics (LEAP), led a core group in establishing a leadership training program. LEAP is a national nonprofit, headquartered in Los Angeles with an office in Washington, D.C. It was founded in 1982 with the mission of achieving full participation and equality for Asian and Pacific Islanders (APIs) through leadership, empowerment, and policy. LEAP's motto is "Growing Leaders"—it runs extensive leadership training programs throughout the corporate world and in AAPI communities across the nation. Audrey Yamagata-Noji and Henry Gee assisted in program development under the auspices of Asian and Pacific Americans in Higher Education (APAHE), a national nonprofit organization launched in 1988 to support the higher education career development of APIs and address issues of concern to API educators and students, such as admissions, tenure, support services, equity, and justice. The Leadership Development Program in Higher Education (LDPHE) was born out of this effort, and Yamagata-Noji and Gee have served as its program coordinators and facilitators since the inaugural class of 1997.

The first major awakening was the discovery that there were insufficient numbers of AAPI vice presidents and deans to even begin to fill the program. Also, recruiting senior administrators was challenging, as many vice presidents and deans believe that they have already "made it" and do not need any leadership training. LDPHE was expanded to include professionals who wanted to move into advanced leadership roles; this has attracted many faculty members, staff, and mid-level managers.

Since 1997, more than 400 people have completed the intensive 3.5-day training seminar. LDPHE graduates are now college presidents, vice presidents, deans, department chairs, and directors, and many have completed advanced degrees. Although individual graduates have been successful, the overall progress in increasing the number of mid- to executive-level leaders has been slow and challenging.

Opportunities to advance into leadership roles in higher education are before us. The looming question is whether AAPIs will be encouraged and supported in pursuing those positions, and considered in filling them. Will colleges and universities embrace a leadership paradigm that fully embodies the richness that comes with diversity and recognizes that leadership profiles cross a wide spectrum of backgrounds, beliefs, and styles? Intentional efforts to support leadership development are imperative. College presidents, chancellors, and other senior executives must support the development of AAPI managers, faculty, and staff. Efforts such as LDPHE need to be recognized as vehicles to prepare AAPI educators for positions of leadership and influence in higher education.

A critical aspect of leadership development for AAPIs is to build on their cultural strengths while providing a safe place to come face-to-face with challenges. Using a continuous improvement model, LDPHE has evolved over the past 15 years. Research from LDPHE (Yamagata-Noji, 2005), coupled with surveys and feedback from participants and mentors, has provided the facilitators with insights into the specific leadership skills that AAPIs can benefit from to become more effective and advance in the profession.

The LDPHE program goals are to—

- Provide a supportive environment for customized development of leadership skills
- Graduate a prepared, knowledgeable, and confident class of AAPI educational leaders
- Create a pool of trained leaders poised to pursue career advancement in higher education
- Teach practical skills using a culturally sensitive, participant-relevant framework
- Develop an enhanced network of Asian and Pacific Islanders in higher education.

To advance in the field, student affairs professionals must be effective and assertive communicators. The stereotyped image of AAPIs as humble, unassertive, reluctant to speak up, and behind-the-scenes workers has had a negative impact on their ability to advance in the profession. Reluctance to affirm or assert one's accomplishments, lack of comfort with making public presentations, and ambivalence about joining in on work-related social opportunities further diminish the advancement opportunities of AAPIs.

LDPHE features well-known speakers whose presentations support the program's goals. Topics embedded in the LDPHE program to strengthen leadership abilities include:

- The 21ˢᵗ Century Leader: Surviving and Thriving in the Third Millennium
- Integrating Asian Pacific Cultural Values and Leadership Roles
- Developing and Promoting Your Leadership Style
- Packaging Yourself for Success
- Mastering the Dynamics of Power: Problem Solving and Making an Impact
- Interviewing for Success—mock interviews
- Mentoring Sessions—one-on-one, panels, small groups

Many AAPIs enter the student affairs field via positions in residential life, student activities, or student life. Others enter as staff in Asian American student centers and other diversity programs. Moving on from these initial positions has been challenging for many of them. Why is this so? To advance, one must be recognized as being knowledgeable and experienced in a wide range of areas. To gain wider experience, one must be willing to take risks, learn new skills, step out of the box, and seek mentoring by those who have walked the same path.

LDPHE addresses three overarching concepts in its culturally relevant approach to leadership development for AAPIs:

- *"Bragging":* Fear of bragging has no place in leadership development. A person must be able to take credit for, affirm, and present his or her accomplishments with confidence. Many AAPIs find it difficult to balance their traditional upbringing, in which humility is seen as a value, with demonstrating readiness for a promotion, new opportunity, new position, or title change. LDPHE addresses the challenge of asserting oneself and focuses on presenting one's abilities and accomplishments through practice dialogues about yourself with key talking points. The interviewing exercises help dispel conflicts about "being humble" and "not drawing attention to yourself."

- *Risk taking*: In her 2010 book, *The Loudest Duck*, Laura Liswood discusses the fear of sticking one's neck out and taking risks. The applicable Chinese saying is "The loudest duck gets shot"; the Japanese say, "The nail that sticks up gets hammered down." This philosophy is ingrained in many AAPIs, so the prospect of "going for it" or volunteering for something that is not guaranteed to be a success can be somewhat frightening. The cultural value of saving face and not bringing shame, dishonor, or failure on oneself, the family, family name, community, or entire ethnic group must be overcome. Individuals who are unable to take risks often work in the shadows, go unnoticed, and do not make career progress. The LDPHE mentors provide excellent insights as they share the risks they have taken to advance and succeed in their careers and personal lives.

- *Communicating*: Student affairs professionals must have strong interpersonal skills and public speaking proficiency. Many AAPIs avoid public speaking and struggle with assertive communication. They may see no need to restate the obvious or repeat what has already been said, so they remain quiet. This communication style leads others to misunderstand and mislabel AAPIs as poor communicators. Student affairs administrators are frequently called upon to make impromptu presentations and intervene in highly charged interpersonal situations with individuals and groups. LDPHE provides a safe and supportive environment where participants can practice and develop assertive communication skills.

In preparing for a new opportunity or career advancement, we are often told to "put your best foot forward." Senior managers who interview AAPI applicants often report, "Their credentials were great, but they shot themselves in the foot during the interview process." Instead of putting our best foot forward, we shoot ourselves in the foot! A critical focus of LDPHE is to assist participants with interviewing skills so they are more confident and polished in presenting themselves. Participants also learn how to seek positions of greater responsibility and how to network professionally to establish key connections that will lead to career opportunities.

One of the most effective aspects of LDPHE is the mentoring component. Some LDPHE participants are unsure about what they do not know and what they need to do. With support from highly respected and experienced mentors, LPDHE participants gain insight, strengthen their self-concepts, and create a career GPS for their future. Mentors include tenured faculty, who coach other faculty on approaching tenure, serving as department chairs, and being influential faculty members. Participants regularly credit their mentoring relationships as one of the most valuable aspects of the program. Having a noted AAPI educator listen, advise, and support can provide an incredible boost to one's self-esteem and professional self-concept.

Another unique aspect of the program is the focus on specific aspects of leadership development relative to Asian American and Pacific Islanders. Feeling a sense of community and support from talking with other AAPIs, participants are able to share, take risks, and grow in an environment of respect for their culture and acceptance of their heritage. Many participants openly share the struggles and challenges they have faced as a result of their ethnicity, language background, and immigrant status, and return to their campuses with cultural pride, a higher sense of self-esteem, and a sense of purpose and direction. For many, acknowledging feelings of pain, anger, and confusion allows them to move forward. Through various programmatic exercises, participants develop insights into the cultural dimensions of their own development and the impact on their leadership styles and leadership journeys.

"You can't plot a course if you don't know where you need to go." With this thought in mind, participants use the resources of mentors and colleagues in the program to plan the next steps in both their careers and personal lives. The program puts significant emphasis on having each participant leave with a plan. In the self-declaratory closing exercise, participants articulate their hopes, dreams, and next steps to others and, especially, to themselves.

Outcomes

The results of the LDPHE program are both measurable and immeasurable. Participants have testified that the program changed their lives, gave them career direction, boosted their confidence, and energized them in their work. These statements have been affirmed by college and university vice presidents and presidents, who report 360-degree changes in LDPHE participants who returned to their campuses as more engaged and effective leaders. Through continuous networking, we have supported LDPHE alumni in all career aspects, from tenure review to interviewing for higher-level positions to earning their doctoral degrees. Faculty alumni of LDPHE seeking support in applying to the ACE Fellows Program have received mentoring assistance from college presidents networked with LDPHE.

Participants are often nominated for the LDPHE program by their college administrators, who recognize leadership qualities the participants do not see in themselves. Faculty members who have been appointed or elected as department chairs are referred to LDPHE to prepare them for their new professional roles, while mid-level managers who can be promoted within the institution are nominated to build greater confidence in exerting their leadership skills. LDPHE participants range from high-level administrators, such as vice presidents and deans/associate deans, to program coordinators/directors and faculty. The goal is not to put every participant on a course to the presidency but to enable all participants to contribute more to their respective institutions, receive greater recognition for their contributions and achievements, create a voice at every level of the institution, and feel more confident assuming visible positions of leadership. At the end of the program, participants share their "next steps" with the entire class. During this exercise, the true impact of the program becomes clear to the individual and to the group, as shown by the following sampling of comments:

"I am ready to begin my next career move to further enhance my leadership and management skills. I will be a living example of one who will change the world. Sometimes your dreams have to be shattered in order for new ones to be built up."

"The Korean in me doesn't usually cry. This has been very transformative. I first thought of this program as a nuisance, but I attended because my vice president nominated me. I wondered why I have been struggling... but discovered that it was because I wasn't asking for help, I just kept working harder."

"I've opened my mind to more possibilities. I've learned to be a bit more forgiving of myself and to advocate for myself. Although I may not have all the steps mapped out, I will walk a little differently from now on."

"When I registered for the program, I never expected that I would be able to develop a roadmap—to find my career GPS. My goals have been crystallized, and I now have a concrete action plan for the next 5 years."

"We aren't strangers to attending conferences, but this program has been moment after moment of heart-touching experiences."

"Someone said that Asians work hard and make us all look bad. That bothered me. So, I got into computers because they wouldn't stereotype me. I have been running away. I've used my family as an excuse not to move up. I've learned that it's okay to be in touch with my culture and not lose myself in the mainstream."

Success Stories

One of the benefits of a long-running program is the ability to track the progress of past participants. The true testimonies are in the career profiles of LDPHE graduates who advanced to a higher position and, in some cases, also completed their doctoral degrees. The following are some examples:

- Frank Chong—from dean of students to college president to deputy assistant secretary for community colleges, U.S. Department of Education
- Lori Adrian—from dean of students to vice president of student services to college president, Coastline College; completed doctoral degree
- Julie Wong—from associate dean of students to vice chancellor, University of South Florida; completed doctoral degree
- Dyrell Foster—from director of student life to dean of student affairs, Rio Hondo College; completed doctoral degree
- Fuji Collins—from director of graduate studies to assistant vice chancellor for student health and wellness, University of California, Merced
- Jocelyn Nakashige—from director of administration and finance, University of California, San Francisco, to senior associate dean, University of California, Riverside School of Medicine
- Gerald Napoles—from dean of students to vice president for student services, Bowling Green Technical College
- Tram Vo-Kumamoto—from faculty counselor to dean of science and math, Chabot College
- Nancy Wada-McKee—from dean of students to assistant vice president for student services, California State University, Los Angeles
- Evette Castillo Clark—from director of student life to assistant dean of students, Tulane University; completed doctoral degree
- Joy Hoffman—from director of multiethnic programs to

director of cross-cultural centers, Whittier College; completed doctoral degree

- Mamta Accapadi—from director to dean of student affairs, Oregon State University; completed doctoral degree
- Mary Ann Takemoto—from director of counseling and psychological services to associate vice president for student affairs, California State University, Long Beach

In addition, six LDPHE graduates—Evette Castillo Clark, Joy Hoffman, Hikaru Kozuma, Sunny Lee, Christine Quemuel, and Julie Wong—have used and developed their leadership skills further by serving as national co-chairs of the Asian Pacific Islanders Concerns Knowledge Community of NASPA.

Each year, participants evaluate the LDPHE program. Speakers and exercises are consistently rated as "superior," and no program component has been rated "poor" in the past 10 years. Most notable are the personal comments, like these:

> "Interviewing skills and practice. Even though I've interviewed regularly over the years, I have never had the kind of practice and feedback that I received at LDPHE. It was practical, challenging, and encouraging."

> "I really appreciated the . . . sense of community when Asians get together. I've spent a lot of time thinking about how I can change my weaknesses—now I know they are not weaknesses, but assets!"

> "Exceeded my expectations! I've never been around so many successful API leaders. They were all so articulate, intelligent, compassionate, and willing to volunteer their time to be here with us."

> "I came in thinking this was a leadership building program. Really, it turned out to be a life-changing experience . . . it gives direction."

> "I learned to be open to hearing criticism because it's for my own good. Likewise, I learned to provide feedback with greater

diplomacy, tact, kindness, and honesty. The mentors modeled this throughout the program. I realized that my values as an API woman and leadership style are actually good, positive, and needed for the workplace. I don't have to sacrifice in full my personhood to be successful and effective."

Three participants in the 2011 LDPHE program shared the following:

"The overall LDPHE experience is such an empowering experience. I learned that leaders are made and that I can be one—yes, even a Filipino immigrant like me, here in the U.S. I did realize that whatever I do, I will do it with the utmost confidence in myself and my cultural identity. With this newfound wisdom, here are things I want to do starting now:

- Be more confident and be the "people person" that I am. (I actually went to three meetings since last week and spoke my ideas with more confidence than I had ever before.)
- Take on new challenges out of my comfort zone. Be more involved in campus and community groups and issues."

"LDPHE was a vibrant, empowering program that allowed me to gain more insight about myself and about leadership and career development than I could have ever imagined taking place in 3-1/2 days. Well-organized with the participation of many accomplished API professionals, LDPHE resonated because it was culturally relevant. As APIs, all of us in attendance—participants and presenters—shared similar challenges and created a strong commitment to form a supportive network."

"The training sessions and the presentations I received through LDPHE were intense and it gave me even stronger affirmation that I have great contributions to make. I want to continue to be challenged professionally so I can take on additional leadership roles. The program gave me a renewed sense of direction and confidence in my expertise and my career path."

Although many participants are from campuses on the West Coast, the program also attracts participants from institutions such as the Maricopa Community College District in Arizona, the University of Houston, the University of North Carolina, the University of Washington, and Wright State University in Ohio. Although the largest proportion of participants listed their ethnic origin as Chinese, Filipino, Japanese, Korean, and Vietnamese, the program has also served Hmong, Cambodians, South Asians, and Pacific Islanders. A considerable number of participants would be considered multiracial, further expanding the diversity within the AAPI population.

The first program in 1997 had 25 participants—including many of the current faculty and speakers. The peak years of 2006 and 2007 had 50 participants per class. Recent economic constraints on higher education have resulted in lower numbers; nevertheless, despite budget cutbacks, institutions have supported 25 to 37 participants in recent years, an indication of the great need for the program and the participants' and institutions' recognition of its importance.

The contributions that LDPHE graduates are making in the field of higher education are phenomenal, as shown in the success stories above. More important, LDPHE continues to support AAPIs in their career and leadership development by providing a comprehensive and culturally relevant approach to leadership training. For AAPIs, attaining higher levels of visible and influential leadership in higher education has been both a pipeline issue and a pipe dream for too many years. As a result of the dedication of the LDPHE program faculty, more than 400 AAPIs are better prepared to break through the glass (or bamboo) ceiling and assume critical positions of leadership.

However, LDPHE facilitators and alumni are aware that leadership training will have limited impact on organizational change unless non-AAPI leaders and institutions share the responsibilities for change at colleges and universities. AAPIs are committed to making these changes, and call on higher education institutions and non-AAPI leaders to initiate and implement more inclusive policies and attitudes.

References

American Council on Education (ACE). (2006). *Minorities in higher education twenty-second annual status report.* Washington, DC: Author.

American Council on Education (ACE). (2007). *The American College President: 2007 Edition.* Washington, DC: Author.

Bridges, B., Eckel, P., Cordova, D., & White, B. (2008). *Broadening the leadership spectrum: Advancing the diversity in the American college presidency.* Washington, DC: American Council on Education.

King, J., & Gomez, G. (2008). *On the pathway to the presidency: Characteristics of higher education's senior leadership.* Washington, DC: American Council on Education.

Liswood, L. (2010). *The loudest duck.* Hoboken, NJ: John Wiley & Sons.

Yamagata-Noji, A. (2005). Leadership development program in higher education: Asian Pacific American leaders in higher education—an oxymoron? In D. Leon (Ed.), *Lessons in leadership* (Diversity in higher education, no. 5, pp. 173–206). Bingley, United Kingdom: Emerald Group Publishing Limited.

PART IV

Working with AAPI College Students

CHAPTER TEN

Factors Related to Native Hawaiian Student Success in College

Lui K. Hokoana and Judy K. Oliveira

In 2005, the Kamehameha Schools published *Ka Huaka'i: Native Hawaiian Assessment*, a report on the educational status of Native Hawaiians. The report cited the following issues that need to be addressed for this group to succeed in higher education:

- On the whole, Native Hawaiian public school students from low-income families score lower on achievement tests, are more often retained in grade school, and are more often required to repeat a grade rather than matriculate from 9th to 10th grade at the end of the school year. They are, therefore, less likely to graduate from high school in 4 years than Native Hawaiian students from more financially secure families.
- The test scores for Native Hawaiian children lag behind statewide

averages by approximately 10 percentile points in reading and math. The achievement gap widens as students progress to higher grades.

- Academic disparities are pronounced in rural regions with very high concentrations of Native Hawaiians.

- The percentage of Native Hawaiian adults who have obtained a bachelor's degree is half the statewide rate (12.6% versus 26.2%).

- Native Hawaiian students at the University of Hawai`i at Mānoa are the least likely of the major ethnic groups to graduate within 6 years. They are the most likely among all students to be working full time while attending school (22.3% versus 17.8% statewide).

The *Ka Huaka`i* findings confirm Benham's (2007, p. 29) assessment that "Native Hawaiians are not faring well in their own homeland." The report and many scholars contend that one way to address this issue is to reinforce cultural identity. Native Hawaiians are the indigenous people of Hawai`i. Like other indigenous U.S. citizens, many have not experienced the American dream. The educational pipeline results for Native Hawaiians are worse than for non-Hawaiians: they have lower test scores and lower transition rates between middle school and high school, are retained in high school more often, and are less likely than non-Hawaiians to graduate, enroll in college, or complete a bachelor's degree in the expected timeframe. It appears that they consistently fall below the average and are deprived of opportunities to engage in academic activities that can provide the widest selection of life choices (Benham, 2007).

Lui's Story

In 1985, I entered the University of Hawai`i at Hilo (UHH) as a freshman. Although I had graduated from a private college-preparatory high school, I was underprepared for college. Not only was I underprepared academically, I was at a loss regarding what I needed to do to survive my freshman year. I saw a faculty advisor who was of no help, as she had just arrived at UHH herself and knew as little as I did about the school. At 18, I believed that I was smarter than almost everybody, so I did my own academic advising. I got a catalog and off I went, creating a course schedule on my own. I wanted to reserve my evenings for the nonacademic/social life part of the college experience, so I scheduled all early morning classes. Although I found it difficult to wake up early enough to arrive on time for my 8:30 a.m. classes in high school, I thought I was a new person. I was in college, so I thought surely I could handle any 8 a.m., 9 a.m., or 10 a.m. class. I could not have been more wrong. At the end of my first semester, I had a 1.5 GPA.

Academic Probation and Introduction to HLDP

To continue at UHH, I had to meet with the academic probation counselor. The counselor tried to rehabilitate me with a "scared straight" tactic, which was ineffective because I feared very few things. I did not follow any of the counselor's recommendations. Fortunately, I had been commiserating with a group of Native Hawaiian students who were involved in the Hawaiian Leadership Development Program (HLDP). They knew about my academic problems and suggested that I see David Sing, the faculty director of HLDP (whom we Hawaiians called Uncle David) to inquire about getting into the program. I scheduled an appointment with Uncle David and was introduced to HLDP.

The program was established at UHH in 1984 by the Committee of Faculty of Hawaiian Ancestry (COFHA), which comprised faculty members from all areas of the college, including student services, instruction, and academic support. The program was designed to address the underrepresentation of Native Hawaiian students in higher education, and the idea was to support Native Hawaiian students who were in academic trouble. There was no money for the program and no special incentive to participate. The 1984 cohort included 10 male students; a year later, only 2 of them were still enrolled at UHH. Although disappointed by the persistence of the first cohort, COFHA did not give up; the second HLDP cohort was a coed group of 20 students. I joined this group in the spring semester of 1986.

COFHA developed the program with the best intentions and on the basis of available research. In retrospect, I believe they were creating the program as they went along. When I participated, it included the following components:

- The HLDP coordinator provided academic advising and helped link students with the support services they needed.
- Every HLDP student was encouraged to take Hawaiian language courses.
- Outside of class, faculty participated with the students in Hawaiian cultural excursions, such as spending the weekend in the beautiful, serene Waipio Valley, working in the taro patches, and restoring the *auwai* (irrigation system). These outings created bonds among students, faculty, and staff.
- Uncle David and HLDP coordinator Faith Mokuau taught a class that was a hybrid of career exploration, leadership development, cultural understanding, and college success skills.
- Successful Native Hawaiians in education, business, and politics appeared as guest speakers.

The final program activity for each HLDP cohort was to plan and host a conference. The twin goals of this activity were (1) to give the students an opportunity to practice leadership in planning and implementing the conference, and (2) to provide a venue for Native Hawaiians to discuss issues related to leadership and education. All the students participated in all aspects of this first conference in 1986; another student and I were selected to lead the planning. The basic premise of HLDP was that a Native Hawaiian student who had a strong foundation in Hawaiian culture would be more successful in college. Thus, Hawaiian culture was embedded at every level of the program.

Graduate Support Program: Operation Kua ʻana

I eventually completed my bachelor's degree at UHH and went on to graduate studies at the University of Hawaiʻi at Mānoa (UHM), the Carnegie Research I campus. I was hired as a graduate student assistant at the Operation Kua`ana program, directed by Ekela Kaniaupio. *Kua`ana* means older brother, and Operation Kua`ana was based on the concept of mentoring: an older brother guiding younger brothers to college success. First and foremost, Operation Kua`ana provided a sense of place for Native Hawaiian students at UHM. This was especially important in 1991, because Hawaiians were seriously underrepresented. Kua`ana was a place where you could hang out with other Native Hawaiians, talk to a counselor, use a computer, or plan and paint the signs for the next campus demonstration. In addition, the program provided peer mentoring, tutoring, and scholarships. The program was well-known for the biannual Kua`ana bash, a huge concert with free food and drink, held primarily to introduce new Native Hawaiian students to Kua`ana.

Operation Kua`ana advisors were not a formal faculty group like COFHA at UHH, but the program was aligned with the Hawaiian Studies program, whose faculty provided mentoring and guidance to Kua`ana students and staff. Kua`ana had a more global focus and did not work exclusively with a cohort. However, like HLDP, it embedded culture into all its program services. A good example is the way Kua`ana approached academic advising. In traditional settings, advising takes place one-on-one on campus; with Kua`ana, it could take place at the remote end of the island, at a beach park in Waianae, with the student and the student's family. The Kua`ana philosophy was similar to that of HLDP— that the Hawaiian culture could serve as a bridge to college success.

First Student Affairs Staff Position: Po`okela

After graduating from UHM, I was hired as director of the Po`okela program at Maui Community College; the program was funded through the Alu Like Native Hawaiian Vocational Education Program (NHVEP). Although they had different names, there was an NHVEP at each of the seven community colleges in the University of Hawai`i system. NHVEP was created by Chancellor Joyce Tunoda in response to a report in 1987 that cited unmet needs of Native Hawaiian students in seven areas: (1) financial problems, (2) personal problems, (3) inadequate childcare, (4) absence of community networking, (5) poor self-image, (6) institutional inadequacies, and (7) insufficient student assessment and monitoring (University of Hawai`i, 1988). Po`okela was created to address these issues in a way that would, it was hoped, lead to success for Native Hawaiians at Maui Community College.

Po`okela provided comprehensive outreach, especially to the rural Maui communities of Hana, Moloka`i, and others. Included in the outreach was academic advising, financial aid and admissions workshops, and family college nights. On campus, Po`okela created a space—a center where Native Hawaiian students could hang out, use a computer, be tutored, and receive other assistance. There was always food and a nurturing presence at Po`okela. Staff held *kanikapila* (music workshops), monthly cultural workshops, and cultural excursions. Po`okela, like HLDP and Kua`ana, used Hawaiian cultural values and experiences as the premise for all its activities.

Does the cultural premise work? Anecdotally, I would say yes, because I and many of my fellow HLDP members successfully completed college. In fact, one became mayor of the Island of Hawai`i. In this chapter, Judy Oliveira and I discuss two studies we conducted to investigate whether Native Hawaiians believe that programs that integrate their culture into program services are important to their educational success, and what other factors might predict college success for Native Hawaiians.

Literature Summary: Native Hawaiians and College

Native Hawaiians and non-Hawaiians have different levels of college preparation. In placement tests, 66% of Native Hawaiians scored below college-level math, compared with 61% of the general student population. In reading, 45% of Native Hawaiians scored below college level, compared with 42% of non-Hawaiians. Fifty-two percent of Native Hawaiians placed below college-level writing, compared with 39% of the general population. Adelman (2004) and other scholars have concluded that students who must take remedial education classes are less likely to be successful in college.

Although limited, the literature on the Native Hawaiian population shows that they have unique characteristics and face many barriers to economic self-sufficiency. Some of these barriers are being addressed in culturally sensitive programs. Higher education is one way to remedy the difficulties the Native Hawaiian community faces every day. Empirical data show that people who attain a college degree earn more money, are more involved in their community, and live longer than those without a degree. Encouraging college success among Native Hawaiian students is a way of addressing the negative environment they face as a group.

The literature provides a glimpse of factors that can increase college success. One factor is students' precollege experience: their high school courses, grades, parents' encouragement, and socioeconomic status (SES). The second fundamental element is student engagement—the more students engage with the institution, faculty, and peers, the greater their likelihood of college success. Data from the 2006 University of Hawai`i Community College Survey of Student Engagement (CCSSE), documents the fact that Native Hawaiians are more engaged in college than their non-Hawaiian peers.

The literature also posits that Native Hawaiians have a lower SES than most non-Hawaiians, but is this enough to explain their low achievement in college? Most researchers say no. Hawaiians' unique political and social history complicates the factors that increase success in college. Understanding how this history affects their views on pursuing a college degree is critical to addressing their specific needs.

Does Culture Matter?

In Hokoana's study, data from quantitative and qualitative measures show the differing perceptions about culture and college success between Hawaiian and non-Hawaiian students attending Windward Community College. Native Hawaiians and non-Hawaiians do not face different barriers to college success, but Native Hawaiian Pell grant recipients are more likely than Native Hawaiians who do not receive grants to believe that they face different barriers than non-Hawaiians. Second, Native Hawaiians and non-Hawaiians seek assistance from similar support networks when they experience difficulty in college. Third, Native Hawaiians, unlike non-Hawaiians, perceive that college programs that integrate their culture and values help them more than programs that do not. Finally, Native Hawaiians, unlike non-Hawaiians, believe that a good understanding of their culture will help them succeed in college.

In Oliveira's study—in which a majority of the students attended colleges throughout the continental United States—the relationship between a Hawaiian sense of belonging and the likelihood of bachelor's degree completion was significant, but it was not a strong predictor of college success. Having a strong sense of belonging might support their ethnic development or it might adversely affect their choice to persist in higher education. Understanding the dynamics of Native Hawaiians and their culture can help us create a framework for programs—such as HLDP, Kua`ana, and Po`okela—that will encourage Native Hawaiian college success.

Other Factors That Determine College Success

Although less than 20% of Native Hawaiians have a college degree, the success of these students shows their ability to overcome barriers. Among numerous factors associated with minority student retention, the three factors that have drawn attention in research focusing on students of Hawaiian ancestry are (1) the effect of family support and encouragement, (2) lack of academic preparation, and (3) concerns about paying for college.

The first factor—parental encouragement—is a protective factor for student retention. For the Hawaiian student, the family is the center of all relationships, and the core values of the Hawaiian way are found in the `ohana (family) (Young, 1980). A lack of parental encouragement can hinder Hawaiian students' success, while parental encouragement may mitigate the risk factors of inadequate academic preparation and lack of financial assistance. In addition, encouragement to attend college has been found to increase the likelihood of minority student completion and is positively related to academic achievement (Jackson, Smith, & Hill, 2003).

Oliveira (2005) studied predictive factors of college completion for Native Hawaiian students. Her study found that parental encouragement was a significant predictor of bachelor's degree completion for Native Hawaiian students. A lack of support and encouragement of a student's college attendance and attainment of a bachelor's degree decreased the probability of completion. The findings were similar for non-Hawaiian students.

The second factor—lack of academic preparation—begins well before college. Inadequacy in the high school curriculum may contribute to low scores on standardized tests for Hawaiian students. Unfortunately, Hawaiian students do not perform as well on these tests as their non-Hawaiian counterparts. In fact, achievement outcomes for Hawaiian students are consistently among the lowest, throughout elementary and secondary school. From 1998 to 2000, the scores of Hawaiian secondary students lagged behind the scores of their peers in other ethnic groups by 11 percentage points for reading and 14 percentage points in math. Longitudinal data suggest that the disparity continues as students get older (Kamehameha Schools, 2002).

The third factor—lack of financial assistance—is unavoidable for many Hawaiian students. Two indicators that Hawaiian families cannot afford college expenses are found in the classification of household incomes and family poverty levels, where high concentrations of low-income and high-poverty households are found among Hawaiian families (Office of Hawaiian Affairs, 2002). Links between financial aid and student persistence substantiate the negative effect of the lack of financial assistance on minority student college completion (Porter, 1991).

Indigenous students are likely to report receiving some form of financial aid to pay for college. In 2007, 39% of American Indians/Alaska Natives and 33% of Native Hawaiians/Pacific Islanders received a Pell grant; as compared to 21% for White students (National Center for Education Statistics, 2008). At the University of Hawai`i in 2010, more than 50% of Native Hawaiians received some form of financial aid as compared to 31% of their non-Hawaiian peers (Yoshimura, 2011).

In the 2008 CCSSE conducted at Windward Community College

(WCC), 83% of Native Hawaiians and 82% of non-Hawaiians reported that an associate's degree was their primary goal. Students in the two groups had similar college aspirations: 74% of Native Hawaiians and 78% of non-Hawaiians said that they planned to transfer to a 4-year college. Forty-five percent of Native Hawaiians and 48% of non-Hawaiians reported working more than 21 hours a week (CCSSE, 2006).

In summary, data from quantitative and qualitative measures show similarities between Hawaiian and non-Hawaiian students at WCC but differing perceptions about culture and college success. First, Native Hawaiians and non-Hawaiians do not face different barriers to college success. However, it is worth investigating why Native Hawaiian Pell grant recipients believe they face different barriers to college, while non-Pell recipients do not hold this belief. Second, Native Hawaiians and non-Hawaiians seek assistance from similar support networks when they experience difficulty in college. Third, Native Hawaiians, unlike non-Hawaiians, believe that college programs that integrate their culture and values help them more than programs that do not (73% versus 43%). Understanding the dynamics of Native Hawaiians and their culture can help create a framework for programs that will encourage Native Hawaiian college success.

Oliveira's study revealed that financial aid was the most likely predictor of bachelor's degree completion for students of Hawaiian ancestry. Parental encouragement and specific opportunities in high school were also significant predictors of completion. These findings support the research discussed in the literature review and affirm the importance of ensuring that these predictive factors are an integral component of policies and programs that address the needs of Native Hawaiian students.

Our Work Today

In 2005, Judy Oliveira was hired to lead WCC's Educational Talent Search (part of the Federal TRIO Programs) to increase college-going among first generation and low-income students. During the latter part of that year, the college joined Lumina's Achieving the Dream (AtD), a national initiative to increase the college success rates of underserved minorities—in WCC's case, Native Hawaiians. AtD has five goals for students: (1) successfully complete coursework; (2) advance from remedial to credit-bearing courses; (3) enroll in and successfully complete gatekeeper courses; (4) enroll from one semester to the next; and (5) earn degrees and/or certificates.

The college held three public forums on achieving the AtD goals; on the basis of feedback from those forums, a plan was developed. The original plan included 52 initiatives; after a year of trying to implement those activities, it was apparent we had been too ambitious. In the second year, we reduced the 52 activities to 4: learning communities, supplemental instruction, financial aid outreach, and first-year experience. Interestingly, all the activities were developed out of the student affairs department, including the first two, which are primarily instructional activities.

Learning Communities and Supplemental Instruction

Learning communities (LCs) were implemented as part of a strategy to get to the kind of teaching that is critical for student success. Although LCs have been around for a long time, WCC did not use the strategy until 2008. LCs pair two or more integrated or nonintegrated courses in a sequence. The first LC at WCC was English 22 and Hawaiian Studies 107. The pass rate for WCC's first LC was poor. The LC was not integrated and, although the teachers had a homogenous group of students based on English 22, they did not bother to change their teaching methods. The next LCs at WCC were integrated, and the pass rates were excellent, surpassing the 5-year average pass rate for each respective class. WCC now offers approximately six LCs each year.

The second AtD initiative to improve teaching was supplemental instruction (SI). SI is sometimes confused with tutoring and, to some extent, some SI sessions are tutoring sessions. The difference is that the tutoring is moved to the classroom. The SI instructor sits through the class with the students and, immediately afterward, holds a study session. The ideal situation is for the SI instructor to teach the concepts using a different methodology to reinforce what was taught in the class. The preliminary data suggest that SI is effective in increasing the pass rates for courses that have traditionally had low pass rates, such as remedial math and English. In 2010, the college offered approximately 50 SI sessions.

Financial Aid Outreach

Oliveira led the AtD financial aid initiative; her planning team consisted of the financial aid officer and the outreach coordinator. The goal was to increase financial aid access from 37% to 50% of all students. To achieve this goal, the team implemented a comprehensive financial aid outreach effort at all feeder high schools through the Scholarship ʻAha (a traditional Hawaiian feast) at the New Year's FAFSA (Free Application for Federal Student Aid) workshop, and by creating a one-stop financial aid center at Windward Mall.

The Scholarship ʻAha is aimed at Native Hawaiian students. The evening is a family affair, where students and their families meet with Native Hawaiian scholarship providers, culminating in dinner. In November 2010, more than 400 people attended the ʻAha on campus and 100 attended the one in Waimanalo, a low-income district with a large Native Hawaiian population and low college attendance. This initiative has been taken statewide, with Scholarship ʻAhas on all islands.

FAFSA workshops help students complete their financial aid applications online. The first FAFSA workshop of the year was held on Saturday, January 2, 2011. The idea was to get students to complete their FAFSAs early so they would be first in line for financial aid that is awarded on a first-come first-served basis. Remarkably, 111 students completed and submitted their FAFSAs at this workshop.

The third initiative was the creation of the Windward Community College Financial Aid One-Stop at Windward Mall. Kamehameha Schools allows WCC to use its storefront at the mall at no cost. The WCC One-Stop is open from November through April on Fridays, Saturdays, Sundays, and Mondays. People can get information about college admissions and financial aid, and a financial aid professional helps them complete the FAFSA and other financial aid applications. More than 800 people used the center in 2010, which was its first year of operation.

The results of the outreach activities were encouraging. The college met its goal of improving financial aid access to 50% and awarded $7 million in financial aid in 2010, an increase of $2 million over 2005.

First Year Experience

First Year Experience (FYE) has three mandatory components for all incoming freshmen: New Student Orientation (NSO), academic advising, and Frosh Camp. NSO is a 1.5-hour workshop that prepares new students to meet with their counselors and register for classes. Each student is assigned to a counselor when he or she is accepted to WCC. They may register for classes as soon as they have attended NSO and taken the placement test; their counselors assist them in this process.

Frosh Camp, a 2-day comprehensive orientation to WCC, is led by peer-mentors. Day 1 includes college success strategies, clarifying college perceptions and misperceptions, and a campus scavenger hunt, with a student club fair during lunch. Day 2 begins with a historical overview of WCC, including learning a chant about the mountain that provides the backdrop to the college. The students meet different faculty via 20-minute "classes," then complete a letter indicating how they intend to demonstrate their commitment to their education. (The letter will be sent to them midway through the semester.) The day ends with a concert hosted by the WCC student government.

The school has collected both qualitative and quantitative data about the success of FYE. Students who attend all three parts of the program persist from one year to the next at 81%, compared with 32% for students who attend only one component.

The final element of FYE, is Frosh Cohorts, which places freshmen into learning communities and is nonmandatory. The first LC class is Interdisciplinary Studies 103, Master Student, taught by a counselor and paired with a course from social sciences, science, humanities, or Hawaiian studies. In addition, the students are enrolled in their respective math and English courses. All Frosh Cohort classes include supplemental instruction. The Frosh Cohort students persisted at 91% from one year to the next.

Student Affairs Can Lead a Campus to Student Success

As the Achieving the Dream initiative was being implemented, something very interesting happened. The instructors wanted to change the way they taught but did not know how. So, as part of the initiative, WCC created a professional development program, with two faculty coaches to assist the instructors in the LC and Frosh Cohort components. Although this is a work in progress, there is richness in having candid discussions about student success with faculty members from English, math, science, social science, humanities, Hawaiian studies, and counseling. Instruction is a critical component in increasing student success; WCC has taught us that student affairs professionals can directly affect teaching at the college.

The AtD initiative gave the authors of this chapter an opportunity to put their theories into practice. Judy's study found that financial aid is an important component of college success. WCC's AtD initiative successfully expanded access to financial aid. Lui's study argued for programs that were aligned with students' values and culture. Native Hawaiian culture emphasizes collective well-being over individual well-being (Meyer, 1998). This emphasis is implied in terms such as 'ohana and hānai (fostering and adoption). It finds expression today in the prevalence of extended family relations and supportive networks in the Native Hawaiian community. Research shows that, like all students, indigenous students achieve superior outcomes when their parents, families, and community actively participate in the educational system (Mokuau, 1990). Thus, for both cultural and educational reasons, many Native Hawaiian educational programs actively cultivate family involvement. Although learning communities, supplemental instruction, financial aid outreach, and first-year experience are traditional western initiatives, the form of these initiatives was unique to the students at WCC. The initiatives were high-touch and student-led, and encouraged a collaborative rather than competitive environment. In addition, the leadership and a majority of the staff are of Native Hawaiian ancestry and familiar with Hawaiian culture.

It is still early for a summative evaluation of the AtD initiatives, but the formative data indicate a strong positive impact on student success. The college has met all its strategic objectives related to student success, and all the AtD initiatives have generated empirical data that suggest that they effectively impact student success. Our experience with AtD is a good example of how student affairs can lead a campus in increasing the educational success of students.

References

Adelman, C. (2004). *Principal indicators of student academic histories in postsecondary education, 1972–2000.* Washington, DC: U.S. Department of Education, Institute of Education Sciences.

Benham, M. K. P. (2007). A challenge to Native Hawaiian and Pacific Islander scholars: What research literature teaches us about our work. *Race, Ethnicity, and Education, 9,* 29–50.

Community College Survey of Student Engagement (CCSSE). (2006). *Engagement by design: 2006 findings.* Honolulu, HI: Author.

Jackson, A. P., Smith, S. A., & Hill, C. L. (2003). Academic persistence among Native American college students. *Journal of College Student Development, 44*(4), 548–556.

Kamehameha Schools. (2002). *Losing ground: Longitudinal trends in Hawai'i: Department of Education test scores for major ethnic groups.* Honolulu, HI: Policy Analysis & System Evaluation (2001–2002: 16).

Kamehameha Schools Press. (2005). *Ka Huaka'i: 2005 Native Hawaiian educational assessment.* Honolulu, HI: Author.

Meyer, M. A. (1998). Native Hawaiian epistemology: Exploring Hawaiian views of knowledge. *Cultural Survival Quarterly, 22,* 38–40.

Mokuau, N. (1990). Ethnic minority curriculum in baccalaureate social work programs. *Journal of Multicultural Social Work, 1,* 57–75.

National Center for Education Statistics. (2008). *Fast facts.* Retrieved from http://nces.ed.gov/FastFacts/display.asp?id=31.

Office of Hawaiian Affairs. (2002). *Native Hawaiian data book.* Honolulu, HI: Author.

Oliveira, J. (2005) *Native Hawaiians' success in higher education: Predictive factors and bachelor's degree completion.* Unpublished doctoral dissertation, University of Southern California, Los Angeles.

Pascarella, E. T., & Terenzini, P. T. (1997). Studying college students in the 21st century: Meeting new challenges. *Review of Higher Education, 21*(2), 151–165.

Porter, O. F. (1991). Where do we go from here? Looking beyond student aid and access to persistence. In J. P. Merisotis (Ed.) *The changing dimensions of student aid* (New directions for higher education, no. 74, pp. 75–90). San Francisco, CA: Jossey-Bass.

University of Hawai`i. (1988). *Native Hawaiian Community College Advisory Council final report.* Honolulu, HI: Chancellor for Community Colleges Office.

Yoshimura, G. (2011, July). Native Hawaiians and financial aid access. Report presented to the Puku`o Council, Honolulu, HI. Retrieved from http://www.hawaii.edu/finaid

Young, B. C. (1980). The Hawaiians. In J. F. McDermott, W. Tsent, & T. Martetzki (Eds.), *People and Cultures of Hawaii* (pp. 25–52). Honolulu, HI: University of Hawai`i Press.

CHAPTER ELEVEN

Redefining Racial Paradigms

Asian American Greek Letter Organizations

in American Higher Education

Anna Gonzalez

On August 2005, Kenny Luong, a California Polytechnic University, Pomona, undergraduate student, died as a result of a pledging event organized by the Lambda Phi Epsilon chapter at the University of California, Irvine (UC Irvine) (Haley, 2009). Founded in 1982, Lambda Phi Epsilon is one of the largest national Asian American fraternities, with approximately 50 chapters, associate chapters, and colonies (Chan, 1999; Chen, 2009). As associate dean of students and director of the Cross-Cultural Center at UC Irvine, I knew members of the chapter and recall their involvement with the Asian American community socially and through philanthropic activities. They were also involved with the Interfraternity Council and Panhellenic organizations in programs such as Greek Songfest, one of the largest events on campus. In the months and years since the death of Kenny Luong, the discourse surrounding Asian American Greek Letter Organizations (AAGLOs) has questioned their relevance in today's more open and desegregated society, as well as the undercurrent of violence that seems to be a part of these groups (Haley, 2009).

Although the first AAGLO, Rho Psi, was founded in 1916 at Cornell University, the dramatic increase of Asian American fraternities and sororities occurred only during the past 30 years. Currently, there are more than 25 known Asian American fraternities and more than 30 sororities. The National Asian Pacific Islander American Panhellenic Association (NAPA), a nongoverning advocacy group, was founded in 2005. Some of these organizations are national, with chapters across the country, whereas many are local or regional. Unlike other Greek letter organizations, little has been written about the history and foundations of AAGLOs. Moreover, popular media accounts lack historical and cultural context, and often reflect the negative and illegal activities AAGLOs allegedly sponsor. Despite the growing number of students who choose to join or form their own AAGLO chapters, the knowledge base of campus administrators, including those of Greek advisors and cultural center directors, has not grown at a substantial pace (Herel, Stannard, Buchanan, & Kim, 2003; Torbensen & Parks, 2009). This chapter discusses how AAGLOs circumnavigate the Black-White racial terrain, redefining racial paradigms to include those who do not fit into either category.

Rearticulating Race in American Higher Education

Over the past four decades, higher education has increasingly provided a laboratory for determining social policies and practices concerning majority and minority populations according to the nation's understanding of race. That understanding is rooted in the history of African Americans under slavery, during Reconstruction, in the period of legal segregation, and in the current period of structural discrimination. It is also based on the civil rights movement and rooted in the struggles of African Americans to realize the promises of the Civil War and *Brown v. Board of Education* to end legal discrimination in this country. It is, therefore, not surprising that the nation perceives itself as having a Black-White racial paradigm (Anderson, 2002; Marable, 1995).

Going beyond this biracial model involves a new and complex understanding of the changing demographics of the country, in which immigration and the increase of other racial minorities have become central facts of the census and of America's imagining of its demographics. The post-1965 immigration of Asians and Latinos to the United States interrupted the Black-White racial paradigm and complicated America's racial dynamic. The complexity of dealing with Asian Americans as a group lies in the fact that, historically and socio-politically, they have been categorized as both Whites and people of color, depending on the situation. The racial ambivalence in the treatment of this group results in a great disservice to the needs of those categorized as Asian Americans in higher education (Bonilla-Silva, 2009; Lowe, 1991; Osajima, 1995; Takagi, 1992; Tuan, 1998).

According to Mia Tuan (1998), Asian Americans are usually placed in the middle of the racial paradigm—positioned as either a dominant or subordinate racial group:

> As racial minorities, Asian ethnics undoubtedly relate to some sentiments that middle-class blacks express. However, Asian-Americans have undergone racialization processes that are different from the processes that black Americans have experienced. That is, the ways in which whites have marked off Asians as "others" are not the same as those for blacks. For Asians, nativism and the stigma of foreignness further compound racial marginalization. Blacks may be many things in the minds of whites, but foreign is not one of them. As far as racial positioning goes, Asians' designation as "model" minorities, the best of those in the "racial others" category, says it all: "racialized other" groups are not equal in the eyes of whites. (p. 8)

Tuan noted that Asian Americans have been pigeonholed as either "honorary Whites" or people of color, while benefiting from neither classification. Asian Americans have become "middlemen minorities"—those who create a niche in commerce as traders, agents, laborers, contractors, and money lenders. This position has allowed them to be used as the buffer between the White elites who dominate the economic system and the customers, who are mainly non-White but are not of the same ethnic background as the trader (Bonacich, 1980; Tuan, 1998).

Dana Takagi (1992) described the inequitable treatment of Asian Americans with regard to admission to highly selective universities and showed flaws in racial policies and misguided definitions of the terms *majority* and *minority*. Takagi found that the admissions policy instituted for Asian Americans differed from that for Whites and non-Asian minorities. Unlike non-Asian minorities and Whites, quotas were placed on admissions of Asian American students. These quotas, as well as harsher criteria directed at Asian Americans during the admissions process, were justified because this group was not a "disadvantaged minority." Officials argued that Asian Americans should not be included in policies implemented with the goal of diversifying colleges and universities, because, they said, Asian Americans do well on their own and do not need any help (Bowen & Bok, 1998; Takagi, 1992).

In 1982, one of American higher education's most prolific researchers on the student experience, Alexander Astin, published *Minorities in American Higher Education*. His exclusion of Asian Americans as a minority group seemed to suggest that this population was somehow different from other ethnic minorities. In fact, one might argue that this invisibility provides tacit acknowledgment that the researchers did not regard Asian Americans as ethnic minorities at all. Similarly, Bowen and Bok's *The Shape of the River: Long-Term Consequences of Considering Race in College and University Admissions* (1998) failed to cover Asian Americans who had been at the center of debates on higher education admissions, both in terms of scholarly discussion and political activism around the issue. Bowen and Bok used a Black-White paradigm for their appraisal of race and college admissions. The authors wrote,

> One reason for focusing on black and white students in this study is that so much of the debate over race-sensitive admissions policies has centered on black-white comparisons. . . . While Hispanics share many of the problems faced by blacks, there are so many differences in cultures, backgrounds, and circumstances within the broad Hispanic category that any rigorous study would need to make more distinctions than are possible within the confines of our database. Native Americans have also endured many handicaps and injustices and have benefited from race-sensitive admissions policies. . . . Asian Americans *differ* [emphasis added] from other minorities in important respects. Unlike the case of blacks and Hispanics, the percentage of Asian Americans in selective colleges and universities is far higher than their percentage in the population at large and continues to increase at the institutions included in this study. (p. xxvii)

Scholars' and institutions' treatment of Asian Americans skews an analysis of race and can be problematic. On the one hand, Asian Americans enhance the "diversity" of student demographics and are, thus, included and sometimes even highlighted when needed to show how diverse the campus is. At the same time, institutions treat Asian Americans as a nonentity and do not include them when discussing critical issues that affect students of color in relationship to White students. In this way, Asian Americans are everywhere and nowhere to be seen at the same time. As Nancy Abelmann (2009) wrote, "Asian Americans offer, by many counts, the one color that does not count. . . . U.S. racial politics teach them that they are somehow different from other college students of color and thus undeserving of race-based programs and policies" (p. 2).

Keith Osajima's research showed that the treatment of Asian Americans by faculty, staff, and students results from the racial politics in higher education that emphasize a Black-White paradigm, as well as the widely held belief that Asian Americans are a model minority (Osajima, 1988; 1995). As with other subordinate groups, the gains made by Asian Americans in the hiring of faculty and staff, as well as the implementation and expansion of Asian American studies programs, have been the result of struggles, demands, and protests by on- and off-campus Asian American activists. However, these struggles are erased in the consciousness of the public and what is seen in racial educational discourse is the success of this particular group. How failure and success are discussed plays into the divisive politics of race and becomes a critical contributor to the invisibility and misrepresentation of Asian Americans in racial discourse.

In the American imagination, being a person of color includes two informal characteristics: (1) being non-White and (2) being unable to make significant gains in American institutions. But one must be able to prove through historical examples the bias experienced because of one's race (Takagi, 1992). The continued promotion of the Asian American community as successful, especially in academia, and the touting of strong family values and a strong work ethic "inherent" in Asian cultures has spurred anti-Asian sentiment on many campuses. In 1996, a UC Irvine student targeted Asian Americans in an e-mail message, saying that there were too many of them, they were ruining the curve, and for that reason he was going to kill them. He was later convicted of a hate crime (Sciupac, 1996). Reports of verbal, written, and physical abuse against Asian Americans come from universities across the country. However, the image of Asian Americans as the model minority has often been the excuse for administrators to ignore these reports and not respond adequately to their needs as victims of racism. According to students, there is a perception that they are passive and will accept a nonresponse from administrators (Greene, 1987; Chan & Wang, 1991).

AAGLOs: Race-ing to Find a Community

The first Greek letter organization, Phi Beta Kappa, was founded in 1776 at the College of William and Mary as a literary and debating society. This fraternal organization flourished, and its impact on collegiate life was such that other chapters and similar organizations spread throughout American colleges and universities (Thelin, 2004). Today, there are more than 350 national social Greek letter organizations, many of which provide leadership development, social activities, and—most important—a sense of belonging for their members. The role of fraternities and sororities in American higher education grew as they became increasingly entrenched in the social, academic, and cultural lives of students (Stuart, 2008; Torbensen, 2009). In fact, Boyer (1987) and Astin (1985) cite Greek life as an example of the cocurricular activities that contribute to students' persistence in college. Fraternities and sororities can bring social status, networks, and academic success to their members (Syrett, 2009).

As Greek life evolved to become part of the mainstream of student life, administrators became more invested in the success of these organizations and their members. As early as the late 19th century, institutions administered or set up systems for membership recruitment events (Thompson & Hardaway, 1950). Chi Alpha Delta, the oldest Asian American sorority, was founded at UCLA in 1928 with the support of UCLA's dean of women, Helen Laughlin (Lim, 2006); over time, colleges and universities established positions of directors and even assistant deans of Greek life. Greek Week became part of the traditional campus events, and university presidents and chancellors recognized Greeks as key student leaders. But as universities recognized and supported these organizations, they were also complicit in the racially and religiously restrictive membership policies and practices of fraternities and sororities. In fact, many universities also had restrictive racial or religious minority covenants in areas such as admissions, housing, and student organizations (Chen, 2009; Torbensen & Parks, 2009).

As historically White universities began to admit more students of color, these students wanted to be a part of organizations to which their White counterparts belonged. Unfortunately, institutional and personal racism prevented most of them from joining these organizations, including fraternities and sororities. Unable to be a part of fraternal organizations, students of color decided to establish their own organizations that embraced the ideals of brotherhood and sisterhood. In 1906, at Cornell University, the oldest African American fraternity, Alpha Phi Alpha, was founded. Ten years later, on the same campus, Rho Psi, the first Asian American fraternity, was founded by a group of Chinese American men (Chen, 2009; Kimbrough, 2003).

In 1929, six Chinese American men at UC Berkeley founded Pi Alpha Phi. This organization has grown into a national fraternity, with members all over the country; it is the oldest AAGLO, as Rho Psi now functions as an alumni organization. As students, all six Pi Alpha Phi founders experienced racism. While Asian Americans were admitted to many California universities as undergraduate and graduate students, they were not allowed to live in the residence halls or join student organizations, including fraternities and sororities. Asian American students wanted to experience the brotherhood and develop networks as they saw White fraternal organizations doing. Their resistance to the racism they experienced and desire for deep and lasting fraternal relationships led them to found their own fraternity (Chan, 1999; Chen, 2009).

Dolores Delgado Bernal's 1997 work focused on student oppositional behavior as part of resistance theory; this theory can be used to describe the way the students who created minority Greek letter organizations were struggling against racism while simultaneously creating like structures. Specifically, the students engaged in "conformist resistance"—they resisted particular roles but did not actively work to change the status quo. Solorzano and Delgado Bernal (2001) noted that this type of resistance is characteristic of individuals who are committed to social justice yet do not critique systems of oppression. The founders of Pi Alpha Phi established an organization that had similarities to fraternities that did not allow them to be members—such as having their own selective membership requirements—but at the same time they have always maintained the importance of their Asian American identity. According to the fraternity's website,

> The Founding Fathers wanted to ensure that Asian Awareness would always be an important part of the fraternity.... Today, the basic premise of the fraternity remains largely unchanged. With

brotherhood as our immutable asset, the lifelong bonds that we develop extend far beyond the university setting. Although the fraternity is open to individuals of all ethnic backgrounds, it still retains its Asian American character. (n.d., para. 2, 4)

The founders of AAGLOs understood through personal experience that America's racist past would not allow them to be accepted as White, no matter how academically or economically successful they might be. Many AAGLO members tried to join other fraternities and sororities, only to discover the barrier of racism (Chen, 2009; Lee, 1955; Ross, 1955). Even when they established their own organizations, structural racism— such as restrictive housing covenants—deprived them of equal opportunities to grow in membership and reputation. For example, the Westwood (Los Angeles) community's restrictive housing covenants that existed from the 1920s through 1968 prevented AAGLOs from purchasing their own fraternity and sorority houses. Without houses, their members had an incomplete Greek life experience and their organizations seemed less desirable to Asian American students who wanted the same privileges that White Greeks had. The lack of their own physical space made it difficult, if not sometimes impossible, for some AAGLOs to establish a permanent presence. Today, of course, it is nearly impossible for any organization to find an affordable house near UCLA. If AAGLOs had been allowed to purchase a house when they were first established, they might have been on UCLA's Greek Row (Chen, 2009).

In the 1940s and 1950s, White fraternities and sororities began to consider the possibility of changing their racially restrictive membership rules. In some cases, national sororities and fraternities—and universities— themselves began to challenge these restrictive covenants. Chapter members of the National Panhellenic Conference (NPC) and the Interfraternity Council (IFC) quietly but firmly began to desegregate their membership by admitting non-Whites and non-Christians. In 1954, the U.S. Supreme Court supported the State University of New York's efforts to eliminate racial and religious discrimination in its membership practices. The university, with the support of the courts, gave all national and local fraternities and sororities until 1958 to rid themselves of these discriminatory admissions practices or cease to exist on campus. Despite the legal rulings, some organizations (particularly fraternities) resisted (Lee, 1955).

The arguments at the various national fraternity conventions in the early 1950s regarding admission of African Americans and Asian Americans are outlined by Alfred McClung Lee in his 1995 book *Fraternities Without Brotherhood: A Campus Report on Racial and Religious Prejudice.* Although the efforts at these pre-civil-rights-era conventions failed to change restrictive admissions policies, a growing minority in the membership argued for more inclusive fraternities. Even having a discussion at this time about including Asian Americans as members of historically White fraternities was interesting, because strong anti-Japanese sentiment lingered from World War II. Ian Ross (1955) suggested that White fraternities had a sense of "confusion" about Asian Americans as a racial group that resulted in inconsistent treatment of Asian Americans compared with other minorities. Perceived differences in national origin and phenotypes of Asian ethnics also resulted in differentiated treatment. Although some Asian Americans were admitted to White fraternities and sororities, most were rejected. The White organizations resorted to a variety of excuses, including the argument that Asians were "sojourners" or "visitors" who were not serious about planting roots and contributing to American society; they were considered "exotic" and perpetual outsiders. The Whites were also confused by the diversity of "Orientals" and the various ethnic groups (e.g., Japanese, Chinese, Indian) that made up this category. However, despite the resistance to desegregating these organizations, the civil rights movement of the 1950s and 1960s, and the increasing number of students of color on college campuses made it inevitable that Asian Americans would be engaged in co-curricular life, whether as members of historically White organizations or in Asian American interest clubs.

As the number of Asian American students increased, so did ethnic and racial organizations that combined their racialized, social, or political interests. The number of culturally based organizations in higher education grew as the critical mass of students of color increased in the 1970s and beyond. Although organizations such as fraternities and sororities began opening their memberships to Asian Americans, this was a challenging time for Greek organizations because of the counterculture movement that was pervasive at many American colleges and universities (Torbensen, 2009). From the 1970s to now, Asian American college students have been featured more and more in the national media, primarily because of the dramatic increase in their numbers compared with other students of color, particularly in highly selective institutions. In the context of increasing numbers and diversity in this population, some Asian American college students were concerned about mainstream political representation, while others struggled against the inequities of the power structure. Asian American students were also concerned about social support organizations such as fraternities, sororities, and ethnic cultural interest clubs (Yamasaki, 1999).

Although the establishment of Asian American studies and affirmative action programs were key to leadership development in college for some Asian American students, others were involved in creating and maintaining Asian American fraternities and sororities, as well as ethnic social support groups. Organizations such as the Nisei Bruins Club (1930s) and Samahang Pilipino (1969), and Asian fraternities and sororities such as Chi Alpha Delta (1930s), Theta Kappa Phi (1959), and Omega Sigma Tau (1966) coexisted and flourished along with the Asian Radical Movement (1969) and the Asian American Student Alliance (1969). And despite the growing reluctance of many social and fraternal organizations to put forth a specific political agenda, AAGLOs continued to embrace their history of resistance against the racial politics of exclusion. In fact, many Asian American cultural organizations and fraternities and sororities were established in large part because of a desire to form a community support system in the face of the exclusionary practices and policies of mainstream groups (Yamasaki, 1999).

Serving AAGLOs

Torbensen and Parks (2009) characterize the available work on AAGLOs as a "paucity of information" (p. 10). Even though AAGLOs have existed in this country almost as long as other minority Greek letter organizations, they lack national organizational structures and frameworks. They do not have governing bodies that work with national offices with paid staff to guide them and provide training for issues such as risk management, member development, and recruitment/rush policies and practices.

Campus administrators may have an understanding of Interfraternity Council and Panhellenic organizations, but AAGLOs are not necessarily part of mainstream Greek life and may not receive comparable services. Even if they are included in the services provided by Greek affairs offices, anecdotal reports suggest that staff members may not have the expertise or knowledge base to serve the unique needs of AAGLOs and may not understand the racialized experience and issues that face Asian American students. At the same time, cultural centers may not have the expertise to serve AAGLOs. The staffs at these centers have expertise and experience to address the unique needs of students of color, but they may not understand the process of fraternity/sorority recruitment or may disapprove of the hierarchical and secretive nature of these organizations.

What, then, does higher education need to do to better serve AAGLOs? First, Greek life staff members need to be trained on the history and issues of AAGLOs. The staff needs to understand and appreciate the racial paradigm that AAGLOs experience. They must also understand that although AAGLOs continue to increase in numbers and membership, they do not have the same institutional structures that historically Black and White groups have, such as governance boards, risk management structures, or even requirements. Greek life staff could support these groups by helping them set up their organizations to be aligned with their mission and to make sure that their activities enhance their educational experience.

Cultural centers must create a welcoming environment for AAGLOs. They must help these students maintain a connection with the larger Asian American community and create opportunities for them to build lasting relationships with other organizations. Meanwhile, AAGLOs should learn about the educational and leadership development opportunities that the centers offer and should pursue and maintain a connection with any Asian American studies programs on campus. AAGLOs can mobilize their members more effectively than many other Asian American groups—they can be great allies and leaders in building a stronger Asian American community on campus.

AAGLOs will continue to grow as the number of Asian American students increases in American higher education. Their existence expands higher education's racialized understanding. As student affairs professionals, we need to increase our understanding of these groups and the students who join them. More important, we need to make sure the organizations understand that we want them to succeed. Showing a commitment to them may mean changing some practices and traditions so that AAGLOs are included in events, on governing boards, and in processes normally reserved for other groups. These changes will have to be explained to other students who have been invested in how structures were initially established and may resist efforts to create a more inclusive community.

This chapter is a brief examination of the racialized positioning of AAGLOs in higher education. Future research can focus on factors such as gender relations, socioeconomic privilege, and pan-ethnic versus ethnic-specific groups in AAGLOs. More research is needed on the relationship between AAGLOs and other minority Greek letter organizations. Examination of these issues will increase our limited knowledge about AAGLOs as well as our ability to work with these organizations to contribute positively to our campuses.

References

Abelmann, N. (2009). *The intimate university: Korean American students and the problems of segregation.* Durham, NC: Duke University Press.

Anderson, J. D. (2002). Race in American higher education: Historical perspectives on current conditions. In W. A. Smith, P. G. Altbach, & K. Lomotey (Eds.), *The racial crisis in American higher education* (pp. 1–22). Albany, NY: State University of New York Press.

Astin, A. W. (1982). *Minorities in American higher education.* San Francisco, CA: Jossey-Bass Publishers.

Astin, A.W. (1985). *Achieving educational excellence.* San Francisco, CA: Jossey-Bass Publishers.

Bonacich, E. (1980). Middlemen minorities and advanced capitalism. *Ethnic Groups: An International Periodical of Ethnic Studies, 2*(3), 211–219.

Bonilla-Silva, E. (2009). *Racism without racists: Color-blind racism and the persistence of racial inequality in the United States.* Oxford, England: Rowman & Littlefield.

Bowen, W. B., and Bok, D. (1998). *The shape of the river: Long-term consequences of considering race in college and university admissions.* Princeton, NJ: Princeton University Press.

Boyer, E. L. (1987). *College: The undergraduate experience in America.* New York, NY: Harper & Row.

Chan, J. (1999). Asian American interest fraternities: Competing masculinities at play. In T. K. Nakayama (Ed.), *Asian Pacific American genders and sexualities* (pp. 65–73). Tempe, AZ: Arizona State University Press.

Chan, S., and Wang, L. (1991). Racism and the model minority: Asian-Americans in higher education. In W. A. Smith, P. G. Altbach, &

K. Lomotey (Eds.), *The racial crisis in American higher education* (pp. 43–68). Albany, NY: State University of New York Press.

Chen, E. W. (2009). Asian Americans in fraternities and sororities: In search of home and place. In C. L. Torbensen & G. S. Parks (Eds.), *Brothers and sisters: Diversity in college fraternities and sororities* (pp. 83–103). Cranbury, NJ: Rosemont Publishing and Printing Corp.

Delgado Bernal, D. (1997). *Chicana school resistance and grassroots leadership: Providing an alternative history of the 1968 East Los Angeles blowouts.* Unpublished doctoral dissertation, University of California, Los Angeles.

Greene, E. (1987, November 18). Asian-Americans find U.S. colleges insensitive, form campus organizations to fight bias. *The Chronicle of Higher Education,* pp. A1, A38–40.

Haley, D. (2009, March 22). The new animal houses. *The Daily Beast.* Retrieved from http://www.thedailybeast.com/articles/2009/03/22/the-new-animal-house.html

Herel, S., Stannard, M. B., Buchanan, W., & Kim, R. (2003, January 23). Fraternity feud's unlikely victim. *San Francisco Chronicle.* Retrieved from http://articles.sfgate.com/2003-01-26/news/17472427_1_drill-team-fraternities-strip-mall

Kimbrough, W. (2003). *Black Greek 101: The culture, customs, and challenges of Black fraternities and sororities.* Madison, NJ: Fairleigh Dickinson University Press.

Lee, A. M. (1955). *Fraternities without brotherhood: A campus report on racial and religious prejudice.* Boston, MA: Beacon.

Lim, S. (2006). *A feeling of belonging: Asian American women's public culture, 1930–1960.* New York, NY: New York University Press.

Lowe, L. (1991). Heterogeneity, hybridity, multiplicity: Marking Asian American differences. *Diaspora 1*(1), 24–44.

Marable, M. (1995). Affirmative action and the politics of race. In M. Marable (Ed.), *Beyond Black and White: Transforming African American politics.* London, England: Verso.

Osajima, K. (1988). Asian Americans as the model minority: An analysis of the popular press image in the 1960s and 1980s. In G. Y. Okihiro (Ed.), *Reflections of shattered windows: Promises and prospects for Asian American studies* (pp. 215–225). Seattle, WA: Washington State University Press.

Osajima, K. (1995). Racial politics and the invisibility of Asian Americans in higher education. *Educational Foundations, 9*(1), 35–53.

Pi Alpha Phi history. (n.d.). Retrieved December 9, 2011, from http://www.pialphaphi.com/v6/?page_id=5

Ross, I. C. (1955). Groups standards concerning the admission of Jews to fraternities at the University of Michigan. *Social Problems, 2*(3), 133–140.

Sciupac, I. (1996, November 11). Graduate student gets hate phone call. *New University,* p. 2.

Solorzano, D., & Delgado Bernal, D. (2001). Examining transformational resistance through a critical race and latcrit theory framework: Chicana and Chicano students in an urban context. *Urban Education, 36,* 308–342.

Stuart, R. (2008, September 18). The next best thing to family. *Diverse: Issues in Higher Education, 25,* 16.

Syrett, N. L. (2009). *The company he keeps: A history of White college fraternities.* Chapel Hill, NC: University of North Carolina Press.

Takagi, D. Y. (1992). *The retreat from race: Asian American admissions and racial politics.* New Brunswick, NJ: Rutgers University Press.

Thelin, J. (2004). *A history of American higher education.* Baltimore, MD: Johns Hopkins University Press.

Thompson, F. M., & Hardaway, C. (1950). Sorority rushing and pledging methods. *The Journal of Higher Education, 21*(6), 321–325.

Torbensen, C. L. (2009). From the beginning: A history of college fraternities and sororities. In C. L. Torbensen & G. S. Parks (Eds.), *Brothers and sisters: Diversity in college fraternities and sororities* (pp. 15–45). Cranbury, NJ: Rosemont Publishing and Printing Corp.

Torbensen, C. L., and Parks, G. S. (Eds.). (2009). *Brothers and sisters: Diversity in college fraternities and sororities.* Cranbury, NJ: Rosemont Publishing and Printing Corp.

Tuan, M. (1998). *Forever foreigners or honorary Whites? The Asian ethnic experience today.* New Brunswick, NJ: Rutgers University Press.

Yamasaki, E. (1999). *Politics in racially diverse contexts: A case study of Asian American students at UCLA* (Doctoral dissertation). Available from ProQuest Dissertations and Theses database. (UMI No. 9940516)

CHAPTER TWELVE

Asian American Mental Health on Campus

Karen Huang

Van Tran, a Chinese refugee from Vietnam, earned a perfect 4.0 grade point average at Hunter College in New York while working full time at a hardware store and helping his sisters adjust to life in the United States. He then earned a doctorate in sociology and social policy at Harvard University and obtained a professorship at Columbia University.

Meanwhile, three Asian American and Pacific Islander (AAPI) students at the California Institute of Technology (Caltech) committed suicide in the summer of 2009. Brian Go was a sports enthusiast and the beloved president of his residence hall who double-majored in computer science and computational mathematics; Jackson Wang was a pianist with the Caltech Chamber Music ensemble; and Long Phan was a graduate student in chemistry.

Although media images of AAPI college students tend to focus on academic *wunderkind* and self-destructive time bombs, the vast majority of

AAPI students are a diverse population who face the same developmental challenges as other college students: finding their place in society, creating a stable identity, establishing mature relationships, dealing with sexuality, negotiating a new dynamic with their parents, and exploring career possibilities.

There are many variations of American culture, Asian culture, and Asian American culture. Studies and discussions must recognize and acknowledge that cultural traditions are complex, heterogeneous, and varying in applicability. Although there is value in identifying and using broad concepts and generalizations, there is also risk in creating and using stereotypes. The intent of the discussion that follows is to enhance understanding of the possible causes and symptoms of AAPI college students' mental health issues; what faculty and staff members can do in response to these symptoms; and how campuses can address and begin to resolve the underlying issues through appropriate policies and procedures. The discussion is not intended to create or use stereotypes.

For many AAPIs, the developmental journey is shaped by an Asian cultural background at odds with mainstream American culture. Social isolation and a lack of social support contribute additional stress for some. To understand the mental health needs of these students, one must understand the experience of being Asian in mainstream America.

Asian Cultural Values

Consider the difference between a culture in which "the squeaky wheel gets the grease" and one in which "the head that stands up gets chopped off." The former reflects a relatively individualistic mainstream American culture that values independence, knowing one's unique internal attributes, and asserting oneself; the latter reflects a relatively collectivistic Asian culture that defines the individual in relation to others and values fitting in and harmonious interdependence with others (Markus & Kitayama, 1991).

A collectivistic orientation toward the self is common in Chinese, Japanese, Filipino, Southeast Asian, South Asian, Hawaiian, and Samoan cultures. Traditionally, the family is the primary social unit, and members are highly interdependent. Rather than aiming for independence and self-expression, members aim to fit in, fulfill mutual obligations, and live up to social role expectations to maintain family harmony and achieve common goals. This sense of family obligation may motivate some AAPIs to avoid risky behaviors (DeBaryshe, Yuen, & Stern, 2001) and pursue academic achievement (Fuligni, 2001).

Parents and children engage in a relationship of filial piety, in which children honor, respect, and obey their parents and other family elders. Rather than talking back, children learn self-restraint, emotional suppression, and self-management—skills that prepare them to live harmoniously with others and subordinate personal desires for the sake of the group. Parents reciprocate in the filial relationship by making significant sacrifices for their children, even at the expense of their own needs and desires.

The traditional AAPI family organization tends to have a hierarchical structure in which members know their respective roles and what is expected of them (e.g., patriarch, elder brother, youngest sister). Elders know that they will be cared for, and the younger generation knows they can turn to the elders for help. Older siblings take an active role in setting an example and caring for younger ones. The potential benefits of this family arrangement include a predictable social order, relative stability, a wide network of communal support, instrumental assistance to family members, and emotional closeness.

A collectivistic definition of self can serve a student well in college. Research suggests that some of the math success of AAPI college students may stem from their tradition of working in study groups (Treisman, 1992). By helping and quizzing each other, they learn the material and identify areas for improvement better than they might if they studied alone. Group study can also provide support, encouragement, and motivation.

In concert with the collectivistic orientation, many Asian cultures tend to emphasize "saving face"—maintaining one's sense of social recognition, prestige, and respect in the eyes of others. Because individuals are highly interconnected with their family members, one member's actions (such as college success or failure, mental health or disorder) can bring either face or shame to all the relatives.

Shaming—the threat of public disgrace and embarrassment—is a common tactic for encouraging conformity and compliance with face-enhancing behaviors. Children are socialized to be attuned to the social judgments of others. This can help them be socially aware enough to avoid being the head that gets chopped off, but it can also lead them to hide their mistakes, pain, and need for help.

Silent Epidemic of Mental Distress

Mental disorders have become increasingly common and severe among college students in recent years (Deschamps, 2009), and this trend applies to AAPI students, although their emotional struggles frequently go unnoticed or are overlooked because of positive stereotyping. Even student affairs professionals appear to hold positive stereotypes of AAPI students (Liang & Sedlacek, 2003).

Research indicates high rates of depression and suicidal feelings among AAPI students, perhaps even higher than those among White American students (Kisch, Leino, & Silverman, 2005). Recently, a spate of AAPI suicides on elite college campuses has highlighted the need for attention to the mental health of AAPI students. For instance, in a decade at Cornell University (1996 to 2006), the majority of student suicides were committed by AAPI students (13 of 21, or 61%), although AAPI students comprised only 14% of the student body (Ramanujan, 2006).

Students of many different backgrounds experience pressures without becoming depressed or suicidal, but for some AAPI students, cultural, societal, interpersonal, and psychological factors can interact to create particularly intense levels of stress.

Social Isolation and Racial Discrimination

The development of healthy, mature relationships is one of the most fundamental milestones faced by college students, but some AAPIs have limited opportunities because of racism and the "model minority" myth.

Especially at a predominantly White college campus that negates ethnicity, some AAPIs can be treated as "different" or "foreign"—outsiders who do not belong. To counter the perception that they "stick to their own kind," some AAPIs avoid socializing with other AAPI students, even to their own detriment. Mainstream White students eating lunch together probably never feel this sort of racial self-consciousness.

Positive stereotyping can create social isolation by leading non-Asians to misunderstand or misperceive AAPIs as enjoying favored status (Wong, Lai, Nagasawa, & Lin, 1998) or not being interested in fun. Positive stereotypes can be the basis of racist satire on college campuses, as in the student-written daily news update regarding Dartmouth's appointment of Dr. Jim Yong Kim as the first Asian American president of an Ivy League school:

> Yesterday came the announcement that President of the College James Write will be replaced by Chinaman Kim Jim Yong. And a little bit of me died inside. It was a complete supplies [*sic*].
>
> On July 1, yet another hard-working American's job will be taken by an immigrant willing to work in substandard conditions at near-subsistent wage, saving half his money and sending the rest home to his village in the form of traveler's checks. Unless "Jim Yong Kim" means "I love freedom" in Chinese, I don't want anything to do with him. Dartmouth is America, not Panda Garden Rice Village Restaurant.
>
> Y'all get ready for an Asianification under the guise of diversity under the actual Malaysian-invasion leadership instituted under the guise of diversity. It's a slippery slope we are on. I for one want Democracy and apple pie, not Charlie Chan and the Curse of the Dragon Queen. I know I sure as shit won't ever be eating my Hop dubs bubs with chopsticks. I like to use my own two American hands. (Goodell, Fidel, & Swire, 2009)

Racist satire in campus newspapers, including the UCLA *Daily Bruin* and *The Campus Press* at the University of Colorado at Boulder, may be a form of backlash against the rising enrollments of AAPIs (Lee, 2008). Filled with Asian stereotypes, they suggest that racism toward AAPIs has morphed into subtle instances of implicit stereotyping, devaluation, and unfairness. One national study found that 74% of Asian Americans have experienced unfair treatment, and 63% of them attributed it to racism (Meyers, 2006).

Being asked, "Where are you from?" or "Where were you born?" or "Why is your English so good?" are not always innocent questions; they are microaggressions—small-scale aggressive acts based on racism—because they can make an AAPI student feel like a perpetual foreigner in his or her own country (the United States) and thereby diminish his or her sense of belonging and equal status with other Americans (Sue, Bucceri, Lin, Nadal, & Torino, 2007). Other forms of microaggression include exoticizing AAPI women as subservient sex objects; treating AAPIs as invisible; stereotyping AAPIs as achievement-driven automatons; and treating Asian cultural values and communication styles as abnormal.

Racial microaggressions and the consequent perception of lowered social status, being treated unfairly, and being disrespected can cause depression, feelings of alienation, physical disorders, behavioral problems, and even suicidal ideation (Gee, Ro, Shariff-Marco, & Chae, 2009; Greene, Way, & Pahl, 2006; Hwang & Goto, 2008). In addition, racism and racist microaggressions may affect American-born AAPIs more than immigrant AAPIs because of their different expectations. Whereas recent Asian immigrants might expect their accents, limited English fluency, and cultural behaviors to make them seem foreign, acculturated AAPIs expect the same rights and acceptance as any American.

The response of student affairs departments to campus racism and their efforts to create a fair and engaging community can profoundly affect the campus climate perceived by AAPI students. For instance, on some campuses, AAPI students perceive an injustice when on-campus fraternities and sororities repeatedly receive preferential funding over ethnic groups. Elsewhere, AAPIs feel empowered by student affairs to speak up and seek fair treatment on campus.

Body Image

During the college years, body image is a central concern for many students, but especially for women. A negative body image can contribute to lowered self-esteem, depression, anxiety, and eating disorders. Limited body image research has studied AAPI women specifically, but recent findings indicate that AAPI women's body image dissatisfaction is the same as or worse than that of their Caucasian counterparts (Grabe & Hyde, 2006; Yates, Edman, & Aruguete, 2004). As AAPI women increasingly aim for the media's "thin ideal," those who internalize this ideal tend to be dissatisfied with their bodies (Nouri, Valente, & Hill, 2010). The collectivistic orientation may also contribute to some AAPI women watching their weight for fear of bringing shame on themselves and their families by being overweight (Phan & Tylka, 2006). Thus, eating disorders and distorted body image may be increasing among AAPI women, but they remain undetected because of the stereotype that AAPIs have no serious problems and because of the false assumption that Asians are naturally thin. In addition to concerns about thinness, many AAPI women express dissatisfaction with their "smaller" breast size (Forbes & Frederick, 2008) and their eyes and faces (Mintz & Kashubeck, 1999), perhaps because they negatively judge their ethnic features in comparison with the Caucasian features that represent beauty in mainstream American culture (Tsai, Curbow, & Heinberg, 2003).

Dating and Sexuality

Through dating and experimentation with romantic relationships, students develop a sense of themselves as sexual beings and clarify their values, sex role identity, and sexual orientation. Cultural differences, mainstream stereotyping, and discrimination can complicate this developmental stage for AAPI students, although in different ways for AAPI men and women.

Mainstream American media consistently portray Asian American men as emasculated, asexual, weak, and socially inept. In American movies, with a few notable exceptions, such as Li Cunxin in *Mao's Last Dancer*, AAPI men rarely play the romantic lead who gets the girl. Even onboard the starship *Enterprise*, the highly rational Spock had a romantic relationship, but the Japanese pilot Sulu never did.

To the extent that students internalize these negative media images, they might treat AAPI men accordingly when choosing whom to date. In one study, respondents rated AAPI men as the least physically and socially attractive of all the race and gender groupings (Jackson, Lewandowski, Ingram, & Hodge, 1997). These stereotypes can also contribute to a rejection of one's own race as potential mates, as when Asian American women prefer White men because they are perceived as more attractive, less patriarchal, and of higher status than Asian men (Fong & Yung, 1995). The result for AAPI men can be deep resentment, intense frustration, self-doubt, and damaged self-esteem.

In contrast, AAPI women students tend to be perceived as attractive dating partners. Some argue that their petite size, presumed femininity, and perceived subservience have contributed to the high rates of White male/Asian female interracial relationships. These perceptions may also underlie an "Asian fetish" or "yellow fever" that objectifies Asian women as submissive sex objects. Certainly, people may feel particularly attracted to a certain set of physical features, such as tallness or slimness, but exoticization that treats AAPI women as objects rather than as people is a form of racism. This type of so-called fetish can range from benign infatuation and relationships based on superficial attraction to harassment and objectification. To the extent that AAPI women internalize these expectations and believe that being attractive requires fulfilling these roles, they may increase their risk of being subjugated, severely limiting their development, and complying with coercive sex. Moreover, these stereotypes of AAPI women have also been implicated in stalking and sexual assault. In one extreme case, three White assailants in Seattle raped two Japanese college women in 2000; they said they targeted them because they assumed that Asian women would be submissive and too ashamed to report the crime (Dundas, 2001).

Culture may also play a role in emotional recovery after a romantic loss.

For instance, a breakup can seem disastrous if an AAPI student has a history of being judged as physically unattractive and romantically undesirable. Rejection by a White partner who is perceived as high status can trigger feelings of ethnic self-hatred and shame. The traditional coping mechanism of suppression can delay grief resolution and reduce help seeking.

Parental expectations can add another layer of complication to an AAPI's dating experience. Traditional Asian parents frequently see dating as a distraction and consider premarital sex fundamentally unacceptable. However, as AAPI students—especially AAPI women—acculturate, their sexual attitudes and behaviors become more similar to those of the White mainstream (Okazaki, 2002). The result can be large rifts with their parents and internal struggles to clarify their own values and attitudes about sex and sexuality.

Academic Achievement Pressures

In Asia, educational achievement is a family affair. Each family member has a role in the quest for the child's educational success. In Korea, for instance, the father provides financial support and the mother is the driving force who "schedules every minute of her child's after-school time at special academies or private tutoring" (Ellinger & Beckham, 1997, p. 624). Even in the United States, immigrant Asian parents are often more actively involved than their non-Asian counterparts in monitoring and guiding their children's academic activities (Chao, 2000). This involvement can provide both assistance and pressure to achieve.

Additional achievement pressure can come from peers and teachers who believe in the model minority stereotype (Schneider & Lee, 1990). As a result, many AAPI students feel intense academic pressure from themselves, their parents, and others. When all work in harmony, the results can be remarkable; if they do not, the results can be painful. Traditional Asian parents often set the bar extremely high, especially in math and science, since they consider academic achievement a given, like sleeping and eating.

However, some AAPI students have neither the talent nor the motivation to excel in math and science.

Another complication is that many traditional Asian parents believe that they have a right—even an obligation—to choose their child's goals (Lee & Ying, 2001). From a traditional Asian perspective, this involvement shows loving care and interest, but from the mainstream American perspective, it is intrusive. As AAPI students acculturate, they sometimes begin to perceive the parental involvement as onerous and the filial duties as burdensome. Some experience their parent's love as conditional on their academic performance and never feel "good enough." For others, academic achievement crowds out other sources of self-worth.

A "bad" grade combined with catastrophizing appraisals ("the B grade means I'll never get into medical school, which means I am a failure") can cause a traumatic rupture in the parent-child relationship and can emotionally devastate some AAPI students. Those with a collectivistic identity who expect to remain close to their parents may feel intense anxiety, guilt, shame, and unhappiness in response to such failure (Lee & Ying, 2001).

Further, these students often have limited coping options. Typically, they would not be able to relieve the stress through rational conversation with their parents. Instead, to avoid shame and humiliation, renewed parental pressure, profound parental rejection, and the withdrawal of financial and emotional support, some AAPI students hide their failure and feelings, a strategy that may escalate the problems.

Coping and Help Seeking

The choice of coping strategies depends on one's beliefs about emotional distress and its causes, and these beliefs are shaped by culture (Tweed & Conway, 2006). The Asian collectivistic worldview emphasizes the belief that life contains suffering that should be accepted and tolerated, and values coping strategies aimed at adjusting the individual's feelings, such as emotional containment rather than expression (Kim & Omizo, 2003).

Depression is seen as internally caused and to be dealt with via social withdrawal and self-criticism (Wong, Kim, & Tran, 2010).

Feelings of shame can also contribute to avoidance of counseling. Although shame, like guilt, triggers negative self-evaluation, it is by definition public, focuses on the entire person rather than a behavior, and often cannot be neutralized by atonement. Thus, shaming may trigger the impulse to hide or escape (Buss, 2001). It can make AAPI students feel so fundamentally bad that they feel too ashamed to accept help.

Negative attitudes toward counseling can be another barrier to treatment. AAPI students might perceive the therapeutic goals as culturally irrelevant or the non-Asian therapist as culturally insensitive or racist. The result of delayed help seeking is that many AAPIs enter treatment in crisis and arrive with symptoms that are more severe than those of other ethnic groups (Chen, Sullivan, Lu, & Shibusava, 2003).

Being an AAPI Therapist in Student Affairs

Although ethnic diversity is increasing among student affairs professionals, the vast majority of practitioners are White (Liang & Sedlacek, 2003). AAPI student affairs staff may have ideas and behaviors that differ from their majority colleagues; they can be important change agents on campus.

With students, AAPI therapists can serve as positive role models, mentors, and educators. By giving presentations around campus, teaching classes, training and supervising resident assistants, eating in the dining halls, and generally being visible on campus, AAPI therapists can counter some of the damaging stereotypes of AAPIs as unemotional and lacking in compassion.

In the counseling context, an AAPI therapist can make counseling seem available and accessible to AAPI students. Just as a therapist who has engaged in competition can make counseling seem more relevant to varsity athletes, an AAPI therapist can enhance a counseling center's perceived accessibility to AAPI students who want a therapist who has dealt with ethnic identity issues, coped with stereotyping, and navigated the demands of individuation and separation in opposing cultural contexts. Research has found that therapist-client ethnic or racial match facilitates the therapeutic alliance and the therapist's credibility (Meyer, Zane, & Cho, 2011), and that multiculturally competent therapists receive higher ratings from AAPI college students than those who are not (Wang & Kim, 2010).

For non-AAPI students, an AAPI therapist might provide an important opportunity to expand their experiences with an ethnic racial minority. An AAPI therapist could also serve as a cultural informant for students who seek to understand cultural differences between themselves and their AAPI classmates. However, an AAPI therapist's ethnicity can be a source of occupational stress. Racist counseling clients sometimes refuse treatment with an AAPI therapist, make comments that indicate their lack of confidence in the AAPI therapist's competence, or engage in the kinds of microaggressions mentioned earlier. In addition, because many AAPI students are in crisis by the time they seek help, AAPI therapists who serve as a primary counseling resource for these students may have more challenging caseloads than their colleagues. Finding appropriate off-campus AAPI counselors and inpatient services for referrals can add to the burden of work.

To encourage early help seeking, campus staff and faculty must be alert and proactive in encouraging referrals. With health centers, advising centers, and other student affairs colleagues, AAPI therapists can establish a network that facilitates access to counseling services. For instance, AAPI students who somatize their stress and depression might seek medical treatment for stomach pains. The medical practitioner can facilitate follow-through with a referral to counseling. Similarly, academic advisors can facilitate a referral for exploratory counseling if the AAPI's issue involves deep struggles with parents.

AAPI therapists can partner with student affairs colleagues to add nuance, challenge traditions and assumptions, and correct misconceptions when campus policies are discussed. As an example, AAPI therapists might help broaden the definitions of and opportunities for leadership and community service. With the dean of students, they might contribute to the multicultural training of resident assistants or provide cultural context for an AAPI student who must go on medical leave. With the student activities dean, an

AAPI therapist can raise questions about the potential for an inherent bias if student organization funding formulas or programs systematically favor groups that are de facto White, such as fraternities and sororities.

With faculty members, AAPI therapists can suggest ways to integrate AAPI psychology into the curriculum and provide useful cultural information about communication styles. Classroom discussion, for instance, feels uncomfortable and intimidating for many AAPI students, who are raised to speak up only when they have something worth listening to and not to think out loud. With admissions staff, AAPI therapists can point out that many of the extracurricular responsibilities of low-income AAPIs—such as caring for extended family members or working at low-wage jobs to help support the family—should not be overlooked in enrollment decisions. An AAPI who is tutoring his cousins may share key qualities with a White student who volunteers as a local elementary school tutor. And with career services, an AAPI therapist can challenge the notion that the "follow your dreams" approach (rooted in individualistic assumptions about human development and actualization) is appropriate for AAPI students, who might be better served by a culturally sensitive solution that satisfies themselves and their parents.

Institutional environments vary in their willingness to value and use cultural information. Some campuses marginalize AAPIs as yet another special interest group that competes against the mainstream student body. In such instances, student affairs colleagues might not welcome the AAPI therapist's cultural consultation. AAPI therapists in such a context may find their knowledge going untapped and may feel underutilized, invalidated, or even invisible. Indeed, a parallel process may exist between the feelings AAPI students have about the campus and the feelings the AAPI therapist has. If AAPI students are experiencing their school as invalidating, alienating, and disinterested in them, chances are the AAPI therapist who is focused on AAPI students will have some similar perceptions.

Cultural traditions may attenuate the AAPI therapist's advocacy for the inclusion of Asian issues in student affairs concerns. As mentioned earlier, Asian cultures value emotional restraint, waiting until the time is right before speaking, making indirect complaints and criticisms, and using a relatively low-key vocal style (Park & Kim, 2008). Unfortunately, rather than intuit the hidden meanings and perceive this style as highly courteous yet emotionally complex, mainstream American colleagues who value forthright assertiveness with obvious emotional expression may judge such communication as opaque, inscrutable, unassertive, and not compelling.

AAPI colleagues who are relatively quiet at meetings because they are waiting for their turn might be misperceived as having nothing to say by those who dive into a discussion; their emotional restraint can be misinterpreted as disinterest or a lack of passion; and their tendency to make complaints through allusion and hints can be misperceived as a fear of conflict, an avoidance of risk, or a lack of leadership. In addition, the cultural tradition of emphasizing team accomplishments while being humble about personal achievements and relying on others to mention them can contribute to AAPI colleagues in student affairs being over-looked for campus recognition and promotion.

AAPI therapists may encounter the same career advancement barriers that other AAPI professionals commonly encounter. For instance, some AAPI women must deal with stereotypes of them as passive and subservi-ent—always assigned to take minutes rather than to run a meeting. They walk a tightrope between reserve and aggressiveness: Speak up but do not speak too much, too quickly, or too shrilly, and smile enough to seem friendly but not too friendly.

Conclusion

On some campuses, AAPI women and men may simultaneously face invisibility on the one hand (e.g., having their true skills and abilities overlooked) and "surplus visibility" on the other (having their mistakes more readily and critically scrutinized because they stand out from the mainstream members of student affairs who have the power and privilege that enable them to judge). Finally, to the extent that AAPI colleagues are left out of the informal social networking that typically occurs among colleagues, they will be disadvantaged in advancing their careers and promoting their ideas about the unique needs of AAPI students.

On some campuses, multiculturalism is integral to the educational enterprise, and hiring for diversity is pursued. In these communities, there is a critical mass of AAPI staff whose cultural knowledge is valued and sought out. With the right leadership, a positive attitude about inclusiveness, and an eye toward cultural nuance, these campuses can provide an engaging community and effective safety net that maximizes mental health and minimizes mental distress among their AAPI students.

References

Buss, A. (2001). *Psychological dimensions of the self.* Thousand Oaks, CA: Sage.

Chao, R. K. (2000). The parenting of immigrant Chinese and European American mothers: Relations between parenting styles, socialization goals, and parental practices. *Journal of Applied Developmental Psychology, 21*(2), 233–248.

Chen, S., Sullivan, N. Y., Lu, Y. E., & Shibusava, T. (2003). Asian Americans and mental health services: A study of utilization patterns in the 1990s. *Journal of Ethnic and Cultural Diversity in Social Work, 12,* 19–42.

DeBaryshe, B. D., Yuen, S., & Stern, I. R. (2001). Psychosocial adjustment in Asian American/Pacific Islander youth: The role of coping strategies, parenting practices, and community social support. *Adolescent and Family Health, 2*(2), 63–71.

Deschamps, K. M. (2009). College student mental health: Current practical, legal, and ethical considerations for student affairs professionals. Educational Leadership and Policy integrative paper. Retrieved from http://www.ed.utah.edu/elp/Programs/MED/CollegeStudentMentalHealth-Deschamps.pdf

Dundas, C. (2001, July 6). Defendant sentenced to 16 years. *The Seattle Times.* Retrieved from http://community.seattletimes.nwsource.com/archive/?date=20010630&slug=kidnapxxxx

Ellinger, T. R., & Beckham, G. M. (1997). South Korea: Placing education at the top of the family agenda. *Phi Delta Kappan, 78*(8), 624–625.

Fong, C., & Yung, J. (1995). In search of the right spouse: Interracial marriage among Chinese and Japanese Americans. *Amerasia Journal, 21*(3), 77–97.

Forbes, G. B., & Frederick. D. A. (2008). The UCLA Body Project II: Breast and body dissatisfaction among African, Asian, European, and Hispanic American college women. *Sex Roles, 58*, 449–457.

Fuligni, A. J. (2001). Family obligation and the academic motivation of adolescents from Asian, Latin American, and European backgrounds. In A. J. Fuligni (Ed.), *Family obligation and assistance during adolescence: Contextual variations and developmental implications* (New directions for child and adolescent development, no. 94, pp. 61–76). San Francisco, CA: Jossey-Bass.

Gee, G. C., Ro, A., Shariff-Marco, S., & Chae, D. (2009). Racial discrimination and health among Asian Americans: Evidence, assessment, and directions for future research. *Epidemiology Review, 31*, 130–151.

Goodell, E., Fidel, E., and Swire, N. (2009, March 5). E-mail on Kim stirs controversy. *The Dartmouth*. Retrieved from http://thedartmouth.com/2009/03/05/news/email

Grabe, S., & Hyde, J. S. (2006). Ethnicity and body dissatisfaction among women in the United States: A meta-analysis. *Psychological Bulletin, 132*(4), 622–640.

Greene, M. L., Way, N., & Pahl, K. (2006). Trajectories of perceived adult and peer discrimination among Black, Latino, and Asian American adolescents: Patterns and psychological correlates. *Developmental Psychology, 42*(2), 218–238.

Hwang, W. C. & Goto, S. (2008). The impact of perceived racial discrimination on the mental health of Asian American and Latino college students. *Cultural Diversity and Ethnic Minority Psychology, 4*, 326–335.

Jackson, L. A., Lewandowski, D. A., Ingram, J. A., & Hodge, C. N. (1997). Group stereotypes: Content, gender specificity, and affect associated with typical group members. *Journal of Social Behavior and Personality, 12*, 381–396.

Kim, B. S. K., & Omizo, M. M. (2003). Asian cultural values, attitudes toward seeking professional psychological help, and willingness to see a counselor. *The Counseling Psychologist, 31*, 343. Retrieved from http://atgstg01.sagepub.com/counselingstudy/Journal%20Articles/Kim2.pdf

Kisch, J., Leino, E. V., & Silverman, M. M. (2005). Aspects of suicidal behavior, depression, and treatment in college students: Results from the spring 2000 National College Health Assessment Survey. *Suicide and Life-Threatening Behavior, 35*, 3–13.

Lee, S. S. (2008, February 28). Satire as racial backlash against Asian Americans. *Inside Higher Ed.* Retrieved from http://www.insidehigh-ered.com/views/2008/02/28/lee

Lee, P., & Ying, Y. (2001). Asian American adolescent academic achievement: A look behind the model minority image. *Journal of Human Behavior in the Social Environment, 3*, 35–48.

Liang, C. T. H., & Sedlacek, W. (2003). Attitudes of White student affairs services practitioners toward Asian Americans. *NASPA Journal, 40*(3), 30–42.

Markus, H. R., & Kitayama, S. (1991). Culture and the self: Implications for cognition, emotion, and motivation, *Psychological Review, 98*(2), 224–253.

Meyer, O., Zane, N., & Cho, Y. I. (2011). Understanding the psychological processes of the racial match effect in Asian Americans. *Journal of Counseling Psychology, 58*(3), 335–345.

Meyers, L. (2006). Asian-American mental health. *APA Monitor, 37*(2), 44.

Mintz, L. B., & Kashubeck, S. (1999). Body image and disordered eating among Asian American and Caucasian college students. *Psychology of Women Quarterly, 23*, 781–796.

Nouri, M., Valente, J. K., & Hill, L. G. (2010). Relations among media exposure, internalization, and body dissatisfaction: Comparing White and Asian-American college females. Retrieved from https://research. wsulibs.wsu.edu:8443/xmlui/handle/2376/2613?show=full

Okazaki, S. (2002). Influences of culture on Asian Americans' sexuality. *The Journal of Sex Research, 39*(1), 34–41.

Park, Y. S., & Kim, B. (2008). Asian and European American cultural values and communication styles among Asian American and European American college students. *Cultural Diversity and Ethnic Minority Psychology, 14*(1), 47–56.

Phan, T., & Tylka, T. (2006). Exploring a model and moderators of disordered eating with Asian American college women. *Journal of Counseling Psychology, 53*(1), 36–47.

Ramanujan, K. (2006, April 19). Health expert explains Asian and Asian-American students' unique pressures to succeed. *Chronicle Online.* Cornell University. Retrieved from http://www.news.cornell.edu/ stories/April06/Chung.ksr.html

Schneider, B., & Lee, Y. (1990). A model for academic success: The school and home environment of East Asian students. *Anthropology and Education Quarterly, 21*(4), 358–377.

Sue, D. W., Bucceri, J., Lin, A. I., Nadal, K. L., & Torino, G. C. (2007). Racial microaggressions and the Asian American experience. *Cultural Diversity and Ethnic Minority Psychology, 13*(1), 72–81.

Treisman, U. (1992). Studying students studying calculus: A look at the lives of minority mathematics students in college. *The College Mathematics Journal, 23*, 362–372.

Tsai, G., Curbow, B., & Heinberg, L. (2003). Sociocultural and developmental influences on body dissatisfaction and disordered eating attitudes and behaviors of Asian women. *Journal of Nervous and Mental Disease, 191*(5), 309–318.

Tweed, R. G., & Conway, L. G. (2006). Fundamental beliefs and coping across cultures. In P. T. P. Wong & C. J. Wong (Eds.), *Handbook of multicultural perspectives on stress and coping.* New York, NY: Springer.

Wang, S., & Kim, B. S. (2010). Therapist multicultural competence, Asian American participants' cultural values, and counseling process. *Journal of Counseling Psychology, 57*(4), 394–401.

Wong, P., Lai, C. F., Nagasawa, R., & Lin, T. (1998). Asian Americans as a model minority: Self-perceptions and perceptions by other racial groups. *Sociological Perspective, 41,* 95–118.

Wong, Y. J., Kim, S. H., & Tran, K. K. (2010). Asian Americans' adherence to Asian values, attributions about depression, and coping strategies. *Cultural Diversity and Ethnic Minority Psychology, 16*(1). Retrieved from http://nro-dd.sagepub.com/lp/psycharticles-reg/asian-americans-adherence-to-asian-values-attributions-about-FC0LZu9bkZ

Yates, A., Edman, J., & Aruguete, M. (2004). Ethnic differences in BMI and body/self- dissatisfaction among Whites, Asian subgroups, Pacific Islanders, and African- Americans. *Journal of Adolescent Health, 34,* 300–307.

CHAPTER THIRTEEN

Demystifying
Mental Health for AAPI Students
on College Campuses

Mary Ann Takemoto
and Diane Hayashino

Todd is a 20-year-old second generation Vietnamese American college student. He is currently on academic probation. He is struggling in his classes and at his engineering internship, and has gradually become distant from friends. His father recently lost his job, and Todd has been driving home on the weekends to help his parents. He has made an appointment with the academic advising center because he has questions about continuing to major in engineering. When the academic advisor encourages him to talk with someone at the university counseling center, Todd replies, "They don't see people like me. Anyway, I'm not crazy. I don't need to talk to a counselor."

College Student Mental Health and Help-Seeking Behaviors

This case study reflects a common scenario experienced by many student affairs staff on college campuses today. As mental health concerns gain increasing attention, significant misunderstanding and misconceptions remain about some issues. Data from the fall 2010 American College Health Association (ACHA) survey found that over the previous 12 months, 84% of students had felt overwhelmed by all they had to do, 46% felt overwhelming anxiety, and 58% felt very sad (ACHA, 2011). In the California State University (CSU) system, the most common conditions for which students seek treatment in counseling centers are anxiety and depression; these findings are consistent with other studies of college mental health trends (Barr, Rando, Krylowicz, & Reetz, 2010; Varlotta & Bragg, 2010). An increasing number of students are presenting with a prior history of mental health treatment (Cooper, 2006), and approximately 25% of students seen at college counseling centers are taking psychiatric medication (Barr et al., 2010).

A number of recent studies have documented an increase in the severity, complexity, and quantity of mental health problems in college students (Benton, Benton, & Perl, 2006; University of California [UC], Student Mental Health Committee, 2006). A UC study reported that 25% of students may be experiencing such problems at any one time (UC, Student Mental Health Committee, 2006). Mental health issues affect the entire campus community, not just those who are experiencing psychological problems. As awareness about mental health issues has increased on both the national and campus levels, student affairs departments have received more calls from concerned faculty, staff, and students about possible mental health issues. Increases in mental health problems are a concern for campus administrators and faculty, because these problems are associated with lower academic achievement (Benton et al., 2006). An effective approach to campus mental health requires collaboration across all segments of the campus community, including faculty, staff, and students.

Some students come to campus with a history of psychological treatment, while others may first experience an emerging mental health problem during their college years. The typical stressors of college—such as moving away from home and being in a more academically competitive environment—can contribute to mental health problems, and the use of alcohol or drugs can trigger mental illness. In Todd's case, we see the effect of family and economic stressors on his academic performance and emotional well-being. In addition to normal developmental issues, Asian American and Pacific Islander (AAPI) students may experience unique cultural or family stressors that can affect their mental health.

An understanding of AAPI college students' help-seeking behaviors and ways of seeking support can help campuses better serve their needs. We know that stress can affect academics, physical health, interpersonal relationships, and socio-emotional functioning. A study by Kearney, Draper, and Baron (2005) of counseling outcomes for ethnic minorities across 40 university campuses found that the AAPI students tended to have low utilization rates for seeking counseling, yet they reported greater distress at intake than comparison groups, including African American and Caucasian students. In a recent national study of counseling center directors, 7% of clients seen at college counseling centers were AAPIs, while 10% were African American and 8% were Latino. The campus demographics in the study were 14.8% AAPI, 8.1% African American, and 10% Latino (Barr et al., 2010).

The low utilization rates should not be used to reinforce the "model minority" myth, which holds that AAPIs do not experience mental health problems. According to the U.S. Surgeon General's report (U.S. Department of Health and Human Services, 2001), which used a community sample of Asian Americans with emotional and psychological problems, 17% of Asian Americans sought professional help; of those, 4% saw a medical doctor, 8% saw a minister or priest, and fewer than 6% sought help from a mental health professional. The multiple settings in which students interact with staff and faculty are opportunities to provide support to a student who otherwise might not seek help, like Todd, who felt more comfortable seeking support from his academic advisor. Campuses can improve these utilization rates by being aware of the types of stressors students typically experience and providing practical information on how counseling and other support services can be beneficial.

What does the term *mental health* mean for AAPI students? The concepts of mental health and counseling have historically been embedded in western values of individualism, emotional catharsis, and self-disclosure. The media have perpetuated the idea that counseling services are for those with very severe problems; they have not emphasized the preventive aspects of counseling. For many Asian Americans, physical and mental health are integrated and holistic, and seeking counseling clashes with traditional Asian values of emotional control, collectivism, and harmony (Kim, Atkinson, & Yang, 1999). For a person raised with a collective "we" rather than "I" orientation, seeking individual counseling might not be viewed as a culturally appropriate treatment option. The concept of "saving face" is familiar to most AAPIs, and many may internalize feelings of shame for seeking help outside their family or community. The stigma of mental health problems has also contributed to the reluctance to seek support; providing outreach and educational materials on the benefits of counseling is essential. In Todd's case, the academic advisor needs to be comfortable exploring Todd's assumptions about counseling and facilitating an understanding of how counseling might positively affect his academic performance and help him save face.

AAPI students might have access to resources and strengths within their communities—forms of support that can help bridge the service delivery gap. The student might be able to rely on a trusted network of family members, respected elders, spiritual leaders, and indigenous healers. Also, a more holistic approach might be available in the community; one that uses herbal remedies, acupuncture, and traditional healers to link body, mind, and spirit (Sue & Zane, 2009). The practice of eastern medicine emphasizes revitalizing the body's functions, maintaining balance, and restoring the body to its natural condition in its environment; these values must be integrated in providing services and affecting health behaviors (Sue & Zane, 2009). Many AAPIs are taught to exhaust these resources before turning to outside resources; this could explain the higher rates of emergency mental health use and longer psychiatric hospital stays (Snowden & Cheung, 1990) among AAPI students.

The family is an important resource and source of support. In a collectivistic culture, when an individual has a problem it is commonly owned by the entire group or family. Yeh, Inman, Kim, and Okubo (2006) conducted a qualitative study of Asian American families' collectivistic coping strategies following the trauma of 9/11. The persons interviewed in this study tended to seek support from family members, church, and members of their own ethnic group rather than seeking outside resources such as counseling. In some cases, the fear of shaming one's family may also serve as a barrier to seeking help for college students. For example, a college student who is experiencing distress in exploring his or her sexual identity may not feel comfortable discussing this with family members. Kim and Park (2009) found that Asian American college students believed that family and extended family members generally held more negative perceptions of seeking counseling than nonfamily members (e.g., professors and peers). Their study demonstrated the importance of social influences, especially family and extended family, to explain the link between Asian values and the intent to seek (or not seek) counseling.

As psychologists working on a diverse college campus, we are aware of the differences among AAPI college students in terms of their racial and ethnic identities, social class status, religion, generation level, and acculturation (changes along norms of the western culture) and enculturation (changes along norms of the native culture). The AAPI student population ranges from first generation recent immigrants to fourth and fifth generation students with varying levels of acculturation. Factors such as acculturation and enculturation have been shown to have implications for practice, including the help-seeking behaviors of AAPI college students (Kim & Omizo, 2006; Miller, Yang, Hui, Choi, & Lim, 2011). Studies have found that the more acculturated and less enculturated a person is, the more likely he or she is to seek counseling (Miller et al., 2011). In Todd's case, it would be important for the counselor to explore his level of acculturation and enculturation to gain a more accurate understanding of the conflicts he is experiencing in his family and to provide appropriate treatment recommendations.

The lack of Asian American psychologists and culturally competent counseling services is another salient factor in the underutilization of services by AAPI students. Only 6.2% of staff in college counseling centers identify as AAPI (Barr et al., 2010). When a student is seeking counseling, a shared cultural background and worldview with the therapist may contribute to a more successful outcome. Bilingual therapists can be very helpful in working with recent immigrant students, who may feel more comfortable speaking to a therapist in their native language.

Common Stressors for AAPI Students

For many students, college may be their first experience living away from home and their support system. Typically, all students experience a normal period of adjustment and transition; they may feel sad, anxious, or frustrated, and may exhibit behaviors such as isolation, withdrawal, difficulty with concentration, and sleep disruption. AAPI students may experience additional stress associated with being an ethnic minority (Wei, Ku, & Liao, 2011). Smedley, Myers, and Harrell (1993) defined *minority stress* as the unique stresses (e.g., first-generation college student, discrimination, racial segregation) experienced by minority students that interfere with their adjustment to college and integration into the university community. College persistence attitudes are essential to retention and graduation rates for ethnic minority students; research by Okamura and Agbayani (1997) has shown that AAPI students have difficulty finding mentors within their own ethnic group to dissuade them from leaving college. For example, if AAPI students experience isolation on campus, in classes, or in building social connections owing to their minority status, their adjustment to college may be negatively affected. This may lead to feelings of discouragement and disconnection, and poor academic performance. AAPI social support groups, student organizations, and mentorship programs can contribute to an increased sense of belonging on campus and can serve as buffers against these stressors.

AAPI college students might also experience difficulty navigating western values and expectations of college along with the traditional cultural values of their families. Intergenerational conflict occurs when differences exist in the rates of acculturation and enculturation among family members, particularly between first and second generations. For AAPI college students, family and generational stressors can lead to conflicts as they make decisions (e.g., area of study, career choice, dating) and balance autonomy with values such as family dependence and filial piety. AAPI students might also be playing the role of "cultural broker" in their families, assisting with communication between their parents and social systems, such as education, health care, legal concerns, and social services; this can affect parental perceptions of control and power. In Todd's case, it would be important to explore his beliefs and expectations about how he is balancing these multiple roles and responsibilities as a student and as a son.

In college, AAPI men and women can experience gender role stress as they attempt to navigate the expectations of their culture of origin and the mainstream culture. Liu and Iwamoto (2006) found that Asian American men under-report psychological problems because they comply with expected gender roles and stereotypes of both Asian and American cultures. In Todd's case, it would be important to explore his gender role identity and expectations. AAPI men typically do not access the services of counseling centers; therefore, it is important to create special outreach programs for this group. AAPI male students may experience conflicts in navigating the gender role expectations between college and family; a counselor can help them gain insight into how to balance these expectations, as well as how these conflicts might be affecting their academic and social functioning (Liu & Iwamoto, 2006). As increasing numbers of AAPI women pursue higher education, mental health services must be sensitive to the intersections of gender and race in the provision of culturally appropriate services to AAPI men and women. The academic experience for AAPI women often differs from that of their male counterparts. Many AAPI women are exploring ways to hold on to traditional values such as filial piety, collectivism, and hierarchical family roles, while also responding to mainstream expectations (e.g., career choice, major of study) (Kawahara & Espin, 2009). Their identities as women are sometimes challenged in college when conflicts occur as they explore "unconventional" areas of study or careers, or when they date someone from a different racial or ethnic background. Giving voice to these experiences through counseling, support groups, and workshops can be healing and transformative for both men and women.

How does the model minority myth affect AAPI college students' mental health? AAPI students who are at risk for academic failure may not get the help and resources they need, because they have internalized this myth and because others do not accurately identify the stressors they are experiencing. Academic stress is a known risk factor for psychological and emotional problems for many AAPI students (Lowe, 2009). The wide discrepancies in academic achievement levels across ethnic groups highlight the need to be more attentive to the heterogeneity among AAPIs and their access to resources; for example, 58.4% of Indian and Pakistani Americans have college degrees, compared with 2.9% of Hmong Americans (Lowe, 2009). In a study by Kim and Park (2009), Asian American students tended to have lower rates of interaction with faculty compared with other racial groups, and they were less likely to have high-quality relationships with faculty. The role of faculty and student service mentors in AAPI academic success cannot be overlooked. Because Todd is struggling academically and questioning his field of study, his academic advisor should determine whether he has any supportive relationships with his engineering faculty. Perhaps, in addition to a referral to the counseling center, Todd might benefit from having a faculty mentor with whom he feels comfortable talking on a regular basis about his academic struggles, career choices, and decision making.

Suicide

The tragedy of a college student suicide affects the entire community, including students, staff, and faculty. The resulting feelings of grief, confusion, anger, and helplessness may affect students in residence halls, classes, clubs, and organizations, as well as staff and faculty who struggle to find a way to comprehend the tragic event. Timely, coordinated responses to a campus suicide are essential, with trained frontline student affairs staff.

Approximately 1,100 American college students die by suicide each year (Jed Foundation, n.d., para. 1). It is the second leading cause of death among college students (Suicide Prevention Research Center, 2006). According to an ACHA health assessment, approximately 6% of college students seriously considered suicide at least once during the previous year, and 1.3% made a suicide attempt (ACHA, 2011). Research shows that students who receive counseling are six times less likely to follow through with suicide (NASPA, 2008). This highlights the importance of early identification and intervention with students who have suicidal ideation, and student affairs staff play a key role in this area.

High rates of suicide among AAPI students at highly selective institutions such as Cornell, Caltech, and MIT have received a great deal of media attention. Several studies have shown that Asian American college students have reported higher levels of suicidal ideation compared with their White counterparts (Kisch, Leino, & Silverman, 2005; Muehlenkamp, Gutierrez, Osman, & Barrios, 2005). In addition, suicide is the second leading cause of death among Asian American women in the 15 to 24 age group, and this is the highest female suicide rate across all major racial/ethnic groups (Centers for Disease Control and Prevention, 2011).

Asian American college students who reported seriously considering suicide identified three problem areas that preceded their suicidal thinking: family problems, academic problems, and financial problems (Wong, Brownson, & Schwing, 2011). Asian American youth who experienced high levels of intergenerational conflict in their families were at a much greater risk for suicidal behavior. This relationship was found to be much stronger among less acculturated Asian American youth (Lau, Jernewall, Zane, & Myers, 2002), among whom family support appears to play a significant role in psychological health. Highly acculturated Asian American youth may have a wider social support network to help create a buffer against stress. Student support services that are visible and accessible contribute to a supportive campus environment; they can include peer advisors, resident assistants, faculty mentors, cultural student organizations, and campus ministries.

The Substance Abuse and Mental Health Services Administration has provided funding to selected colleges and universities to prevent suicide and reduce mental health problems among college students. Project OCEAN (On Campus Emergency Assistance Network) at CSU Long Beach is a federally funded program that centers on increasing awareness of mental health and providing suicide prevention training to faculty, staff, and student leaders. This program uses QPR (Question, Persuade, Refer) training for frontline staff and students to increase their ability to respond to suicidal students. Nearly 2,000 students, staff, and faculty have been trained in QPR to date, helping to create and expand a safety net for at-risk students at CSU Long Beach.

Promoting Psychological Wellness

Attention has focused recently on a wellness approach to promote positive mental health among college students. This proactive approach originates in community psychology and focuses on prevention and education. It takes into account the individual as well as the systems he or she is part of, such as a residence hall, health center, recreation and wellness center, campus police, dean of students, career center, and student organizations. Wellness programs can be offered outside the traditional campus counseling center in places where AAPI students congregate, such as a multicultural center or Asian American resource center. This approach empowers students, staff, and faculty to participate in developing a campus that promotes psychological health.

The visibility of counseling center staff is an essential part of campus prevention efforts. Efforts to reduce stigma and normalize the need for and use of psychological services are especially important for AAPI students. Educational programs targeting families can help reduce negative social norms related to help seeking (Kim & Park, 2009). Ensuring that these educational and orientation programs are provided in languages spoken by the families is crucial. CSU Long Beach has developed a brochure for all parents of incoming freshman that specifically addresses mental health concerns, and counseling center staff are active participants in parent orientation programs. Marketing mental health programs as "support groups" or "workshops" may make them more acceptable to AAPI students because of the educational focus. Developing culture-specific approaches such as meditation, tai chi, biofeedback, and acupuncture may be helpful for some AAPI students; they can be used alone or in conjunction with traditional counseling services. Partnerships between the counseling center and other campus units—such as the multicultural center, ethnic studies department, housing, student health center, women and men's centers, and student activities—can lead to innovative joint programs and successful referrals. These campus partnerships are important because AAPI college students, owing to their cultural values, are more likely to seek academic, career, or health-related services than personal counseling (Kim & Park, 2009).

Recommendations for Student Affairs Staff Serving AAPI Students

To provide a supportive environment for AAPI students to reach their goals, student affairs must take a multifaceted approach. As AAPI students are a heterogeneous group and may present with different mental health concerns, ongoing training and education to understand the diversity of this community must be a priority for campuses. Another priority is ongoing needs assessment of the factors likely to affect mental health for AAPI ethnic groups in different situations: different geographic locations, public versus private institutions, different campus sizes, and various demographics. The importance of hiring multiculturally competent mental health professionals who can effectively provide culturally sensitive and congruent services cannot be overemphasized. Wang & Kim (2010) highlighted the importance of multicultural training for existing staff members to work effectively with AAPI students. Increasing the number of AAPI psychologists who reflect the ethnic and racial demographics of the campus is essential: The number of AAPI psychologists in college counseling centers should be comparable with the AAPI student population on the campus.

Student affairs professionals also need to prioritize and reinforce stronger relationships between the university and local AAPI communities by actively seeking opportunities for partnership with community groups. Increasing service learning opportunities for students to work in AAPI communities can contribute to stronger relationships between the university and the communities they serve. Creating opportunities for networking among the various student groups and organizations on a campus benefits cross-ethnic coalitions and initiatives. AAPI staff and faculty organizations on campus can develop and maintain mentoring opportunities, provide student advocacy, and support community building. It is essential that counseling centers and other departments remain up to date in the use of outreach technologies, including social marketing and websites.

Another area in which student affairs can play a role in college student mental health is that of AAPI leadership and visibility. There is a shortage of AAPI leaders in higher education and student affairs and, thus, a need to continue to build professional networks across racial and ethnic groups. Organizations such as Leadership Education for Asian Pacifics, Inc. and Asian Pacific Americans in Higher Education are valuable for support and growth, and for their ability to help AAPIs enter the fields of counseling and higher education.

AAPI Psychologists

The authors' personal and professional identities as Asian American women psychologists influence the work we do with students and staff on our campuses. Counseling center psychologists play a variety of roles, including providing individual and group counseling, consultation to departments, outreach presentations to student groups, mentoring students, trainings (with staff and interns), research, teaching, committee work, and serving as liaisons to academic and student service departments. The diversity in what we do as psychologists on our campuses is one of the highlights of our work, as we are able to nurture our strengths through the multiple roles that we play.

The multicultural movement in counseling and psychology has led to improved awareness, knowledge, and skills in working with ethnically diverse groups in a culturally appropriate and respectful manner. As psychologists on college campuses, we have opportunities to participate in collaborative projects with colleagues from various disciplines and departments. The interaction with students—being a part of their academic and personal development through college and beyond—is an honor and a privilege. In addition to our work with students, we are aware of the importance of making an impact on the system, which includes campus climate and organizational-level policies. To best serve our AAPI students, we must continue to work from a model of social justice that values equity, empowerment, and collaboration across the systems that affect students.

References

American College Health Association (ACHA). (2011). American College Health Association-National College Health Assessment II: Reference Group Executive Summary (fall 2010). Linthicum, MD: ACHA.

Barr, V., Rando, R., Krylowicz, B., & Reetz, D. (2010). Association for University and College Counseling Center Directors (AUCCCD) Annual Survey. Retrieved from http://www.aucccd.org/img/pdfs/directorssurveymonograph2010.pdf

Benton, S. L., Benton, S. A., & Perl, M. F. (2006). Key issues for faculty regarding college student mental health. In S. A. Benton & S. L. Benton (Eds.), *College student mental health: Effective services and strategies across campus* (pp. 121–138). Washington, DC: National Association of Student Personnel Administrators.

Centers for Disease Control and Prevention. (2011). Retrieved from http://www.cdc.gov/women/lcod

Cooper, S. E. (2006). Counseling and mental health issues. In S. A. Benton & S. L. Benton (Eds.), *College student mental health: Effective services and strategies across campus* (pp. 151–167). Washington, DC: National Association of Student Personnel Administrators.

Jed Foundation. (n.d.). *For campus professionals*. Retrieved from https://www.jedfoundation.org/professionals

Kawahara, D., & Espin, O. (2009). Asian American women in therapy: Feminist reflections on growth and transformations. *Women and Therapy, 30*(3–4), 1–5.

Kearney, L., Draper, M., & Baron, A. (2005). Counseling utilization by ethnic minority college students. *Cultural Diversity and Ethnic Minority Psychology, 11*(3), 272–285.

Kim, B., Atkinson, D., & Yang, P. (1999). The Asian values scale:

Development, factor analysis, validation, and reliability. *Journal of Counseling Psychology, 46*(3), 342–352.

Kim, B., & Omizo, M. (2006). Behavioral acculturation and enculturation and psychological functioning among Asian American college students. *Cultural Diversity and Ethnic Minority Psychology, 12*(2), 245–258.

Kim, P., & Park, I. (2009). Testing a multiple mediation model of Asian American college students' willingness to see a counselor. *Cultural Diversity and Ethnic Minority Psychology, 15* (3), 295–302.

Kisch, J., Leino, E. V., & Silverman, M. M. (2005). Aspects of suicidal behavior, depression, and treatment in college students: Results from the spring 2000 national college health assessment survey. *Suicide and Life Threatening Behavior, 35,* 3–13.

Lau, A. S., Jernewall, N. M., Zane, N. & Myers, H. F. (2002). Correlates of suicidal behaviors among Asian American outpatient youths. *Cultural Diversity and Ethnic Minority Psychology, 8,* 199–213.

Liu, W., & Iwamoto, D. (2006). Asian American men's gender role conflict: The role of Asian values, self-esteem, and psychological distress. *Psychology of Men and Masculinity, 7*(3), 153–164.

Lowe, S. (2009). A frank discussion on Asian Americans and their academic and career development. In N. Tewari & A. Alvarez (Eds.), *Asian American psychology: Current perspectives* (pp. 463–481). New York, NY: Lawrence Erlbaum.

Miller, M., Yang, M., Hui, K., Choi, N., & Lim, R. (2011). Acculturation, enculturation, and Asian American college students' mental health and attitudes toward seeking professional psychological help. *Journal of Counseling Psychology, 58*(3), 346–357.

Muehlenkamp, J. J., Gutierrez, P. M., Osman, A., & Barrios, F. X. (2005). Validation of the positive and negative suicide ideation (PANSI) inventory in a diverse sample of young adults. *Journal of Clinical Psychology, 61*(4), 431–445.

National Association of Student Personnel Administrators (NASPA). (2008). Profile of today's college student. Retrieved from http://www. naspa.org/divctr/research/profile/results.cfm

Okamura, J., & Agbayani, A. (1997). Pamantasan: Filipino American higher education. In M. P. Root (Ed.), *Filipino Americans: Transformation and identity* (pp. 183–197). Thousand Oaks, CA: Sage.

Smedley, B. D., Myers, H. F., & Harrell, S. P. (1993). Minority-status stress and the adjustment of ethnic minority freshmen. *Journal of Higher Education, 64,* 434–451.

Sue, S., & Zane, N. (2009). The role of culture and cultural techniques in psychotherapy: A critique and reformulation. *Asian American Journal of Psychology, S*(1), 3–14.

Suicide Prevention Research Center. (2006). Retrieved from http://www. sprc.org

Snowden, L. & Cheung, F. (1990). Use of inpatient mental health services by members of ethnic minority groups. *American Psychologist, 45*(3), 347–355.

University of California (UC), Student Mental Health Committee. (2006). *Report of the University of California Student Mental Health Committee.* Retrieved from http://www.universityofcalifornia.edu/ regents/regmeet/sept06/303attach.pdf

U.S. Department of Health and Human Services. (2001). *Mental health: Culture, race, and ethnicity—A supplement to mental health: A report of the surgeon general* (DHHS Publication No. SMA 01-3613). Washington, DC: U.S. Government Printing Office.

Varlotta, L., & Bragg, M. (2010). *Select committee on mental health: Report to the CSU Board of Trustees.* Retrieved from http://www.calstate. edu/bot/agendas/may10/edu-policy.pdf

Wang, S., & Kim, B. (2010). Therapist multicultural competence, Asian American participants' cultural values, and counseling process. *Journal of Counseling Psychology, 57*(4), 394–401.

Wei, M., Ku, T., & Liao, K. (2011). Minority stress and college persistence attitudes among African American, Asian American, and Latino students: Perception of university environment as a mediator. *Cultural Diversity and Ethnic Minority Psychology, 17*(2), 195–203.

Wong, Y., Brownson, C., & Schwing, A. E. (2011). Risk and protective factors associated with Asian American students' suicidal ideation: A multicampus national study. *Journal of College Student Development, 52,* 396–408.

Yeh, C., Inman, A., Kim, A., & Okubo, Y. (2006). Asian American families' collectivistic coping strategies in response to 9/11. *Cultural Diversity and Ethnic Minority Psychology, 12*(1), 134–148.

PART V

AAPI Role Expectations

CHAPTER FOURTEEN

My Journey in Student Affairs
Living on the Edge

Julie Marianne Wong

I had accomplished all my goals. Get a PhD. Check. Become a dean of students. Check. Buy a house. Check. Get involved in the community. Check. I was thriving in my role as dean of students at a large public research university with a diverse student body. I had my dream job and loved every minute of it. I was involved in several new initiatives and had developed strong ties with students, faculty, and staff. I chaired the largest bi-national arts and cultural design competition, linking two countries through art, culture, and open space; developing connections with local and international leaders; and becoming known in the community.

Life was good. Professionally, I had reached the highest level I desired. The role of dean of students was the perfect blend of student interaction and staff development. Socially, I had developed strong relationships on campus and in the surrounding community. Financially, I lived a comfortable life in a beautiful home in a nice neighborhood. I enjoyed my public speaking events, being a voice for students, supervising directors in student affairs, and working collaboratively across campus.

At a national conference, I noticed a table for Semester at Sea. Colleagues who had served as staff on Semester at Sea told me I would love it and treasure the experience for the rest of my life. I bonded immediately with the woman who would be dean of students on the next voyage, and she encouraged me to apply. My biggest challenge would be to get the time off work.

Although my life was fulfilling, I knew I would regret not doing this. I had not taken a semester abroad as an undergraduate, so Semester at Sea would be a chance to make up for that lost opportunity. Traveling around the world in a community with faculty, students, and staff would fulfill a lifetime dream to travel with the world as my laboratory.

I submitted my application, was interviewed by the woman I had met at the conference, and was offered the position. I felt as though I had won the lottery! This was an exciting opportunity to work with a veteran of Semester at Sea—someone from whom I would learn a great deal.

My mom was excited about the countries I would see; remote villages I would visit; families I would meet; and global community service in which I would participate. My aunt saw a student on a plane in a Semester at Sea sweatshirt and asked, "Was it as good as everyone says?" He replied, "Better!" My aunt was sold. I was born and raised in the United States, but my Asian roots and cultural values run deep. Even though I was an adult, my family's approval and blessing to do Semester at Sea were important to me.

Since I had my family's blessing, I arranged a meeting with my supervisor to discuss an unpaid leave of absence. I prepared for the meeting by creating a plan to delegate my responsibilities among my staff and to use the money the department would save on my salary to start a new initiative that needed funding. I was a bit nervous going into the meeting and curious to know how he would react. A few years earlier, as associate dean of students and director of student activities, I had applied to Semester at Sea and was denied a leave of absence, because my supervisor could not see letting me take so much time off work. Now, several years later, as dean of students, I believed that Semester at Sea would rejuvenate and enhance my work in student affairs as I learned about other cultures, participated in community service, and developed strong relationships with students. When I returned, I could serve as liaison for students who were interested in study abroad opportunities.

I made the pitch to my supervisor about the great opportunity to make me a better dean of students, one who was more globally and culturally aware. He responded that in my position as dean of students, I was at too high a level to be gone for such an extended period. So the answer was no. I was disappointed, and this was a reality check for me as an Asian American. I had always believed that if you worked hard, you would be rewarded. My life revolved around my position, and it was a big part of my identity. The fact that I was denied an unpaid leave of absence to pursue this dream was like a dagger in my soul. I did not understand how my loyalty to my position and the university were not reciprocated.

I called the dean of students and told her I would not be able to accept the Semester at Sea position. Knowing how much I wanted to go, she suggested that I think about it. I replied that there was nothing to think about, because I had a house payment and could not simply quit my job. She had to form her team, and I did not want to hold up the process. She said I did not sound like myself, and she could wait a few days to form her team. She asked me to take the weekend to think about it.

It was the longest weekend of my life. I called a colleague who had gone on Semester at Sea in the middle of her PhD studies. Her advisor told her that it would ruin her career in higher education and that she would have to choose another advisor to work with her when she returned. She decided to go anyway, and it turned out to be one of the best experiences of her life. She was confident that no matter what situation I was in after the Semester at Sea, everything would work out in the end. I asked, "What about my house?" She replied, "It's just a house." I asked, "What about my stuff?" She said, "You'll figure out a place to store it; it's just stuff." She asked, "What are you afraid of?" I didn't know how to answer that question. It just seemed crazy to leave a job you love not knowing what the future might hold. When I thought about it, I admitted being afraid of losing control of my life by giving up my house, a steady income, and the prestige of being dean of students. The Asian cultural values of hard work, honor, and respect were my internal struggles. My colleague said I could look for a job when I returned from Semester at Sea and suggested several options: I could move in with my parents after the voyage, then look for a job. I could look for a job at sea through the Internet access on the ship. Or I could do a light job search now and ask for a later starting date. Two other colleagues who had left their jobs to go on Semester at Sea offered similar advice: "Julie, you will get a job." One of them had moved in with her brother after Semester at Sea and quickly gotten three job offers. None of the people I talked to had any regrets about going on Semester at Sea, and all said they would do it again without hesitation.

I was still scared to give it all up. I called my mom, who urged me to travel the world before I became tied down with responsibilities. She went around the world before she married my dad and had always encouraged me to see the world. Not surprisingly, she loved the idea of Semester at Sea; in fact, she wanted to join me for part of the trip as a senior continuing education participant. She knew how excited I was about this program and how I was struggling with the decision to leave the job I had worked so hard to get. When I told her I was scared, she pulled out Christopher Logue's (1969) poem "Come to the Edge" and read it over the phone:

> Come to the edge.
> We might fall.
> Come to the edge.
> It's too high!
> COME TO THE EDGE!
> And they came,
> and we pushed,
> And they flew. (pp. 65–66)

Mom said, "Live. Choose to live your life! Go to Semester at Sea." With mom's blessing, I had nothing holding me back, but I still hesitated. A friend who had known me personally and professionally for more than 18 years said, "Julie, if the one thing in your life that you would regret is not going to Semester at Sea, then go! Don't let anyone take away your dreams or prevent them from happening." He asked what held me back. I realized that it was my ego. I loved being dean of students and didn't want to lose my rock-star status. He laughed and said, "Julie, you will be a rock star on Semester at Sea. Whether or not you go to Semester at Sea is up to you. You have the power and control to make this happen." My head was spinning. The people who cared about me most knew my heart and what was important to me. They fully supported me. After much soul searching, I decided to live on the edge and follow my dream. I called my Semester at Sea supervisor and accepted the position. She was overjoyed and said I sounded like my old self.

The next day, I met with my supervisor and told him that so far I had accomplished all my goals, and I did not want to live my life with any regrets. Sadly and with much emotion, I told him I would be submitting my letter of resignation. He was stunned. Although he knew how important this was to me, he said he would never do it himself and that he did not think it was a good move for my career. After the meeting, I felt lighter and taller, as though a huge weight had been lifted off my shoulders. I made a big decision and took my life back into my own hands. I was captain of my ship. I felt free as a bird out of a cage. I was not living to please anyone but myself. I was pursuing a lifelong goal. It felt amazing.

I put my house up for sale and thought about how I would inform my staff. We had worked together for 4 years. Things were humming, and we had several new initiatives in the works. I was happy and thriving in my work. When I told my executive assistant of my decision, she said, tearfully, "Julie, I'm not crying because you're leaving. I'm crying because very few people in this world have an opportunity to truly follow their dreams. I'm happy for you."

Before the next staff meeting, I placed a miniature lighthouse on each agenda. I started the meeting by explaining my dream of traveling around the world in community. The lighthouse symbolized the light I found to follow my dreams, the light of knowledge and learning while at sea. My staff was surprised—and happy for me. They believed that I would be more marketable when I returned.

Although I was on cloud nine and light as a feather, a sense of responsibility motivated me to do a light job search with the goal of finding a position as vice president of a small liberal arts college in my home state of California that would allow me to start after I returned from Semester at Sea. Amazingly, such a position became available, and I applied. I did not even get an interview. Lesson learned: Never put all your hopes and dreams into one option. On to Plan B. Applying for the first senior student affairs position gave me the momentum to apply to other positions at that level. I applied at a large private East Coast university and was invited for an interview. They needed to fill the position right away and were unable to give me a late start date, so we parted ways. I was not disappointed, because I did not want to worry about the new position while I was on Semester at Sea. I applied for a director of student life position with a similar result. This happened a couple more times, and I could not have been happier. I bought a new suitcase, started packing, and got an international cell phone.

Then something told me to apply for a senior student affairs position in the Rocky Mountain region, a position I had previously passed up because I did not want to live in the middle of the country in an area with few people of color. I had always worked in large, diverse urban campuses in cities and towns with a presence of Asian Americans, African Americans, and Chicanos/Latinos. But I listened to the voice inside and sent in my application.

To my surprise, I was invited for a phone interview. I did extensive research on the campus. I dressed up for the interview, compiled a list of questions to ask the committee, and prepared answers to questions I thought they would ask me. This was a big job, and I wanted to be at my best for the tremendous opportunity. At least a dozen members of the 15-member selection committee were on the phone interview. The questions varied, and I answered them confidently and spoke freely. It is a great feeling to interview for a job when your dream job is waiting in the wings. I knew I would be just as happy if I did not get a campus interview; my heart was already embarking on Semester at Sea.

After the interview, I hung up the phone and asked myself, "Who was that?" I was so confident that I was afraid my answers might have sounded a bit sarcastic, but as it turned out, the committee thought I was enthusiastic. A strange thing had happened to me when I quit my job: I had become myself—confident and authentic. I was not saying what I thought the selection committee wanted to hear, nor was I afraid of speaking from the heart. I stressed my views on diversity. My research on the university had informed me that it lacked a diverse student body. I boldly stated that an increase in diversity would greatly enhance the role and responsibility of a flagship public university.

I was one of five finalists invited for a campus interview. It pays to be yourself! This was an honor. I needed to prepare for this amazing opportunity. My director of housing and residence life was from the area and knew the campus, community, and state. He also knew the student experience, because his brother and sister attended the university. My neighbor was from the area; from him, I learned about the state from a business perspective. A colleague from NASPA–Student Affairs Administrators in Higher Education had recently been promoted to vice president of student affairs at another large university in the state and was a great resource on the politics, demographics, and university system.

I did extensive research on the university and the division of student affairs. This was my first interview for a senior student affairs position. I was excited, and I had nothing to lose. My dream job waited in the wings. I was in a good place in my life.

I arrived the night before the interview, rented a car, and drove around the area. My first appointment was dinner with the provost, who was warm and personable. He asked me what I was passionate about and how I would work with other colleagues, including the new vice chancellor for diversity. As diversity was my passion, I discussed the importance of a strong partnership between student affairs and academic affairs. He was aware of my Semester at Sea plans and said they were willing to continue my candidacy. This was the only campus I interviewed with that was willing to consider my Semester at Sea plans, and that impressed me. The conversation was smooth, and I began to like the people and the place. I enjoyed the restaurant we were in and tried to envision myself living in the city.

After 2 days of nonstop interviews with the chancellor, cabinet members, vice chancellors, deans, student leaders, student affairs staff, faculty, and selection committee, I was still excited. I enjoyed meeting the campus community and maintained a high level of enthusiasm throughout the process. I was impressed with the down-to-earth and personable reception I received, and I felt completely at ease with myself. I was asked about my leadership style, how I dealt with change, and my thoughts and vision for student affairs. As I was being interviewed, I was also interviewing the campus. Was this a place where I wanted to spend a significant portion of my life? Were these the people I wanted to work with? Did my future supervisor care about me as a person? Would I be happy here? Would I be able to make a difference on campus and be respected for my knowledge and experience? Was the campus student-oriented? Would I be allowed to have a late start date?

On the last day of the interviews, a private meeting with the senior legal counsel—a Latina/Mexican American—was added to my schedule. She asked whether I had any questions or concerns she could answer as a woman of color in senior leadership. She was open and honest about her experience at the university, and I saw her as a potential role model and mentor. I appreciated her effort to reach out and give me the space to ask questions about her experience as a woman of color in a predominately White institution. We discussed Semester at Sea and possible options, such as starting the job early, going to sea, then returning to the job.

The final late addition to my schedule was a private meeting with the university chancellor. We discussed Semester at Sea and how I might manage it. The chancellor was personable, and he mentioned how he almost worked with Chang Lin Tien, the former chancellor of my previous institution who worked in the same research area he did. Although I had had an earlier half-hour meeting with him, he was impressed with my résumé and wanted to be sure that all my questions were answered before I headed back to the airport.

When the provost later called to inform me that I was their top candidate and they wanted to offer me the job, he also stated that they needed me to start in the position right away. The university was about to go through its accreditation process. They had just done a major reorganization of the division, and unfortunately could not wait until I returned from Semester at Sea.

I thought I had been clear about Semester at Sea. But although they might have considered it, they believed that three-and-a-half months was too long, given the impending accreditation review. This was a huge opportunity to become the vice chancellor of student affairs at a flagship university. My colleagues advised me to take the job, as did my mom and my friends. I could go on Semester at Sea at another time, and I would be crazy not to take this position. My NASPA mentor said this was a "plum" position. I was leaning heavily toward taking the position but still thought about my dream of going abroad in community. If I didn't do it now, I might never go.

The provost did not say I could not go to Semester at Sea, he just said I was needed right away. I asked him, "Is there a possibility to go on Semester at Sea 3 or 4 years down the road, when things are more calm and organized?" He said, "Absolutely; we just need you now. Three years down the road is doable." I asked for this in writing, and the letter offering me the position included a statement that I could apply for an unpaid leave of absence after my third year.

I accepted the position and have not looked back. I am often asked when I will go on Semester at Sea. I know I will go some day, but not right now. It would be difficult to leave my position for three-and-a-half months. I absolutely love being a senior student affairs officer and have no regrets about taking this position. Maybe I'll do Semester at Sea when I retire.

Transition to Senior Administration

In the past I had not really aspired to a senior student affairs position, fearing that I would lose contact with students and thinking the position would be too political. I loved being dean of students, yet there were moments when I wished I had the power to make changes within the division. Surprisingly, my transition to the senior position was smooth. My experience in housing and residence life provided me with a rich foundation in community, facilities, crisis management, and supervision. I had invaluable broad-based student affairs experiences in student conduct, recreation services, counseling and psychological services, student government, orientation, clubs and organizations, community service, Greek life, leadership development, and gay, lesbian, bisexual, and transgender issues. Although I had not supervised enrollment management, parent relations, the environmental center, student legal services, alumni relations, the health center, the student union, career services, and veterans affairs, my leadership, supervision, and student development skills were transferable.

One of the biggest changes in moving from direct student services into senior management was the shift from a focus on students to a focus on the entire campus. Cabinet meeting topics typically included tenure, research, student behavior, athletics, capital campaigns, lawsuits, branding, human resources, and statewide legislation. A pleasant surprise in cabinet meetings was that these topics often revolved around students. Undergraduates were the majority of the student population; thus, enrollment, orientation, parent relations, and student housing were significant topics. Campus operational and policy issues were discussed at weekly vice chancellor meetings. As a senior leader, I attended meetings of the Deans Council and the Chancellor's Executive Committee, which included the cabinet, deans, university communications, human resources, staff council, faculty council, and athletics.

Lessons Learned

I am now in my second senior student affairs position—at a young, growing urban university. However, I learned some important lessons in my first position at the senior level:

1. Although I miss contact with students, I have grown as a professional and understand that being at the table to represent student issues and concerns is just as important. Part of my role as a senior student affairs administrator is to educate the campus on the role of student affairs and the service and development opportunities it provides for students.
2. My experience in student affairs with a variety of departments has been invaluable and significant. My portfolio and experience at other institutions prepared me for the senior position.
3. Organizational fit is extremely important. I have learned that my values must be in line with those of the institution. I am fortunate in that my current and former institutions are student focused and place an important value on the student experience.
4. Never underestimate your ability to move to the next level. I love the challenge and opportunity to set a vision and direction for the division, including hiring the senior leadership team and reorganizing the division. The tremendous responsibility of the senior student affairs officer is accompanied by pride and satisfaction in making changes to serve students better and the privilege of being privy to the many great things happening within the university, including its challenges and direction.
5. I have discovered that I love development and fundraising, even with no previous experience. In my first position as a senior student affairs officer, I had a development team dedicated to raising funds

for student affairs. This was a huge growth area for me, and I have enjoyed the trainings on development, as well as actually meeting and cultivating donors.

6. Developing partnerships around campus is both invigorating and time consuming. A significant portion of my time at the senior level is spent cultivating relationships at lunches or dinners with a variety of constituents. A large part of being a senior student affairs officer is being visible at campuswide events and developing meaningful and purposeful partnership.

7. Communication is important. I am learning to balance internal and external involvement. Meeting with folks around campus and succeeding at fundraising means a lot of meetings outside the division. It is essential to communicate constantly with your leadership team, directors, staff, and students.

8. Developing relationships with other senior student affairs administrators around the country has been invaluable. My former chancellor's best suggestion was that I bring two colleagues to the campus to analyze the organizational culture and my division. I also invited an organizational development consultant and a seasoned vice president of student affairs to meet my staff and colleagues and get a feel for the campus culture. I have continued my relationship with these people, whose wisdom and guidance were critical in my first 2 years in the position. I regularly attend conferences and professional development opportunities for senior-level administrators, which has allowed me to expand my network and meet supportive colleagues who are dealing with similar challenges.

9. It was important for me to live and work in a predominately White community, to learn that I could be effective in a variety of environments. My previous experiences had been in diverse urban communities. In my first senior student affairs position, I was typically the only Asian American or person of color in the room at a given time. I understood the importance of my role as a senior administrator and rarely turned down an opportunity to welcome or recruit new

students to campus. As one of the few administrators of color, it was important to be visible to faculty, staff, and the community. My visibility in the Asian American community increased when I initiated a monthly Asian American faculty and staff lunch, and organized the first Asian American alumni affinity group.

10. I have found my voice and become comfortable in my own skin as an Asian American. The moment I quit my job to follow my passion of traveling around the world in community, I changed. I no longer worked to please others. I now work for what I believe in: I believe that education is the great equalizer in society; I know that relationships built in student affairs are transformative; and I believe in developing students to become the next generation of global leaders. I believe in students and the work of student affairs to facilitate positive communities to create change in the world. I became myself in a new way. I did not worry about what other people felt or thought. I trusted my instincts. I began to listen to myself and what I believed in.

11. In my evolution as a leader, I plan to develop a strong foundation in student affairs and focus on developing my staff so they can reach the next level in their own careers.

Reflections as an Asian American in Student Affairs

My career in higher education has been a combination of good fortune and purposeful experiences. I did not plan to be a senior student affairs administrator. I was fortunate to have colleagues who challenged me to advance in my career when my cultural value of humility made me reluctant to apply for positions at higher levels. Three experiences had a significant effect on my confidence and preparation as an Asian American administrator in higher education:

1. LEAP (Leadership Education for Asian Pacific Americans) aims to increase the pipeline of Asian Americans in senior-level admin-

istration. My participation in LEAP's Leadership Development Program in Higher Education was a game changer in my career, because every session was designed with an Asian American lens and filter. The most incredible part of the experience was being in a room with successful, influential Asian American college presidents and vice presidents who supported the program as mentors and facilitators. I could see myself in a senior leadership role when I met Asian Americans in executive positions and heard their stories. I did not have to explain myself—people intuitively saw my strengths as a leader and the value I bring to an organization as an Asian American.

2. The NASPA Alice Manicur Symposium for Women Aspiring to become Senior Student Affairs Officers was significant as I built a network of women administrators of color with whom I continue to be in contact. The experience encouraged me to prepare and plan for the next level in my career, as opposed to just letting it happen. Hearing the stories of women in senior administration and learning from their experience was invaluable.

3. Co-chairing the NASPA Asian Pacific Islanders Concerns Knowledge Community has been crucial to my professional involvement with NASPA, which has been the foundation of my growth as an Asian American administrator in student affairs and has led to presentations at national conferences, serving on committees, networking, mentorship, and lifelong friendships.

My journey in student affairs has been an adventure, full of life lessons and self-discovery. I will always remember that I landed my first senior student affairs position because I was not afraid to follow my dreams and live on the edge.

Reference

Logue, C. (1969). *New numbers*. London, England: Jonathan Cape.

CHAPTER FIFTEEN

Footprints of Hope and Opportunities

A Student Affairs and Family Legacy

Kevin J. Gin and Hal G. Gin

Student affairs professionals carry with them a general set of values and approaches to life. How do these values and approaches compare with their paradigm when held against the context of Asian and Pacific Islander (API) cultural and family heritage? Family history, culture, and traditions influence and shape our legacies. This chapter examines the relationship of a father and son working in student affairs while comparing and contrasting their definitions and experiences as a family legacy. Convergent and divergent patterns of identity development and growth emerge, as well as reflections on family heritage, the meaning of legacy, and the effect of cultural values on their identity as student affairs practitioners.

Our Journeys

The path traveled to a destination defines a journey. Separate courses can intersect. They may parallel. They sometimes diverge. At other times they converge. More often, paths share qualities that are neither identical nor incongruent but weave in a pattern that reflects our individual life experiences. Journeys are gateways to discovery. They are the introspective narratives that simultaneously facilitate growth and validate history.

We are two student affairs practitioners, separated by a generation of experience and knowledge. We are also father and son. We wrote our stories independently and without consulting each other. This is the first time we have seen our words together. Our lives have been melded into one in this chapter. We were guided by a prompt to reflect on the importance to our profession of our legacy as Asian Americans. How do we define our values? Where does culture inform our work? And what does heritage mean in student affairs? The result is a glimpse of history and our hope for the future in student affairs. This is the impact of legacy.

Hal Gin: A Generation of Hope and Opportunity

The Chinese proverb "A journey of a thousand miles begins with the first step" holds significant meaning in understanding my historical and cultural roots. I am indebted to my ancestors, who unselfishly labored so future generations could enjoy a life with hope and opportunity. Over centuries, the teachings of the Chinese philosopher Confucius have influenced China's history, cultural, social, and educational beliefs. Confucianism is considered to be the cornerstone of my traditional culture. Confucian values include reverence for the past and respect for elders, and places significant importance on family. These beliefs have guided and motivated many Chinese families, including my own.

Historical and narrative accounts revealed my family as well-to-do landowners who settled in Loc Chung, near what is known today as Kaiping City in the Guangzhou Province. This province is near the mouth of the Pearl River in Southeast China; Guangdong (Canton) is the provincial capital and one of the oldest port cities of China. For centuries, Guangdong was the port from which most Chinese emigrants disembarked for the United States.

As a young man in his early 20s, my paternal grandfather was the first of my family to arrive in the United States, after leaving the ancestral village at the turn of the 19th century. The voyage took over a month. He crossed 7,000 miles of the vast Pacific Ocean on a crowded clipper ship. Although the Chinese Exclusion Act regulated the immigration of Chinese to the United States at that time, he qualified to enter the country as a "son of a merchant," although it is unclear how he managed to qualify under that category. For more than 40 years, he enjoyed the freedom of traveling numerous times between the United States and China. It was customary for Chinese men in America to return home every 7 years with their wealth to provide for the family. With his savings in the form of gold coins, my grandfather returned on numerous occasions to provide for his family in China.

In March 1938, my parents were married in my father's ancestral home. It was an arranged marriage; these were still common and were viewed as a means to perpetuate and ensure the survival of the family. In October 1939, my grandfather escorted my father to the United States onboard the *SS President Coolidge*. The purpose of this trip was similar to his quest nearly 40 years earlier: to seek better opportunities for the family. Their plan was to return to China with their earnings at a later time.

During World War II, my father served in the United States Air Force; he was honorably discharged in November 1945. After World War II, the U.S. government expressed its gratitude to the many Chinese Americans who had served in the armed forces by relaxing immigration restrictions. This made it possible for the veterans to bring their wives to the United States. My father took advantage of this benefit: He left for China in April 1947 and returned to America in February 1948 with my mother.

My parents endured their share of personal sacrifices and hardships. They adopted the work ethic of their ancestors, with the determination of establishing a strong foundation for the family and their future grandchildren. In 1955, they decided that starting their own business was the best way to control their destiny. They opened a corner grocery/liquor store named Gin's Liquors, which they proudly and successfully ran until their retirement in 1990. This mom-and-pop store became a landmark in Oakland, California's, Chinatown in the 35 years that my parents owned the property. Throughout those years, they operated the store on a 14-hour day and rarely closed the business for more than a day at a time. Like many of their Asian acquaintances who immigrated to the United States, my parents lived a simple and modest life. They were frugal, budgeted their money, and invested wisely.

My paternal grandmother left the ancestral village before the communist takeover of China in 1949 and spent over a decade in Hong Kong. In 1963 she immigrated to the United States. Her arrival marked the first time in more than 60 years that three generations of the Gin family were living together under the same roof. She passed away in 1975 at the age of 91.

My parents prized education. They hoped that their children would become doctors or dentists, or would enter a related medical profession. They believed that my generation would enjoy a quality of life better than theirs. I graduated from high school in 1968 and continued my education at a local community college. My brother and I started college with the intention of pursuing studies in the medical field. We did not want to disappoint our parents. However, our interests soon shifted away from the life sciences and into the social sciences. Rather than a career in the medical sciences, I envisioned a career as a hospital administrator. In January 1971, I transferred to California State University, Hayward (now East Bay), where I majored in sociology with plans to pursue a master's degree in public health with an option in hospital administration.

As a new student, I attended a daylong orientation for transfer students. Besides a few administrators, student volunteers staffed the program. The thought of volunteering with this unit excited me. I also realized that, if selected, I would receive the benefit of priority registration for my classes. Shortly after submitting an application to the Student Affairs Office, I was notified that I and 25 other students had been selected to serve. I volunteered for 2 years and discovered how much I enjoyed helping students learn, grow, and develop. I found myself gravitating toward a career in student affairs.

In 1974, I started my career in student affairs as a special programs adviser. I assisted with various programs and services, including new student orientation, parent programs, disabled student services, the Women's Resource Center, crisis hotline, volunteer services, and adult re-entry services. After completing my undergraduate degree in sociology, I continued on to complete a master's degree in public administration and a doctorate in educational leadership. In the 30 years following my first student affairs assignment, my career included responsibilities for student life, career development, housing and residence life, student government, and judicial affairs.

Being involved and participating in professional organizations such as NASPA–Student Affairs Administrators in Higher Education were important factors in my success in the field throughout my career. When I was a young professional, my vice president for student services introduced me to NASPA. He enthusiastically supported my participation on committees and my attendance at regional and national conferences. My first NASPA assignment was in 1970, when I was invited to serve on the Northern California Continuing Education Committee. From then until my retirement in 2005, I had the privilege of serving in numerous NASPA regional and national leadership positions, including regional vice president. I have connected with some of the finest colleagues and friends in the profession, many of whom are my role models and mentors.

My interest in and commitment to education continued after my retirement. I was appointed to serve on the seven-member board of trustees of the Chabot-Las Positas Community College District in 2006—I was the first Asian American to serve on the board in the district's 44-year history. I had the privilege of serving as president of the board in 2009; as one of my priorities, I sought to bring issues relating to Asian student populations to the attention of the district.

I sorely miss my mother and father, who passed away in 1995 and 2006 respectively. They were the links to my past and the holders of my family's history. I am fortunate that my parents kept many of the family keepsakes. Photographs, documents, and handwritten journals chronicle many significant events in their lives. These mementos are priceless to me. They provide me with historical perspective and are the footprints of the legacy they left behind. My parents taught me to believe in myself, to honor my ancestors, and to never tarnish the family name. My values, moral compass, and actions reflect the quality and richness of their legacies.

As college-educated parents, my wife and I placed great value on education for our son and daughter. We deliberately chose not to interfere with their selection of academic disciplines, because we wanted them to have the freedom to explore opportunities without parental direction or pressure. Our son, Kevin, enjoyed a successful undergraduate experience majoring in environmental science. Similarly to the way I launched myself into student affairs as a student orientation assistant, Kevin led campus tours and other group activities for new and prospective students at the University of California, Berkeley. After receiving his bachelor's degree, he astounded us by announcing student affairs as his career of choice. After completing a graduate degree in higher education and student affairs in 2009 at Colorado State University, he began his career in student affairs with a position in student activities. He continues to grow and explore the field as a young professional, creating his own legacy through his journey and exploration.

From the family pioneers of the early 19th century (who left China in search of a better life) to my parents (who labored to build a foundation for the future), creating opportunity has been at the core of my family. My ancestors' footprints have led to new hope for current and future generations. The story continues to be written and will be for generations to come. There is nothing more powerful than our past, and it will guide our journey into the future.

Kevin Gin: Legacy of the Past, Hope for the Future

My last name is Gin. It is the same as my father's. It is the same as my father's father. It is the same as generations of my ancestors, going back 4,000 to

5,000 years. This is something that I have known my entire life. It is an inherent part of who I am, as a child, a student, a family member, and a professional. My family name was one of the first words I learned how to say and write in my native Chinese language. It is my most important possession.

As an indication of the importance of a last name in Chinese culture, the surname traditionally comes before the first name. A name is something to be proud of and protected. As a third-generation Chinese American, I was raised to protect my name, to honor it, and to represent everything that it stands for. In the years before I knew anything about student affairs, I developed a paradigm of how to shape my personal and professional identity. Everything I know today and the values by which I define myself stem from the importance of my family name.

My last name is Gin. As far as I know, I am one of only two Gins in the field of student affairs in higher education. It is rare for me to go anywhere, talk to anyone, or write anything about student affairs without someone recognizing my last name. This is unusual, because I have only been in the field for 5 years. In 5 years, I have attended graduate school, secured my first professional position, and only recently embarked on my journey as a practitioner in the field. I am still an entry-level professional. I have a lifetime of experience ahead of me. So why do people recognize my name? The other Gin I am aware of in this field is Hal Gin. He happens to be my dad. And we are a father-son legacy in our profession.

I was never supposed to end up in student services. Much like many of my Asian friends, I had childhood aspirations of working in medicine. The expectation was that, as a Chinese American male, I would achieve and conform to the rigid cultural standards of academic and professional success as a doctor, lawyer, or engineer. I never reacted to this symbolic weight with skepticism. I envisioned a future as a medical professional and allowed that expectation to guide me in my development of classroom passion. I studied hardest in my biology classes, measuring myself against peers who had similar aspirations. I acquired an interest in chemistry and hoped to attend a university with a strong reputation in the life sciences.

I considered myself book smart and possessing classroom savvy. Excelling on paper and meeting expectations were sources of pride.

These reactions and perceptions were not a result of any parental pressures to fit a mold. Nor were they the result of strict discipline or nostalgic desires by my family to instill traditional Chinese values in my life. On the contrary, my family did not want me to carry a burden to conform in a way that was not true to myself. But I wanted to be like my other Asian friends and peers. I acted, behaved, and felt the way they did. My emotions, perceptions, and cultural expectations evolved as ways for me to feel accepted. My friends' academic lives were rigid. Parents set lofty expectations for success and professional achievement, and they were forced to live in the context of traditional Asian expectations to become a doctor, lawyer, engineer, or businessman. I began to realize that I was not the traditional Chinese kid I thought I was when it came to academic and professional achievement. I started to think about how the stories of my peers were different than mine. I realized that I lacked those familial pressures and that my life was not like their lives. I was somewhat shaken by these realizations, and they helped shape the person I am today.

As a college student, I began to reexamine my career goals and aspirations. The attraction of a career in higher education started to outweigh my lifelong interest in science. After spending hours in research laboratories and weeks on field excursions, I realized that the idea of working in the environmental sciences did not fill me with passion. In contrast, my time as a campus tour guide at the University of California, Berkeley, Visitor Center, involvement on the campus Program Board, and work at the Cal Alumni Association increased my desire to dedicate my energies to creating vibrant campus life. I wanted to be able to pass the experiences I was afforded as a student on to others and to advocate for access and diversity on college and university campuses. I realized that, as a student advocate, I would be able to help enrich the college experience and create social change through empowering campus populations. I also wanted to honor the mentors and peers who encouraged me to achieve as a student by entering a profession in which I could help inspire and transform others for a life of purpose.

My parents' reaction to my sudden career change was unlike that of many of my Asian peers. In the Chinese language, *student affairs* has no direct or literal translation. Because of this, many of my Chinese peers who also decided to enter the field found it difficult to explain to their families what their future would be. It is even more difficult to explain in the Chinese language what it means to get an advanced degree in "student affairs in higher education." My dad was different. Because of his direct familiarity with the field, he was happy that I was able to define a path that I was interested in and passionate about pursuing. Both my parents understood what a life in student affairs meant when it came to jobs, salary, and professional development. My dad was especially excited and supportive. He was able to share more than 25 years' worth of perspective, advice, and insight on what I could expect in the years ahead. His knowledge spanned everything from conference etiquette to balancing personal time, and that wisdom guides me in my journey and development as a professional.

The importance of a name in student affairs extends beyond a singular reputation. Reputations are fragile. They take a lifetime to build but only seconds to destroy. I believe I have a responsibility to honor the work that has come before me by continuing to build a future that reflects my name. That impetus grounds me in the profession. My work extends beyond my own identity. A consciousness of my heritage informs my decisions and ethics, and fosters motivation. It pushes me toward the achievement of excellence to create a personal legacy.

A name is defined by its history. It is impossible to quantify the value of someone's name. It is the definition of who he or she is. It is the culmination of a lifetime of decisions and accomplishments. It is instantly recognizable. This principle drives my approach and philosophy working in higher education. My responsibility is to continue a tradition of distinction in service, learning, and growth. My name guides me as a lifelong learner. The interconnectedness of this relationship affects my growth and magnifies the past.

The infusion of Chinese American culture in my philosophy as a student affairs practitioner has not only influenced me as a professional but has also strengthened my core values and guiding principles. My cultural identity acts as a compass for my journey. Drawing on my heritage infuses a well-structured value set that dictates how I work with students and evolve as a professional. Introspection affords me the opportunity to critically examine higher education through a lens I can simultaneously understand and challenge.

My only regret is that I did not follow in my father's footsteps at an earlier age. Our personal and professional relationship has shaped my life, both in and out of higher education. I do not doubt that my father's values and his training as a student affairs practitioner influenced my upbringing and continue to infuse my outlook and philosophical paradigms. The bond and relationship we share creates stability and confidence in my work and my progression as a student and practitioner.

Framing student affairs through relationships with my family and culture has given me the opportunity to rely on a congruent value set derived from a strong and stable facet of my identity. I believe that I have inherited these values through common and shared experiences stemming from the influence of my family and heritage. They will always be present in my life, and I am thankful for the strength they afford me. Because my last name is Gin. And this is my legacy.

Different Generations, Common Values

It is difficult to quantify the effect we have had on each other's lives. It has been both surreal and joyous to share in the growth of our lives, as father and son and as student affairs professionals. We are separated by the years between us but united by the parallels in our stories. We are proof that student affairs is not just the hours we spend in the office, but the philosophies and ethics that grow out of our values. Our stories continue to evolve through our struggles, successes, and mutual desire to honor the past while projecting into the future. This is what defines our intergenerational hope. It is the sum of our experiences. It is the impact of our relationships. And we are not just father and son: we are mentor and mentee, and we are colleagues in student affairs.

CHAPTER SIXTEEN

Redefining Success

*Asian American Women Negotiating
Multiple Roles and Identities*

Sunny Lee

As a young professional in graduate school and in entry-level positions, I began adopting a culture of student affairs that I greatly enjoyed. Because I felt fortunate to have found a career I was so passionate about, I rarely questioned the long hours that were considered the norm in student affairs. Then I became a new mother and realized that I was unprepared for this profound convergence of my professional and personal lives. How was I to balance my multiple roles as a nursing mom, a midlevel manger of my department, and a PhD student? I had underestimated the transformative nature of motherhood and realized that I had given very little thought to how I would succeed in all my various roles. In this chapter, I share my reflections on the elusive work-life balance issue as well as the stories and insights of three Asian American women in student affairs who are in a similar season of their lives. We are all mid-career, raising young children, and crafting our lives as we make sense of our changing values and definitions of success.

I was born in Seoul, Korea, in the early 1970s; I was the first-born daughter of a first-born son. My mother told me that when I was born, my paternal grandmother did not visit us at the hospital because she was upset that I was a girl. She blamed my mother for not producing a son as the first grandchild. Ultimately, like other first-generation Asian American women, I reacted to patriarchy and sexism by working to be even better than a first-born son.

In my mid-30s, I married, started a PhD program, obtained my first managerial position, and had a child. I began to look around for examples of how others were "doing it all." Fortunately, my supervisor—a senior-level leader of my division—was a mother to a young child and I felt very supported by her. However, among dozens of midlevel leaders in the division of student affairs, only a few other women seemed to be combining careers and young children, let alone doctoral work. Given the lack of role models, I began looking to the literature for answers. In the course of higher education research, I discovered very little on the topic of women and multiple roles, and what does exist focuses mostly on the experiences of White women. Most published material on women, family, and higher education is about women faculty and the challenges that exist as the tenure timeline collides with the maternal biological clock (Armenti, 2004; Drago and Colbeck, 2003; Perna, 2001; Ward & Wolf-Wendel, 2004).

In the literature on women in higher education, very few studies include student affairs professionals who are women (Belch & Strange, 1995; Marshall, 2009; Marshall & Jones, 1990; Nobbe & Manning, 1997). None of these studies focus on the experiences of women of color, or even include many women of color in their samples. One study examines the lives of four Asian American women administrators through their narratives related to race, gender, and discrimination (Ideta & Cooper, 1997/2000). Two of the women were in academic affairs and two in student affairs.

The women encountered discrimination in the workplace as a result of both their race and gender, and used these negative experiences to invest more of their personal and professional efforts into working against discrimination in higher education. Renn and Hughes's (2004) *Roads Taken: Women in Student Affairs at Mid-Career* features a range of reflective and experiential chapters, including several by women of color. The stories illustrate that women often choose not to—or simply cannot—separate their professional and personal lives.

While struggling and juggling my multiple roles, I wondered what it was like for other Asian American women in student affairs who find themselves in this position. At student affairs conferences and surveying the higher education landscape, I saw very few Asian American women role models in senior-level student affairs positions. My peers and I noticed that many of our female role models from the baby boomer generation had made difficult choices regarding careers and family. Many of the women in top-level student affairs positions (e.g., vice president) were single or married with no children. Those with children typically had had them early in their careers. This is consistent with the findings in the literature about executive women in general (Hewlett, 2002). When women choose to bear children later in life, in mid-career, their lives can become filled with chaos, uncertainty, and stress as they navigate their careers while raising young children (Fochtman, 2011). Is having it all a myth, like the objectionable "model minority" myth, or is it possible to fulfill these roles without feeling as though we are making significant sacrifices in our professional or personal lives, or both?

A wise mentor once told me that we could have it all, but not all at the same time. Is there such a thing as a superwoman? Levinson and Levinson (1996) defined *superwoman* as a woman who can do it all with grace and flair. What are the costs and benefits of being a woman who juggles multiple roles? How does our Asian American identity intersect with our gender and other multiple identities as we navigate our personal and professional lives? How do we make our public and private lives more seamless, holistic, and integrated? To gain deeper insights into these questions, I interviewed three Asian American women. I selected three women in different parts of the country who are at mid-career, have or are pursuing a doctorate, and are mothers.

My conversations with these three inspiring women resulted in the following themes and perspectives gained from their experiences and insights. The three women are in traditional and heterosexual-normative marriage relationships. Their experiences are not meant to be generalized to a larger population of Asian Americans, women, or Asian American women. I have used pseudonyms in sharing their narratives of how they navigate their multiple roles. A value of most Asian cultures is the concept of "saving face," meaning it is not acceptable to share details of personal experiences with people outside the family or a close circle of friends. I am, therefore, grateful for the transparency and honesty of the three women and their willingness to share their stories.

Kaila, Anita, and Jenny

Kaila is fourth-generation Japanese American and second-generation Filipina, and the director of the women's center at a doctorate-granting university on the West Coast. She is in her early 40s and is the mother of a 6-year-old son and 2-year-old daughter. Kaila says she "fell into" the field of student affairs accidentally when she became a master's degree student in American studies at the campus where she works. Her graduate assistant-ship at the women's center became a professional position, with increasingly progressive responsibilities. She has served as director for 13 years. Kaila started her PhD program in education administration soon after marrying. She is currently in the middle of writing her dissertation while working full time and being an active parent to her two young children.

Anita is second-generation Indian American, in her mid-30s, and dean of student life at a large public university in the Northwest. She has a PhD in higher education administration and has been in her current position for 2 years. She has a 3-year-old daughter. Anita says that, growing up, she was "every stereotype that one could apply to an Asian American." She graduated from high school second in her class, with enough Advanced Placement credits to start as a senior in college in a premed major. However, she was not prepared for college and initially performed poorly. She became an orientation advisor, which motivated her to do well in school. She did not want to fail and go home for the summer and face her parents. Anita has breadth and depth of student affairs experience, including residential life and multicultural affairs.

Jenny is second-generation Korean American and works as a program coordinator of student life at a large public university on the East Coast. She is in her mid-30s and has 3-year-old and 6-month-old daughters. She is a full-time student affairs professional, a mother, and an advanced PhD student in education at the university where she works. She commutes an hour to and from work. Like Anita, Jenny entered student affairs as a result of undergraduate student involvement. She worked at the campus office of volunteer community service and eventually became the lead student program director. Like Anita, she began college as a premed student, attempting to fulfill the dreams of her immigrant parents. During her senior year, in a conversation with the office staff director, she realized that she could pursue a career in student affairs; she enrolled in the master's degree program in education with a student affairs track at her university.

Motherhood = New Identity

When asked how they prioritized the multiple roles in their lives, all three women ranked being a mother as their top priority. For all three, being a wife or partner was next, followed by their various other roles of worker, professional, or student. All three women were clear that although being a professional was not their most important role, that did not mean that the quality of their work was diminished. On the contrary, they talked about how being a mother had a positive effect on their role in student affairs. Kaila said, "Before [having children], I was Kaila, director of the women's center. Now I'm Matt and Eva's mom. I love that name, I love that identity." Anita said, "To me, motherhood is a way of life. When I introduce myself, I say my full-time job is mother, and in my free time I'm dean of students. I don't mean to diminish my professional role, but it's a deal-breaker if you ask me to compromise motherhood." Jenny said being a mother was her top priority, followed by being a partner to her husband, followed by her role as a professional. She said, "I'm not completely interested in being career-driven. I don't want my career to be the driving force of what happens with my family."

Benefits and Challenges

All three women talked about how being a mother has enhanced their role as a student affairs professional. For Kaila, having children deepened her commitment to her work in violence prevention and gender equity. As the mother of a son, living in a community where Filipino men are often stereotyped as perpetrators of sexual violence, her work in education and prevention is more personal and meaningful than ever before. Her role as a mother has enhanced her effectiveness at work and the way she leads. She said parenthood has made her more honest, real, and direct: "When you have kids, you can't fake anything at all." She believes that she has gained new skills in speaking and framing ideas. She discussed how becoming a parent gave her new perspective on her work on social justice and relationships. "I used to be, 'Are you down with the movement or not?' Now I see even more shades of gray than I did before. Something totally changed in the way I interact with people." Kaila explained how she gained valuable perspective when she took 6 months of maternity leave and the center seemed to run fine without her. This helped her recognize that she did not always have to be on every committee or be involved in every aspect of the work. She said it was a good check for her ego to see that things ran smoothly without her presence. She believed that this was a valuable lesson for her to create a more healthy and balanced life.

Anita relates her work in creating equitable learning environments for students to child development literature she has been reading about her toddler daughter. She said, "Being an administrator on campus helps me be a better mother, and striving to be a better mother helps me be an amazing administrator and professional, and I see those things daily." She said that in her previous work on multicultural affairs and advocacy, she was sometimes more concerned about being right than about being in a relationship with people. She said she now approaches her work in social justice with more care by prioritizing relationships. Jenny described feeling nourished intellectually by working with good colleagues and friends. She said that while she would like to spend more time with her children, she knows that she needs the intellectual stimulation provided by her work and studies. "I think I'm still growing in ways that are important to the person I am. I think I'm still growing because of my career."

In addition to the benefits of combining motherhood and professional work, all three women were candid about the challenges they have experienced in juggling multiple roles. Kaila and Jenny talked about the lack of time they have had to devote to their doctoral studies and the pressures they felt as they worked on their dissertations. They talked about the challenge of ensuring that they spent enough quality time with their partners and children. Anita talked about being exhausted and her need to get enough rest. Jenny talked about the push-pull of wanting to participate in additional committees and projects while desiring to put her family first and finding time for her academic work. She discussed her role in her family, including helping her mother who lives nearby, and the occasional pressure she feels about fulfilling unspoken cultural expectations of relatives.

Redefinition of Success

For the three women, combining motherhood with their other identities meant redefining success. They all talked about how much they worked before they had children. They adopted the extended hours as culturally normal in student affairs, along with self-imposed pressures and expectations. Now, as parents of young children, they are less willing to spend extra hours away from their kids. Instead, they are redefining success and excellence, and leading to create that culture in their sphere of influence.

The women were clear that they were able to function in their multiple roles because of the support of partners and supervisors. All three women said that their partners contributed equally to household chores and childrearing. Anita's husband does most of the cleaning, but she does most of the meal preparation; although she is a feminist and a progressive woman, she says there is something within her to carry that role. Kaila's husband has a more flexible schedule as a faculty member, and Jenny's husband works much closer to their home, which enables him to handle more child care responsibilities.

All three women said their supervisors have been supportive of their role as working parents. Kaila said her supervisor pressures her to finish her dissertation and provides the means to do so by giving her a flexible schedule so she can conduct research and write. Jenny adopted a 4/10 work schedule during the summer months, which allowed her a full day each week to focus on writing. Anita says she blurs weekdays and weekends, and will take time off during the week to tend to family matters because she works many evenings and weekends attending student programs and events. She takes her 3-year-old daughter to many events when it is appropriate. This practice is modeled by her supervisor, the vice president for student affairs, who brings his son to campus events; it helps create a campus culture that is accepting of family. All three women talked about how they support work-life balance with their staff members, whether they are parents or not. They recognize and value that their staff have various responsibilities outside the workplace, such as care of elderly parents or other family members. Jenny said, "I think it's good for student affairs people, even if they don't have children. I think it's important for them to know they need to seek balance, too. For me, balance is tangible because I have these people [her daughters] who are relying on me, so I need to leave the office by a certain time."

For Anita, making it all work includes working from home 1 day a month and arranging her work week to make sure she has enough time with her family. If she works weekends, she takes flex time during the week. She said that before her current job, she did not envision the possibility of a dean of students role for herself. In fact, she had decided that she was going to be a stay-at-home mom, because she could not imagine going back to working the 12-hour days that are typical in residence life and multicultural affairs. However, when she was invited to interview for her current position, she had an experience that made her feel that this could be a place where she was welcomed as a working mother. When Anita asked her interviewers for a freezer so she could pump and freeze her breast milk to take back to her 3-month-old daughter, they were so accommodating and supportive that she felt reassured about her potential working environment. Until that point, she had not told her interviewers that she was a new mother, because she believed it might work against her.

When I asked Anita what's next for her, she said, "I feel I'm building habits that will help me sustain myself personally and professionally so that I can imagine the possibility of a vice presidency. I want you to know that that's very different from 'Wow, I don't even want to move on from this field, because it won't work because of my lifestyle before.' The great news is that I won't go back to an unhealthy lifestyle. It just won't happen, because I know differently now." She added, "Rethink the social norms that you live by. I think I'm a pretty progressive woman, but I internalized social norms that I wasn't even willing to admit to myself. Have the honest conversation about those things and surround yourself with people who are willing to have that honest conversation with you."

Becoming the Role Models

There are very few Asian Americans in senior-level leadership positions in higher education, especially women who are simultaneously raising children and devoting the hours often required for a demanding executive role. Kaila shared an observation about the women from the baby boomer generation who had to choose between their careers and families to move up in the field. She believes that the message often passed down to her generation of women is "Either suck it up and do it because I did, or give it up [family or career]. There's no in-between." She said, "No one talks about the benefits of having a family."

None of the women were willing to give up their families as their number-one priority to advance their careers. For Kaila, prioritizing her children meant that the family would not move for job promotions, which is often necessary to advance in the field. Before they had children, she and her husband were willing to move anywhere for the right job. After the birth of their son, they could not imagine leaving a community that loved their son as much as they did. She said, "Okay then, if we're going to stay here, how can I stay here and not feel like I sacrificed anything? It took a lot of conversations . . . it was a family decision." She explained that while they thought they were on one track, having children changed their minds completely. Kaila talked about the importance of sharing these diverse experiences and stories with younger professionals at conferences. Although younger professionals may not feel that certain experiences will apply to them, it gives them a variety of options to choose from through-out the course of their professional and personal lives. She says, "We need to create the way" and demonstrate different ways of navigating our careers and our lives.

For Jenny, work-life balance meant taking a different position in her department that provided more predictable working hours and not as many weeknights and weekends. After working 4 years in multicultural affairs and advocacy, she was feeling burnt out from the nature of the work and its long hours into the nights and weekends. She applied for a 9-to-5 position that enabled her to start the PhD program and think about a family. When I asked Jenny what she would want younger professionals to know about her story, she said, "Give yourself grace, know what you need to feel nourished, because you're in so many roles of serving others. Student affairs is about serving others. Being a mother is about serving and facilitating the growth of these little people. I think for Asian American women, for women who are doing work in and for the community, it's even more important to nourish yourself."

Anita reflected on her experience with her first-generation mother, who worked two to three shifts as the single income earner of her household while Anita was growing up. Her mother did not understand why Anita worked such long days. She would ask, "What's the point of a graduate degree if the quality of your life is so poor?" Anita used to be defensive and resistant to such comments; however, now she understands what her mother was trying to say. Anita shared that striving for work-life balance should not be the goal—it is happiness that we should strive for, and work-life balance is too low a bar. Anita said, "We talk about our elders in the profession—Asian American women or women in general, men of color. They didn't make sacrifices so we could make the same sacrifices. If we're making the same sacrifices they were making, then there's something wrong. We should be building." Anita reasons that we—the younger generation—should not have to make the same sacrifices our parents had to make. There should be progress, and progress would be indicated by fighting battles that are different from those of our predecessors.

Reflections

A common cultural norm in student affairs is long hours that are not compensated and a high value on lots of face time at work. These values put working parents who are responsible for caring for children and those who have responsibilities for other family members at a disadvantage. Student affairs can continue to attract and retain diverse high-quality professionals if we rethink what is considered normal practice in the field.

Hughes (2004) noted that we have been trained in student affairs to think that "more is better" when it comes to our careers. The stories of these three women demonstrate that while they are juggling multiple roles, they are able to make their lives work because of intentional decisions they have made along the way, as well as the institutional support systems that are in place. Although the women are high-achieving and successful in their careers, they are very clear that their priority is children and family. All three have managed to craft their work and personal life to support what is important to them.

McKenna (1997) warned that women cannot renegotiate the traditional workday if they do not speak up for what they need, and Pipher (1994) discussed how silence and lack of advocacy on such issues have hurt women. In the absence of an alternative voice, Pipher noted the work environment will continue to be based on false assumptions, the largest of which is a supervisor's expectation that the traditional workday will work for everyone. If women and men continue to be silent on these issues, the status quo will remain. In Kropf's (1997) research for *Catalyst*, she found that the largest obstacle for women in making other work arrangements was their buying into the "success culture" value system. They feared the effect alternatives would have on their careers.

The literature shows that although women have made up a large part of the American workforce since the 1970s, careers and institutions are still structured in ways that privilege White men with stay-at-home wives who handle the child-rearing and household responsibilities (Acker, 2000). Career development literature in the 1990s called for businesses and organizations to change their structures to better accommodate the multiple roles of women (Shapiro, Ingols, & Blake-Beard, 2008). Recent literature asserts that for organizations to retain women, especially women with children, the nature of careers must change.

Blackhurst (2000) found that a glass ceiling exists for women in student affairs: Women are disproportionately represented in middle management versus senior-level positions. Women in student affairs reported that it is much more common to have worked for a man who had children than for a woman who had children (Fochtman, 2011; Nobbe & Manning, 1997; Renn & Hughes, 2004). A woman who works as a senior-level administrator is more likely to be single or childless. Today, two-thirds of all students in student affairs graduate programs are women (Taub & McEwen, 2006). Considering the higher representation of women in the profession, we cannot ignore issues related to work-life balance. Kaila, Anita, and Jenny have supportive partners and supervisors, but this is not always the case for women.

To nurture the leadership development of Asian American women and to prime the pipeline for future leaders, the wholeness of our lives should be supported. Asian American women experience many of the same challenges and rewards as other working mothers, in addition to the challenges of race and racism unique to being women of color. If higher education is serious about increasing diversity at the highest positions, we need to question what is considered normal regarding expectations and productivity. Owing to the nature of our field, we will continue to put a high value on face time and fostering interpersonal relationships in the workplace. However, the lives of these three women illustrate more creative ways to foster success. By focusing on outcomes versus input of time, we can shift the definition of excellence. Motherhood taught the interviewees to let go and to be much more efficient with their time. Because of the institutional support they enjoy, they are able to thrive in their professional roles without compromising motherhood as their number one priority.

Student affairs professionals are often the agents of change on college campuses. Surely, we can envision and implement creative solutions to retain qualified diverse professionals in student affairs and encourage their career development. Job sharing, flex-time, part-time schedules, sabbaticals for student affairs professionals, subsidized child care, private rooms for nursing or pumping, and an automatic family leave policy are examples of the possibilities for our profession—not just for parents but for anyone who is caring for others, such as elders or ill family members. These policies should be available to both women and men, to enable men to contribute equally to household management.

To further advance the pipeline of qualified diverse candidates to key leadership positions in higher education and student affairs, we need to challenge some of the cultural norms we take for granted in our field. The student affairs profession was founded on and continues to center on fostering the holistic development of students (American Council on Education, 1937, 1949). Those who advocate work-life balance in student affairs observe that while we promote this value for our students, we rarely practice it in our own lives, resulting in a lack of congruence between what we say and what we do. By aligning our values with our practice, we can make great progress in creating equitable working and learning environments that are truly inclusive.

References

American Council on Education (ACE). (1937). *Student personnel point of view.* Washington, DC: Author.

American Council on Education (ACE). (1949). *Student personnel point of view.* Washington, DC: Author.

Acker, S., Wyn, J., & Richards, E. (2000). Making a difference: Women in management in Australian and Canadian faculties of education. *Gender and Education, 12*(4), 435–447.

Armenti, C. (2004). May babies and post-tenure babies: Maternal decisions of women professors. *Review of Higher Education, 27*(2), 211–231.

Belch, H. A., & Strange, C. C. (1995). View from the bottleneck: Middle managers in student affairs. *NASPA Journal, 32*(3), 208–221.

Blackhurst, A. (2000). Effects of mentoring on the employment experiences and career satisfaction of women student affairs administrators. *NASPA Journal, 37*(2), 573–586.

Drago, R. C., & Colbeck, C. (2003). *The mapping project: Exploring the terrain of U.S. colleges and universities for faculty and families.* College Park, PA: The Pennsylvania State University.

Fochtman, M. M. (2011). High-achieving women: Navigating multiple roles and environments in academic and student affairs. In P. Pasque and S. E. Nicholson (Eds.), *Empowering women in higher education and student affairs: Theory, research, narratives, and practice from feminist perspectives* (pp. 85–103). Sterling, VA: Stylus.

Hewlett, S. A. (2002, April 1). Executive women and the myth of having it all. *Harvard Business Review, 80*(4), 66–73.

Hughes, C. (2004). Introduction to "I've arrived": It's the journey, not the destination. In K. A. Renn & C. Hughes (Eds.), *Roads taken: Women in student affairs at mid-career* (pp. 135–141). Sterling, VA: Stylus.

Ideta, L. M., & Cooper, J. E. (1997/2000). Asian American leaders of higher education. In J. Glazer-Raymo, B. K. Townsend, & B. Ropers-Huilman (Eds.), *Women in higher education: A feminist perspective* (pp. 259–268). Boston, MA: Pearson Custom Publishing.

Kropf, M. B. (1997). Part-time work arrangements have considerable impact on today's workplaces. *Catalyst.* Retrieved from http://www.catalyst.org/press-release/5

Levinson, D. J., & Levinson, J. D. (1996). *The seasons of a woman's life.* New York, NY: Ballantine Books.

Marshall, M. R., & Jones, C .H. (1990). Childbearing sequence and the career development of women administrators in higher education. *Journal of College Student Development, 31*(6), 531–537.

Marshall, S. M. (2009). Women higher education administrators with children: Negotiating personal and professional lives. *NASPA Journal About Women in Higher Education, 2*(1), 188–221.

McKenna, E. P. (1997). *When work doesn't work anymore.* New York, NY: Dell Publishing.

Nobbe, J., & Manning, S. (1997). Issues for women in student affairs with children. *NASPA Journal, 34*(2), 101–111.

Perna, L. W. (2001). The relationship between family responsibilities and employment status among college and university faculty. *Journal of Higher Education, 72*(5), 584–611.

Pipher, M. Q. (1994). *Reviving Ophelia.* New York, NY: Ballantine Books.

Renn, K. A., & Hughes, C. (Eds.). (2004). *Roads taken: Women in student affairs at mid-career.* Sterling, VA: Stylus.

Shapiro, M., Ingols, C., & Blake-Beard, S. (2008). Confronting career double blinds: Implications for women, organizations, and career practitioners. *Journal of Career Development, 34*(3), 309–333.

Taub, D. J., & McEwen, M. K. (2006). Decision to enter the profession of student affairs. *Journal of College Student Personnel, 47*(2), 206–216.

Ward, K., & Wolf-Wendel, L. (2004). Academic motherhood: Managing complex roles in research universities. *Review of Higher Education, 27*(2), 233–257.

CHAPTER SEVENTEEN

The Effect of AAPI Community Involvement on Career Progression in Student Affairs

Connie Tingson-Gatuz

O ver the past few decades, Asian American and Pacific Islander (AAPI) professionals have contributed to the student affairs profession in both generalist and specialist roles, with increasing scope of responsibility. In addition to holding these positions, professionals are often called on to contribute to broader AAPI community projects, such as national scholarship reads, leadership development programs, and community-based projects that serve students. For 20 years, I have had the pleasure of working with fellow AAPI professionals in both higher education and nonprofit sectors devoted to meeting the diverse needs of AAPI college students. National college scholarship programs, national student leadership development programs, and regional student organization activities have provided annual opportunities for me to connect with colleagues in unique ways.

Board of Advisors to the Midwest Asian American Student Union

The Midwest Asian American Student Union (MAASU) was established in 1989 to support the Asian Pacific Islander American (APIA) community and to promote political unity among Asian American students in the Midwest. MAASU helps schools establish APIA student organizations, cultural centers, and Asian American studies programs; promotes leadership among APIA students through Leadership Retreat, Spring Conference, and other programs; addresses the educational needs of APIAs and provides scholarship information for APIA students; develops and maintains communication with APIA student organizations through e-mail, newsletter, and networking; encourages APIA students to work toward social change by providing a forum for social consciousness; and unites and strengthens the APIA community against all forms of oppression (Midwest Asian American Student Union, 2012). Fifteen years after being part of the original founding membership, I and several colleagues served on the board of advisors to support the student leadership. As members of the board, we provided insight and guidance on all aspects of managing the nonprofit organization serving the APIA community.

APIA U

Seeing a need to develop leadership among AAPI students, the Organization of Chinese Americans established APIA U (formerly called Next GenerAsian)—a leadership training program for APIA student leaders—in 1999. The program focuses on the development of leadership and organizational skills that are relevant to APIAs on campuses and in communities; it uses a leadership training program that involves hands-on exercises, small-group discussions, and presentations led by qualified APIA facilitators. The 1-day training assembles 60 students from each region and focuses on self-awareness, team building, and direct action organizing. Participants are given the opportunity to challenge themselves, share experiences, and develop leadership tools so they can serve effectively as catalysts for change (Organization of Chinese Ameicans, 2012). In collaboration with two colleagues, I developed the critical APIA Leadership Framework Model to provide a theoretical framework for the program. Over the past decade, I facilitated APIA U trainings and served as the trainer of trainers.

Gates Millennium Scholars Program

Established in 1999, the Gates Millennium Scholars (GMS) program was initially funded by a $1 billion grant from the Bill and Melinda Gates Foundation. The Asian and Pacific Islander American Scholarship Fund administers the GMS program for the AAPI community, providing the scholars with personal and professional development through leadership programs and academic support throughout their college attendance. GMS strives to support minority students with excessive financial need as they enter higher education. A select group of APIA high school seniors are admitted to the program and receive financial support and leadership development opportunities. The four primary goals of the GMS program are: (1) significantly reduce financial challenges for APIA students possessing strong academic and leadership potential; (2) impact the number of APIAs in fields where minorities are underrepresented; (3) promote leaders representing diverse populations at all levels of higher education; and (4) increase the levels of graduate students in specific disciplines (Asian and Pacific Islander American Scholarship Fund, 2009).

In addition to helping students, AAPI student affairs professionals can leverage their experiences with the GMS program to progress in the field and their careers, as noted in the following quotes:

> "Being part of the MAASU Board of Advisors and the GMS read helped me feel that I can contribute to the advancement of Asian American representation in higher education. These

opportunities demonstrated to me that my solitary work at the University of Missouri is part of a greater whole that helps my community and helps me to provide mentoring to future leaders. These experiences reinvigorated me to keep my efforts and idealism high."

"In the GMS read, I was surrounded by fellow student affairs staff who have similar goals in creating programs and opportunities for students within a social justice agenda. It not only allowed me to feel supported within a network of individuals but also allowed me to create further professional goals and gave me ideas of where I would like to be professionally in the future. The read also allowed me to share my experience as one of the few Pacific Islanders in student affairs and highlight the need to create greater cultural competencies among student affairs stuff so they can become stronger advocates for all students."

"I am better skilled and versed in the broader concepts of the AAPI diaspora, especially in the realm of higher education. I have also learned that forcing your kids to learn the violin or cello may not be a bad thing after all. I love being involved with GMS and being surrounded by other professionals who share a similar position on the philosophical spectrum as it relates to educational opportunity and access."

"The GMS read broadened my knowledge base about issues around access to higher education in the APIA community. Though I came to the read with experience in working with Asian American students, my understanding of challenges within certain smaller communities was limited. I worked at a highly competitive and selective law school at the time—I left the GMS read with a heightened sensitivity to the obstacles faced by so many who do not have direct access to higher education and require substantive financial support."

"Being involved with community-based organizations as a GMS reader and a SEARAC [Southeast Asia Research Action Center] board chair has definitely given me professional development skills and competencies. It has expanded my knowledge base of educational issues of APIAs such as the Pacific Islanders and given me the confidence to interact with elected officials and other policymakers to advocate on behalf of our APIAs and other immigrant youth. These two skills . . . allowed me to actively engage my Southeast Asian American community with the UMass-Lowell system."

Personal Benefits

These experiences provided personal benefits. As my competencies increasingly developed, my responsibilities in the programs escalated. Ultimately, my career progression was affected and enhanced. I grew from opportunities to be mentored and from mentoring others. My network of colleagues who could serve as professional references and from whom I learned of new career opportunities expanded significantly. My level of exposure to other aspects of these organizations increased, along with my perspective on their scope and structure. Sometimes I received financial compensation for my services, but much of the time I was a volunteer. In either case, I benefited from an infusion of ideas to increase student involvement and a wide range of insights in areas from college student development to programming.

Impact of Peer Mentoring

AAPI professional peers influence one another to become increasingly involved in our respective communities, both on and off campus. Our leadership roles in the AAPI community and connections to other community members become personal investments akin to family ties. The strong sense of membership in the AAPI community promotes a culture of personal connectedness to one another. Peers inspire one another to serve the community with a heightened sense of purpose and choose collective over individual action while serving in leadership roles.

Relationships that AAPI professionals develop with their peers enable them to speak candidly about personal topics. Unrestricted conversations promote strong interpersonal ties among colleagues that strengthen their commitment to each other and to the larger community as they share their experiences in different roles. Interpersonal connections are established when multiple parties exchange information and engage in active listening, communicating, and understanding.

AAPIs take advantage of the opportunities for give-and-take with each other. They are committed to each other through a collective understanding even when they disagree. They value being with peers who have different perspectives and appreciate opportunities to examine and evaluate new ideas so they can make decisions that are in the best interest of the group.

Inspired by colleagues who have had similar experiences, some take action to explore their racial and ethnic identities. Together, they share challenges involving identity, which strengthens their bond. In one instance, a colleague's thinking about his cultural identity shifted when a peer shared a common multiracial background to which he could relate. Through examples set by other peers, he developed strategies to deal with the identity crisis he was experiencing as a multiracial professional. The commitment to challenge racism and oppression motivates these professionals to serve the community.

Inspired to model such behaviors, AAPI professionals have transferred what they learned from their peers to involvement in their communities and to raising awareness of key issues. Peers provide significant motivation to attend community activities and offer suggestions for involvement with increasing responsibility. Consistent attendance and participation over time has enabled many AAPIs to be elected to formal leadership positions in community organizations. AAPI professionals influence one another to maintain high levels of involvement in the community. They provide mutual support in the face of challenge. I have witnessed and benefitted from AAPI professionals who work to maintain a strong foundation for the organization so that new members find support when they enter the institution. AAPI peers seek role models and serve as role models to others. Although community service continues to be the primary focus, community members encourage their peers to assume more responsibility.

Impact of AAPI Leadership on Serving the Community

Increased involvement through leadership roles can create a sense of obligation and commitment to the community that increases one's feeling of connectedness. AAPI professionals can be inspired by peer leaders who are perceived as productive and personable in their formal leadership positions. AAPI professionals observe leader behaviors that push them to seek purpose in their decision to become actively involved in a racial and ethnic organization, and in their respective member roles they stimulate others to advocate for the community.

AAPI professionals have worked to create a structure built on the concepts of unification and service. They offer a collective vision of building meaningful relationships with members across multiple organizations in the AAPI community. Although these organizations have varying agendas, AAPI leaders can help them find common ground.

Service to the AAPI community has enabled members of various organizations to engage with the community in meaningful ways. AAPI professionals are needed to lend their expertise in AAPI nonprofit organizations. The experiences of peers provide valuable knowledge on how to navigate the system—they can describe incidences in which they acted on their desire to meet community needs. The process of organizing advocacy efforts has taught valuable lessons nested in service to the community. AAPIs can continue to develop a strong sense of empowerment and a willingness to take risks on behalf of others who are too fearful to advocate for themselves.

Collective Over Individual Action

AAPI professionals have promoted more collective than individualistic perspectives on service to the community. The strong ties among AAPI professionals supporting each other provide a backdrop for collective support. When no meaningful relationships exist among colleagues, efforts to achieve effective collective action can bog down. Sometimes AAPIs must decide not to let differences interfere with achieving goals. Compromise is encouraged for the greater good of the community, as opposed to focusing on individual goals.

Encouragement and support for ideas motivates and inspires us to give more. Community-building efforts are solidified by AAPI peers who mentor others. Together, they establish personal investments in each other and ties to the broader racial and ethnic community. Individual and collective purposes serve as motivation to increase community involvement. Having personally benefitted from involvement in community organizations and having witnessed countless other AAPI colleagues progress throughout their careers, I believe broader involvement in community-based organizations contributes to the development of invaluable professional competencies that prepare AAPI professionals for generalist and specialist roles in student affairs.

References

Asian & Pacific Islander American Scholarship Fund. (2009). *Gates Millennium Scholars*. Retrieved from http://apiasf.org/scholarship_gms.html

Midwest Asian American Student Union. (2012). *Board of Advisors*. Retrieved from http://maasu.org/about

Organization of Chinese Americans. (2012). *APIA U: College Leadership Training Program*. Retrieved from http://www.ocanational.org/index.php?option=com_content&task=view&id=53&Itemid=62

PART VI

Looking Forward

CHAPTER EIGHTEEN

Voices from the Future

Karlen N. Suga

Other chapters in this volume present the research, insights, and journeys of Asian, Pacific Islander, and Desi American (APIDA) higher education professionals. The words *trailblazer*, *legacy*, and *impact* are used to describe the accomplishments of the current generation of APIDA presidents, vice presidents, deans, and directors. Beyond the impact of their work for students and college campuses across the nation, these men and women have mentored and inspired the next generation of APIDA administrators.

What is the next generation of APIDA student affairs administrators hoping to accomplish, and what lessons have they learned from those who came before them? A group of 15 new and midlevel professionals representing varying years of experience, program areas, and APIDA ethnicities were asked those very questions. The result is the perspective that follows on what the future might hold for APIDA professionals in student affairs.

Background and Methodology

E-mail surveys were sent to 37 new professionals and graduate students who identify as APIDA and are affiliated with NASPA–Student Affairs Administrators in Higher Education and the American College Personnel Association. Fifteen people responded. The survey included the following questions:

- How many years have you been in the higher education profession?
- What functional area(s) of higher education do you have experience in?
- What are your career aspirations?
- In what ways have your career aspirations been influenced by mentors in the profession? Please make special note of any who identify as APIDA.
- As you progress through your career in student affairs, what are some key contributions you hope to make?
- What do you think is the legacy of the APIDA student affairs professionals who have come before you? What have you learned from them?

The Next Generation

The 15 professionals who responded to the survey represent a wide range of years of experience, APIDA cultures, and higher education functional areas. The average professional experience was 4.8 years, and many cited work done in undergraduate and graduate school as part of their journey. Ethnically, Asian, Pacific Islander, and South Asian American perspectives were represented in the response pool. The majority of respondents were affiliated with public and private institutions in the eastern and western United States, although some attended and worked at institutions in the Midwest, specifically Missouri and Illinois. They represented a wide variety of functional areas in student affairs, such as residence life/housing;

multicultural affairs; lesbian, gay, bisexual, and transgender student support; student activities and organizations; career services; retention programming; and academic support/advising. Before their first professional position, respondents cited graduate and undergraduate experience in all these areas, as well as alumni affairs, admissions, Greek life, and orientation programming.

Career Aspirations

With regard to career aspirations and who influenced them, responses centered on two major themes: influencing change and building successful careers. A key goal shared by the majority of respondents was the desire to focus their energy on influencing change that affects students' lives and the greater campus community:

> "[I'd like] to empower students to find their passion, vocation, and be agents of change post-college."

> "Whether I am a department director or assistant dean of students, I would like my job responsibilities to still focus on some aspects of diversity, social justice, and leadership."

> "I'm hoping to take on a leadership role that will allow me to enact change."

> "I have been involved with managing, creating, and developing living and learning communities, so a position that works with this focus is appealing."

Some respondents expressed a desire to rise to higher administrative roles, pursue doctoral work, and continue to build on the existing body of knowledge regarding APIDA students and professionals:

> "My long-term goal is to become a dean of students or VP [vice president] of student affairs and, depending on my guidance, possibly become one of the first API college presidents."

"[I'd like] to get my doctorate and begin exploring areas of assessment and research in the field. I would love to teach someday or work up to an upper-level position as an assistant VP or dean."

Some respondents acknowledged the realities and challenges of pursuing upper-level positions, and uncertainty about what the future holds for them:

"I draw my energy from the students, so if there is less interaction with them, I could forecast that my energy would decline and my motivation would not be what it should be to work in our field."

"Now with a family, I am being more cognizant of striking a healthier work-life balance."

"At this point of my career, my career aspirations change constantly. There are days where I think I would be happy to become a university vice president of student affairs, and there are days where I think about leaving higher education altogether. I think a common theme for me is growth and change."

Inspiration and Impact of Mentoring

Not surprisingly, today's new and midlevel APIDA student affairs professionals have benefited from the support of mentors who identify as both APIDA and non-APIDA. As one professional said, "My career aspirations have been shaped by the mentors that I have [had]." Although the number of APIDAs in leadership and mentoring roles has increased on campuses across the nation, non-APIDA mentors are also valued and continue to have an effect on the lives of up-and-coming professionals. Many of those who responded to the survey credit their mentors with validating and playing a role in their identity development, and helping them navigate the politics of their identity in the profession:

"I used to think that the parts of me that have been so deeply ingrained by my upbringing would be a barrier to ever becoming a senior student affairs officer.... [Now I] realize that I need to come to terms with the notion of simultaneously being a leader who happens to identify as APIDA."

"[Because of my mentor,] I became more in tune with learning about my identities and what it meant to be a person of color in a profession that was predominantly White."

"[As a student,] I was exploring my identity as a Korean American adoptee and they [my APIDA mentors] took me in, connected me to the Asian American Student Association, and were my first models of effective mentorship in student affairs."

Others credit mentors with providing support and inspiring them to think critically, learn from experience, and pursue their passion:

"[My mentor] has been the type of mentor who helps you learn the nuances of the work environment, such as campus politics, as well as the role and treatment of professionals of color in our field."

"Some [of my mentors] were a reflection of what I could achieve ... others were there to guide and support me as I looked to develop my awareness and knowledge."

"In addition to simply seeing APIDA professionals in prominent positions, I have also had the fortune of finding strong and consistent mentorship from APIDA professionals who have given me the confidence to believe in myself and find a place to be a leader in this type of work."

"I have learned that success is not about going up in rank but finding a position where I am content and doing good work."

It is clear that the next generation of APIDA student affairs professionals are preparing themselves for greatness. All those who responded have earned masters' degrees, and many are planning or considering doctoral work. They are already leaders on their campuses and in their professional and personal communities, as indicated by their positions, their ability to influence decisions, and the respect they have earned. They continue to work toward their goals. When asked about what they hope to contribute to the student affairs profession, their responses mirrored the impact of their mentors and other successful APIDA student affairs professionals. A key theme in these responses was that of continuing to open the door and pave the way for others—professionals and students alike—and to contribute to the existing body of knowledge on the community:

> "I would like to help make the way for APIDA folks to get in [student affairs] and also to break down stereotypes about our community."

> "I hope to be able to provide more access to higher education for students from historically underrepresented communities and outreach to those individuals about being a change agent in their communities."

> "I definitely would like to do more to share my experiences with students, colleagues, and communities that could benefit."

> "[I want to promote and be a part of providing] access and education about college to underrepresented students and equity in services."

> "I . . . hope to produce research regarding issues revolving around South Asians and Pacific Islanders, because there is not a lot of information out there that disaggregates the cultural differences of these communities."

Our profession is about the lives and experiences of students. Many responses centered on the desire to make students' experience on campus positive and to make learning meaningful:

> "I hope to be able to continue to build relationships between student affairs and academic affairs, ensuring that both sides of the university understand the importance of the ever-changing needs of students."

> "I hope to make a difference in how diversity, multiculturalism, and global citizenship are viewed, especially in more traditional/conservative cultures."

> "Implementing programs that can help students holistically—personally, professionally, financially, and overall well-being."

> "[I want to] make a difference in a student's life, whether it is through leadership development, help with career/internship choices, help to network and build relationships, [or creating] . . . community."

> "My goal is to continue to share my passion for the profession and inspire others to make a difference in the work that we do for students."

> "I also hope to come up with some way of changing campus culture so that all students feel safe and welcome to be who they are."

Not surprisingly, respondents expressed a desire to "pay it forward" by mentoring students and up-and-coming professionals:

> "My mentors were the people in my life who made me believe in myself and my potential, [and who] drew me back to college. I hope to be that kind of mentor to students."

> "Mentoring young professionals is a contribution . . . I would like to make."

Legacies

As with stories told within a family, the stories of past and current APIDA professionals can give up-and-coming professionals a sense of pride and belonging to the profession and the culture. Through relationship building and mentoring, new professionals acquire a sense of the personal and professional struggles and successes of those who have gone before. The lessons passed down from those already successful in the field are not lost on the new generation. A key part of the legacy of APIDA student affairs professionals, thus far, has been paving the way for the success of the generations to come:

> "[Their legacy is] really making way for us to be here today. Particularly in our professional organizations, these folks have often been the only ones at the table and yet have worked to break down walls and create space so that we as APIDA folks can connect and support each other."

> "Look out for the marginalized and . . . break down the silence on all college campuses."

> "They have paved the way for the rest of us, and . . . given us higher standards and goals to meet."

> "Unrelenting sacrifice and dedication to lay a foundation and groundwork for present and future generations."

The impact of past APIDA professionals on students' lives and experiences has provided new professionals with a sense of legacy:

> "Our students trust them, and I know if they continue to trust me, I must be doing something right."

> "Each one teach one. . . . If I can truly influence the life of one student positively, then I know that I have given back to my community."

"[To] have a high work ethic and standard of care to serve students."

Although all these contributions are meaningful, arguably one of the most important parts of the legacy of APIDA student affairs professionals is to strive to achieve, support, and succeed, and to continue to bring others along for the ride:

"Creating a sense of belonging, family, and support while challenging each other to think outside the box and be better professionals and individuals."

"The APIDA legacy is one that is unique because of the diversity and richness of [the community]. I have learned that through perseverance, hard work, and love for the profession, a student affairs professional in the APIDA community can accomplish great things!"

"I think APIDA professionals convey the dual message that it is possible to be movers and shakers in this field, yet we cannot lose sight that, proportionately, there still aren't enough APIDA leaders obtaining senior-level roles."

Challenges

The road traveled by successful APIDA student affairs professionals has not been a smooth one, as acknowledged by those who will shape the future of the profession. The work already done has built a solid foundation for future successes, but challenges and barriers remain for both students and professionals. APIDA stereotypes—such as being submissive, lacking leadership and communication skills, and being talented in the sciences—continue to pose challenges for those who want to move up in the profession. Professionals who live by APIDA collectivist cultural values find it counter to those values to bring attention to their individual accomplishments rather than those of the group, so they tend to experience difficulty when it comes to being promoted. Many of those interviewed for this chapter said there is still an overall lack of APIDA professionals in the field, particularly at higher administration levels such as president and vice president. The lack of APIDA and multiethnic or multiracial role models in these positions motivates the next generation one new professional said,

> "The lack of APIDA staff in general during my experiences pushed me to want to go into student affairs and obtain higher education in that field and be a mentor to others as I have had during my time as an undergrad."

And some ethnic groups considered to be part of the API or APIDA identity group are less represented than others, which can make it even harder for both students and up-and-coming professionals to find people who share their values and can serve as role models. As one survey respondent said,

> "As a first-generation Thai-American with close ties to my heritage, I find that Thai professionals in the field of student affairs are quite rare. (I know absolutely none on my campus and have yet to meet any in the field.) This fact is very apparent to me in my daily interactions with colleagues, and the sensation is extremely lonely when I allow myself to think about it and feel the weight of it. It saddens me to feel like I'm the only one on campus."

Programs such as the NASPA Undergraduate Fellows Program (NUFP) are designed to provide mentoring and resources to students who, as undergraduates, express interest in the field. These programs give students access to both APIDA and non-APIDA mentors and senior student affairs officers, who can offer perspectives from various points in the profession. For the APIDA community, programs such as NUFP and the mentoring that occurs at all levels continue to be important, as they encourage young professionals to pursue senior leadership positions in all aspects of higher education.

A significant challenge facing new APIDA student affairs professionals and higher education in general is the changing landscape of the student population. According to the 2010 U.S. Census, the APIDA population has increased by 43% since the 2000 census (Humes, Jones, & Ramirez, 2011). This percentage growth is the fastest of all minority ethnic groups. Over the years, there has been a growing perception that the APIDA community is overrepresented in higher education, and some question the need for affirmative action and minority-serving activities directed at and including APIDA students. As an enrollment management professional, I have observed that many articles and essays that report enrollment statistics for minorities exclude Asians as a whole. The perception that APIDA students are being served at higher rates is flawed, because socio-economic status and rates of educational attainment vary greatly among APIDA cultures and groups. A report from the National Commission on Asian American and Pacific Islander Research in Education (CARE, 2010) shows that the percentage of Cambodian, Hmong, Laotian, Tongan, Samoan, Guamanian/Chamorro, and Native Hawaiians earning a bachelor's degree or higher ranged from 9% to 18%. Of the ethnic groups identifying as APIDA, Asian Indians reported the highest rate of degree attainment at 69%, followed by Pakistanis at 55%. Furthermore, the number of students identifying as multiracial is increasing. APIDA professionals will need to continue to advocate on behalf of their own communities, as those before them have done.

Analysis and Personal Reflection

The next generation of APIDA student affairs professionals is goal-oriented and student-centered. As shown in the many functional areas represented in the survey group, they are bringing a wide variety of perspectives. Although a number of them plan to develop an area of specialty, many are advised by mentors, fellow professionals, and graduate program advisors to explore diverse areas of the field to strengthen their future market-ability and upward mobility. Another characteristic of the new generation of APIDA student affairs professionals, as indicated by the responses to this survey, is their gratitude and awareness of the work previously done on their behalf and that of students to ensure a smoother path. It appears certain that they will endeavor to have a similar impact: to mentor, engage, and serve the communities they are a part of to ensure a bright future for other APIDAs. They seem to have a realistic perspective—that while much has been done to pave the way, more work still needs to be done.

The responses of my peers motivated me to reflect on my own goals and journey. I am a fourth-generation Japanese American, born and raised in Hawai`i, and now living and working in the Pacific Northwest. Like many who want to enter student affairs as a career, I was inspired and supported by mentors at both the undergraduate and graduate levels. Although my mentors as an undergraduate student were not APIDAs, they helped me celebrate and validate who I was culturally and personally. They believed in me when I did not believe in myself and supported me through the challenges that came my way. When I made the move from the unique cultural landscape of Hawai`i (where I was part of the majority culture) to Colorado (where I was truly a minority), an APIDA mentor helped me navigate my new perspective and life. I continue to be mentored by both APIDA and non-APIDA professionals who inspire and encourage me to think outside the box and trust my professional and personal instincts; challenge me to be in a constant state of improvement; and communicate their belief that I am making a difference. In my world of enrollment management, this means I am opening the door to the very experiences in college that shaped me as a person. It excites me to know that my peers working in residence life, student activities, career services, academic advising, alumni relations, and other student affairs fields will help fill the lives of prospective college students with meaning, learning, and fun. As one of very few Asian American women in my field, I know my role is to advocate for APIDA students who seek access to higher education, and to encourage and mentor up-and-coming APIDA professionals who seek to follow a similar path. I recognize that the path will not always be smooth. Knowing that I will continue to face both personal and professional challenges, I am comforted that I will have a peer group and mentors who will support and advise me through difficult times. Ultimately, I share the sense of purpose with the peers who shared their stories with me: to make a difference in the lives of college students.

The Future

Although it is impossible to know what the future holds for the next generation of APIDA student affairs professionals, one thing is certain—that future is bright! As a fellow new professional, I am inspired and validated by the insights of my peers who participated in this survey, and I share their desire to honor and contribute to the inspiration and legacy passed down to us, as we continue to pave the road for generations to come. Our goal is to make a difference in the lives of students and ensure that their experiences are positive and their futures bright. Collectively, we will continue to build on the legacy.

References

Humes, K. R., Jones, N. A., & Ramirez, R. R. (2011). *Overview of race and hispanic origin: 2010* (C2010BR-02). Washington, DC: U.S. Department of Commerce, U.S. Census Bureau. Retrieved from http://www.census.gov/prod/cen2010/briefs/c2010br-02.pdf

National Commission on Asian American and Pacific Islander Research in Education (CARE). (2010). *Federal higher education policy priorities and the Asian American and Pacific Islander community.* Retrieved from http://apiasf.org/CAREreport/2010_CARE_report.pdf

Epilogue

Amefil Agbayani and Doris Ching

We set out on a journey to publish the first book on Asian Americans and Pacific Islanders (AAPIs) in higher education student affairs. In our search for educator-colleagues who could relate experiences and insights on the small but significant, diverse, and rapidly growing community of AAPI professionals and students on college and university campuses, we discovered narrators of stories that inform, and we identified researchers and scholars whose analyses and studies probed deeply and challenged current perceptions, even among those within the group. Their research, observations, and personal experiences create a call for action to change the environments at institutions that have neither provided sufficient support and resources to AAPI students, faculty, and staff nor encouraged their voices to be heard. The reflections in this volume of AAPI student affairs professionals reveal their struggles to develop their identities and address the intersection of more than one identity that may be subject to discrimination, including the intersection common to all: being a member of the AAPI minority race and, simultaneously, a professional in student affairs, which is often in the lower echelon of the college or university hierarchy.

Connections, interconnectedness between generations, and legacy emerge as themes in the chapters, as does continuing the hope, dreams, and new opportunities for growth and success for generations that follow. These themes reflect the AAPI values of family, culture, and tradition. The authors are unanimous in their belief that the "model minority" myth continues to exist on campuses and that it hinders the delivery of resources to AAPI students and professionals who need them. Higher education needs to heed the 2010 report of the National Commission on Asian American and Pacific Islander Research in Education (CARE), which states that campus policies must be based on facts and data, not on myths.

The publication of this book marks the launch of a new mission to increase AAPI voices and enlighten campuses on the important contributions of AAPI student affairs professionals to the educational success of college and university students. The platform is set for the discussions that must occur if campuses are to become the truly diverse and equitable places they strive to be.

AAPI Representation in Higher Education

It is fitting that the journey begins with the wisdom of Bob Suzuki, whose accomplishments as an AAPI scholar and university president, involvement in civil rights issues, commitment to social justice, and advocacy of diversifying college campuses have been an inspiration for decades.

Howard Wang and Robert Teranishi's research and data provide a solid foundation for perspectives on AAPIs in higher education administration, faculty, and student affairs. Teranishi was principal investigator for the CARE project, which focused on the position of AAPIs and the heterogeneous groups within the AAPI community related to higher education policy and priorities.

AAPI Racial Identity Formation

Sumun and Vijay Pendakur work to build practitioner-allies for APIA college students by radicalizing notions of APIA racial identity through the lenses of Critical Race Theory and Racial Formation. They argue that a radical understanding of race and history can help us reposition and reframe APIA college student identity, moving away from the model minority myth. Pendakur and Pendakur offer a concrete set of action items for practitioner-allies to advocate effectively for the multiplicity of unique risks and needs held by today's APIA college student.

Mamta Motwani Accapadi proposes a new way of contextualizing Asian American identity and addressing identity-relevant needs of the growing AAPI student population through a polycultural model that engages practitioners to understand identity development in a holistic manner that considers multiple social identities, or intersections, and allows authentic insight into one's identity development.

Sara Furr, Bernard Liang, and Stephanie Nixon hypothesize that the experiences and needs of multiracial and multiethnic Asian Pacific Americans (APAs) are affected by various factors; they explore how involvement in higher education can enhance or inhibit multiracial identity development. Since the 2000 U.S. Census allowed individuals to identify in more than one race category, the numbers of multiracial, mixed-race, and biracial APAs have increased substantially in the community and in higher education.

In a scholarly personal narrative, Raja Bhattar shares insights on the effect of race and sexual orientation on student affairs educators' personal and professional experiences. These professionals need role models as they struggle to be authentic. The author's own reflections and those of other professionals are analyzed through the prism of broader models and perspectives of development.

Strengthening AAPI through Organizations and Leadership

Cynya Michelle Ko studies the challenge of developing students as leaders for social change on campuses, in professions, in communities, and in the world. Ko examines Asian American and Pacific Islander student organizations and explores how AAPI student organizations have been learning environments for Asian Americans to develop into leaders for social change.

Monica Nixon, Glenn DeGuzman, and Sunny Park Suh trace the groundbreaking history of the Asian Pacific American Network (APAN) as it celebrates its 25th anniversary. Asian American student affairs professionals worked in relative isolation on their campuses for decades. Motivated by the need to support one another, early professionals laid the ground for connections. In 1987, the American College Personnel Association established APAN to meet the needs of a growing and changing demographic of APIA student affairs professionals.

Hikaru Kozuma and Karlen Suga discuss the 2010 Legacy Project on the history and evolution of NASPA–Student Affairs Administrators in Higher Education's Asian Pacific Islanders Concerns Knowledge Community (APIKC), which supports the development of Asian Pacific Islander Desi American (APIDA) professionals and students. The project underlined the importance of intergenerational connections and knowledge of the history and development of organizations to enhance personal growth and facilitate connections.

Audrey Yamagata-Noji and Henry Gee discuss the dearth of AAPI leaders in recognized administrative roles, especially executive-level positions, in American colleges and universities. Leadership challenges and strategies are presented to help create a voice at every level of the institution, including the presidency, while increasing the pipeline of prepared leaders through the Leadership Development Program in Higher Education. Leadership training that is specific to the needs of Asian Americans and Pacific Islanders is clearly needed and warranted, given the meager 0.5% increase in the number of AAPI university presidents as documented in the American Council on Education's Profile of College Presidents, 1986 and 2006.

Working with AAPI College Students

Unlike other Pacific Islanders in the United States, Native Hawaiians are an indigenous people. Because of their unique status, strategies designed to enhance their chances for success in college have been combined with Hawaiian culture. Lui Hokoana and Judy Oliveira discuss what Native Hawaiian students believe about the effect of culture-focused services and programs and other factors on their college success.

Anna Gonzalez relates the dramatic increase of Asian American Greek Letter Organizations (AAGLOs) over the past 40 years. As the number of AAGLOs grew, campus administrators, advisors, and cultural center directors did not keep pace. AAGLOs circumnavigated the Black-White racial terrain of colleges and universities in order to redefine racial paradigms to be inclusive of those who do not fit into either category.

In her analysis of AAPI mental health on college campuses, including suicides, Karen Huang urges student affairs practitioners to understand and address stressors that contribute to mental health concerns in this diverse population. Negotiating cultural norms of collectivism in a society of individualism, striving to fulfill parental expectations for achievement, coping with racist microaggressions, and living in invalidating campuses can impede psychological health and lead to distress and disorders.

Noting that AAPI students have lower utilization rates of counseling services and greater distress at intake than other students, Mary Ann Takemoto and Diane Hayashino point to the need for competent multicultural services and clinicians who are sensitive to AAPI issues. College stressors can cause or exacerbate mental health issues for AAPI students, who may face cultural and family conflicts, pressures to excel, financial problems, and language difficulties.

AAPI Role Expectations

When Julie Wong was denied a leave of absence to participate in Semester at Sea, she chose to leave her job and live her life. She writes that it was "the most empowering decision in my life and opened up a path to finding my voice, confidence, and going against the traditional AAPI cultural values of obedience, and challenging the importance I place on . . . titles and material things. It's a story of finding me. Finding my voice. Finding the warrior in me."

A father and son, Hal Gin and Kevin Gin, relate student affairs professionals' values and philosophies to AAPI cultural and family heritage, comparing definitions and experiences as a family legacy. They describe their identity development and growth related to heritage, legacy, and cultural values as student affairs practitioners. The experiences and lessons of one generation offer dreams, hope, and opportunities for the next generation.

Noting that student affairs is a profession based on values of education and human development—congruent with AAPI values and emphasis on family—Sunny Lee examines the positive and negative outcomes for an AAPI woman as she negotiates role expectations in her attempt to "have it all" in career and family. Themes, insights, and reflections of AAPI student affairs professionals shed light on how AAPI women balance—or fail to balance—cultural norms, expectations, and values of profession and family.

Connie Tingson-Gatuz observes that AAPI professionals are often called on to participate in external community projects, such as scholarship reads, leadership development programs, and nonprofit community-based efforts. Although little is known about the effect of community involvement on the career progression of AAPI professionals, she speculates that AAPI professionals can leverage these experiences to progress in the field.

Karlen Suga observes the active participation of Asian Pacific Islander and Desi American (APIDA) student affairs professionals and their continued contributions to the field through research, advocacy, and practice. She discusses the hopes, dreams and goals of APIDA-identified

NASPA Undergraduate Fellows, graduate students, and new professionals as they commence their professional journey in student affairs.

Conclusion

Among the many complex and interrelated issues higher education institutions must deal with—including globalization, workforce development, academic excellence, technology, affordability, and social justice—a need exists for dialogue to explore options and expedite action to revise policies, devise new procedures, and bring about changes to meet the needs and address the concerns of AAPI students and student affairs professionals. The engagement of colleges and universities in the process will show their commitment to diversity, equity, and excellence. The promise of higher levels of effectiveness and commitment to diversity and equity in all aspects of the institution will be the reward.

> Diversity on college and university campuses is no longer a projection: it is a reality. In the context of compelling issues in the United States and abroad—changing demographics, immigration, health disparities, civil rights, and diversity in the marketplace, to name only a few—diversity provides powerful opportunities and serious challenges. In approaching these challenges and opportunities, institutional stakeholders must ask: How can we build our institutions' capacity to be effective, high-performing places where diversity thrives?... Today's diversity imperative extends far beyond student success (although student success remains critical).... We must bring people from diverse backgrounds together at every level on campus, from the president's cabinet to administrative units, to student affairs, to ethnic studies, to women's studies and beyond. (Smith, 2009, p. 14)

Our society acknowledges the importance of diversity; however, AAPIs are usually invisible or excluded from conversations, research, and policies related to diversity and equity in higher education. Only in 2007 did Congress create a new minority funding category of Asian American and Native American Pacific Islander serving institutions, and only in 2011 was the Asian Pacific Islander American Association of Colleges and Universities formed. Other organizations that advocate equity for minorities in education have much longer histories, including the National Association for Equal Opportunity in Higher Education (established in 1969), which supports historically Black institutions; the American Indian Higher Education Consortium (1972); and the Hispanic Association of Colleges and Universities (1986). Moreover, in 1999, these three organizations established a coordinating group called the Alliance for Equity in Higher Education.

The emergence of the pan-ethnic AAPI term has many benefits, and its use by government and other groups continues to grow. Among the many reasons AAPIs lack visibility is that inclusive terms such as AAPI are relatively new and not yet fully accepted or regularly used by the media, policy makers, or even AAPI groups themselves. Before the 1965 immigration law reform, a majority of Asian Americans in the United States were born here; now, there is much more heterogeneity within the AAPI category. The majority of AAPIs are foreign born, from many different countries, have low incomes and little education, are less familiar with English, and identify with their ethnic group or country of origin. A major challenge for AAPIs is inequity among the groups. The older, more established Chinese and Japanese groups are often privileged, while newer, smaller groups—such as Southeast Asians, South Asians, and Pacific Islanders—are marginalized. The various AAPI groups (including their multiracial and multiethnic members) will have to reach out to the newer, smaller, or disadvantaged groups so they can coalesce on common issues to support or oppose, such as language access, discrimination, and others. AAPI pan-ethnic identity will continue to be "an efficacious but contested category, encompassing not only cultural differences but also social, political, and economic inequalities" (Espiritu, 2008, p. 135). An ethnic-specific identity and a pan-ethnic AAPI identity are not mutually exclusive and can be beneficial. Much work is needed to present accurate disaggregated and aggregated data, analysis, and recommendations for consideration by both AAPI and non-AAPI communities, organizations, and policy makers.

We conclude this book with a call for higher visibility and a stronger voice for AAPIs, encouraging more research and increasing AAPI representation and leadership in higher education. There is an obvious lack of research on AAPIs conducted by scholars, policy makers, community groups, and, particularly, AAPI student affairs professionals. AAPI student affairs professionals have multiple roles to fulfill, including research and dissemination of that research to give voice and visibility to critical issues in higher education. The insight and perspectives of these professionals must become a regular part of scholarship, practice, and policies. Encouraging undergraduate and graduate students and student affairs professionals to conduct research on AAPI issues will require institutional resources and rewards.

Policy makers and responsible campuses must address the projected growth and underrepresentation of AAPIs as a group and for specific AAPI subgroups in higher education. Many faculty and administrators will be retiring in the next decade. Institutions often overlook talented AAPIs and others whose leadership styles are different from the styles of current leaders. Replicating the demographic background of today's faculty and administrators is not advisable. Institutional discrimination, benign neglect, leadership stereotypes, and traditional networks must change. Institutions need to redefine leadership so that qualities such as cross-cultural competence, collaboration, and humility are considered strengths. Generational retirement issues and the increase in the AAPI population offer a critical opportunity to actively and intentionally include AAPI talent on our campuses.

The responsibility and rewards for identifying and supporting diversity and including talented AAPI students and AAPI student affairs professionals must be shared by all. AAPIs must not work in isolation, and they must work actively with every racial and ethnic group. AAPIs must form alliances with other groups seeking equity, such as African Americans, Hispanic Americans, and Native Americans. Effective institutions will make these changes because it is beneficial to do so. But the changes will only be accomplished as a result of efforts to make the characteristics, status, and aspirations of AAPIs and the AAPI subgroups visible by developing more AAPI leaders and disseminating more research that will enable our voices to be heard.

References

Espiritu, Y. L. (2008). Asian American panethnicity: Challenges and possibilities. In P. M. Ong (Ed.), *The state of Asian America: Trajectory of civic and political engagement* (pp. 119–136). Los Angeles, CA: LEAP Asian Pacific Public Policy Institute.

National Commission on Asian American and Pacific Islander Research in Education (CARE). (2010). *Federal higher education policy priorities and the Asian American and Pacific Islander community.* Retrieved from http://apiasf.org/CAREreport/2010_CARE_report.pdf

Smith, D. G. (2009). Reframing diversity as an institutional capacity. *Diversity and democracy, 12*(2), 14–15. Retrieved from http://www.diversityweb.org/DiversityDemocracy/vol12no2/vol12no2.pdf

The Authors

Mamta Motwani Accapadi, dean of student life at Oregon State University, served on the faculty and as an administrator in Asian American, ethnic, and women's studies at The University of Texas at Austin, Schreiner University, and St. Edward's University. She received a BA in microbiology and an MEd and PhD in higher education administration from The University of Texas at Austin. Her academic areas are social justice education, Asian American identity, and the intersectionality of race and gender.

Amefil "Amy" Agbayani, director of student equity, excellence and diversity at the University of Hawai`i at Mānoa, is recognized nationally for her leadership and strong voice for women, civil rights, immigrant rights, workers' rights, Filipinos, and equity and diversity in higher education. She was born in the Philippines and received her undergraduate degree from the University of the Philippines and her PhD from the University of Hawai`i.

Raja G. Bhattar is director of the Lesbian Gay Bisexual Transgender Campus Resource Center at the University of California, Los Angeles. He holds an MEd in higher education and student affairs from the University of Vermont and a BA in psychology from Boston University. He has served in leadership roles with NASPA–Student Affairs Administrators in Higher Education and the Consortium of Higher Education LGBT Resource Professionals. Raja's research interests include assessment of social justice ally development, South Asian queer identity formation, and holistic identity development.

Doris Ching served as vice president for student affairs, associate professor, and associate dean of education at the University of Hawai`i. An advocate of equal rights for all students, she initiated numerous programs to promote student success. She was the first Asian American and Pacific Islander and first woman of color to be elected president of NASPA–Student Affairs Administrators in Higher Education. She received her EdD from Arizona State University, and her BEd and MEd from the University of Hawai`i at Mānoa.

Glenn DeGuzman is assistant director, student conduct services, at the University of California, Berkeley. He has taught undergraduate and graduate courses at UC Berkeley, Colorado State University (CSU), and San Jose State University, and has held administrative positions at Evergreen Valley College and CSU. His bachelor's degree is from UC Santa Barbara, master's degree from CSU, and doctoral degree from the University of La Verne. He is a former chair of the American College Personnel Association Asian Pacific Network.

Sara Furr, assistant director of multicultural student success at DePaul University, has a passion for social justice and students as change agents. She has presented at conferences on identity development and power, privilege, and oppression. She was previously at Loyola University Maryland, Mount St. Mary's University, and Fordham University. Her bachelor's degree is from the University of North Carolina, and her master's degree is from the University of South Carolina.

Henry Gee, vice president for student services at Rio Hondo College for eight years, co-facilitates the Leadership Development Program in Higher Education, in collaboration with Leadership Education for Asian Pacifics.

He was previously at Santa Ana College and Azusa Pacific University. His roles in NASPA–Student Affairs Administrators in Higher Education include regional vice president, national chair of the Educational Equity and Ethnic Diversity Network, NASPA Foundation Board of Directors, and the James E. Scott Academy Board. He was also a long-standing board member for Asian Pacific Americans in Higher Education.

Hal G. Gin retired from California State University, East Bay. He is a member of the Chabot-Las Positas Community College District Board of Trustees and was previously the first AAPI president/chair of the board. His bachelor's and master's degrees are from CSU East Bay, and his doctorate is from the University of San Francisco. He has served on the NASPA and NASPA Foundation boards of directors and is co-founder of the Hayward and Yixing (China) Sister City Committee.

Kevin J. Gin is coordinator of clubs and events at Berklee College of Music in Boston. He received his bachelor's degree from the University of California, Berkeley, and his master's degree from Colorado State University. He is NASPA Region I's representative to the Asian Pacific Islanders Concerns Knowledge Community. He has presented at regional and national conferences on undergraduate student retention, identity development, and family legacies.

Anna Gonzalez is associate vice chancellor for student affairs at the University of Illinois at Urbana–Champaign. She has served as associate dean of students at the University of California, Irvine, and sailed four times with the Semester at Sea Program, three times serving as the dean of students. In July 2012, Anna will become the senior student affairs officer for Lewis and Clark College. She is secretary-treasurer for the Association for Asian American Studies and past chair of the NASPA Undergraduate Fellows Program board. Anna received her degrees from Loyola Marymount University (BA) and Claremont Graduate University (MA, PhD).

Diane Hayashino is a licensed psychologist and training director of counseling and psychological services at California State University, Long

Beach, where she also lectures in the graduate program in educational psychology, administration, and counseling. She received her bachelor's degree from the University of California at Davis and her doctoral degree in counseling psychology from the University of Oregon.

Lui K. Hokoana is associate vice president for student affairs at the University of Hawai`i. His previous position was vice chancellor of student affairs at Windward Community College. He has planned, developed, and implemented numerous programs to address the higher education needs of Native Hawaiian students. He received a BA and MA from the University of Hawai`i and an EdD from the University of Southern California.

Karen Huang is manager of leadership assessment at Korn/Ferry International, one of the world's largest recruiting firms. A licensed psychologist, she served as staff psychologist at Stanford and Lehigh universities and taught at Stanford, Lehigh, and the University of California, Berkeley. She co-authored the first true multicultural psychology textbook. Her PhD and AB with honors in psychology are from UC Berkeley. She completed her pre- and postdoctoral training at Harvard Medical School sites and is a member of Phi Beta Kappa.

Cynya Michelle Ko is the director of Asian Pacific Student Services at Loyola Marymount University. Her undergraduate experiences as a student leader at the University of California, Irvine, led her to Columbia University, where she served under the office of the Dean of Students and completed her MA and EdM and successfully defended her doctoral dissertation on the influence of APIA student organizations on the development of leadership for social change. She serves on the board of directors for the Asian Pacific Community Fund and Project by Project.

Hikaru Kozuma graduated from Middlebury College, where he later served in residence hall director and housing director positions. His MEd in higher education administration is from the Harvard Graduate School of Education. He was director of residential programs at Columbia University and is executive director of student affairs at the University of Pennsylvania.

He co-chaired the NASPA Asian Pacific Islanders Concerns Knowledge Community.

Sunny Lee is assistant ombudsperson for students at the University of California, Berkeley. She has served as dean of students for Semester at Sea, director of student life and cultural centers at California State University, Pomona, and has worked in multicultural affairs at the University of California, Irvine, and Pomona College. She co-edited *Working with Asian American Students* (Jossey-Bass, 2002). She earned a BA at UC Irvine, an MEd at the University of Maryland College Park, and is completing a PhD at Claremont Graduate University.

Bernard "Bernie" Liang is director of student activities at Seattle University. He previously worked at the University of Washington, Tacoma; Susquehanna University; and Willamette University. He holds a bachelor's degree in business from The Pennsylvania State University and master's degree in student development administration from Seattle University. His interests include outdoor experiential leadership, student identity and leadership development, and intersections of identity.

Monica Nixon is director of multicultural affairs at Seattle University and a doctoral student at the University of Washington. Her previous positions were at Colgate University, the University of Puget Sound, and the University of Virginia, where she earned an MEd in counseling and a BA in English. She is past chair of the American College Personnel Association Asian Pacific American Network and currently serves on the NASPA Undergraduate Fellows Program board.

Stephanie Nixon is director of residential programs at Columbia University. She previously worked as a residence life, student conduct, and student center administrator at Willamette University and the University of Virginia, where she earned her bachelor's and master's degrees and taught leadership and multicultural education. Her interests include student identity development, bystander intervention, student activism, and college access.

Judy K. Oliveira is director of two TRiO Educational Talent Search projects at Windward Community College. She has been involved in numerous programs that support college access and financial aid for Native Hawaiian students and underrepresented minority students. She is an active board member of the Native Hawaiian Education Association. She earned a BEd from the University of Hawai`i at Mānoa, an MEd from Gonzaga University, and an EdD from the University of Southern California.

Sumun Pendakur is director of Asian Pacific American student services at the University of Southern California (USC). She holds a BA from Northwestern University, an MA from the University of Michigan, and an EdD from USC. From student activist to award-winning student affairs educator and researcher, she has been committed to access and equity for all. Her interests include Critical Race Theory, intersectionality, and lesbian, gay, bisexual, transgender, and queer advocacy.

Vijay Pendakur is the director of the Office of Multicultural Student Success at DePaul University. He holds a BA from the University of Wisconsin–Madison and an MA from the University of California, San Diego. He also works as a social justice educator and blogger and is currently pursuing his doctorate in education at DePaul University. His interests are Asian American history, Critical Race Theory, postcolonial theory, color-blind racism, and post-race politics.

Karlen N. Suga is an assistant director of undergraduate admissions at Pacific University in Oregon. She previously served as admissions counselor at Colorado State University (CSU). A native of Hilo, Hawai`i, she earned a BA in communication at the University of Hawai`i at Hilo and an MS in student affairs in higher education at CSU. She is a past national co-chair of NASPA's Asian Pacific Islanders Concerns Knowledge Community.

Sunny Park Suh is a former class dean at Columbia University and currently a full-time mom. A graduate of Mount Holyoke College, she holds an MEd and EdD from Teachers College, Columbia University. Her dissertation was the first study of Asian Pacific American (APA) administrators nationwide. Her expertise includes APA administrators, women's studies, minority affairs, and minorities in engineering. She is a former chair of the Asian Pacific American Network.

Bob H. Suzuki, president emeritus of California State Polytechnic University, Pomona, instituted programs to diversify the curriculum, students, faculty, and administration. He received the American Council on Education 2010 Reginald Wilson Diversity Leadership Award for extraordinary contributions to higher education. He earned BS and MS degrees in engineering at the University of California, Berkeley, and a PhD at the California Institute of Technology. A civil rights advocate, he helped desegregate the Pasadena public schools and was among the first scholars to debunk the Asian American model minority stereotype with his seminal journal article on the subject.

Mary Ann Takemoto is associate vice president for student services at California State University, Long Beach. She previously served as director of counseling and psychological services at Cal State Long Beach; associate director of the counseling center at the University of California, Irvine; and a lecturer in Asian American studies at UC Irvine. Her PhD in clinical psychology is from Indiana University and her BA is from Barnard College, Columbia University.

Robert T. Teranishi is associate professor of higher education at New York University (NYU). He is also principal investigator for the National Commission on Asian American and Pacific Islander Research in Education (CARE); co-director of the Institute for Globalization and Education in Metropolitan Settings; and a faculty consultant to the Ford Foundation's Advancing Higher Education Access and Success. In 2010, he received NYU's Martin Luther King, Jr. Faculty Award and was named one of the top up-and-coming leaders by *Diverse Issues in Higher Education.* In 2011, he was appointed by the U.S. Secretary of Education to the Department of Education's Equity and Excellence Commission.

Connie Tingson-Gatuz, is vice president for student affairs and mission integration at Madonna University in Livonia, Michigan. Previously, she directed retention programs at Michigan State University (MSU) and the University of Michigan. She received the 2010 Henry Gee Outstanding Mentor Award from the NASPA Asian Pacific Islanders Concerns Knowledge Community. As a consultant and speaker, she has worked with colleges, universities, and community-based organizations in the United States, South Korea, and the Philippines. She holds a BA in political science, an MA in university administration, and a PhD in higher education administration from MSU.

Howard Wang is associate vice president for student affairs at California State University, Fullerton. His MS in clinical microbiology is from the University of Wisconsin–Madison and his doctorate in higher education administration is from the University of California, Los Angeles. He is a frequent consultant to universities in China; associate editor of publications on global student affairs; and a member of Congresswoman Loretta Sanchez's Asian and Pacific Islander Americans Advisory Committee and the California State University Asian American and Pacific Islander Initiative.

Julie Marianne Wong is regional associate vice chancellor for student affairs at the University of South Florida St. Petersburg. She previously worked at the University of Colorado Boulder; University of Texas at El Paso; University of California, San Diego; Chapman University; California State University, Los Angeles; and University of California, Berkeley. Her bachelor's degree is from San Jose State University, MA from Michigan State University, and PhD from the University of Southern California.

Audrey Yamagata-Noji, vice president for student services at Mt. San Antonio College, co-facilitates the Leadership Development Program in Higher Education in collaboration with Leadership Education for Asian Pacifics. She is serving her sixth elected term on the Santa Ana Board of Education and is a founding member of Asian Pacific Americans in Higher Education, for which she serves on the board of directors. She has worked for 32 years as a community college faculty member and administrator.

Index

Americans and Pacific Islanders, xxiii

Presidents of colleges. *See* College presidents

Project OCEAN (On Campus Emergency Assistance Network) at CSU Long Beach, 260

Proposition 209 banning affirmative action in California, xvi

Psychologists. *See* Counseling services; Mental health

Public schools, AAPI students and personnel in, 6–10, 8–9*t*

Q

Queer sexuality
Asian American identity and, 77
Desi queer, 109–118. *See also* Desi queer professional in student affairs

Quemuel, Christine, 189

Quota system for immigrants, 130

R

Racial differences. *See also* African Americans; Diversity
college attendance, 173
college minority programs and, 39, 134
college presidents, 174
leadership programs, participation of academic officers in, 178
multicultural networks and subcommittees, 146
NASPA membership, 19–23, 20*t*, 22*t*, 158
NEEED membership, 160
"person of color," meaning of, 218
racial paradigm, placement of Asian Americans in, 215–216
underrepresented, programs for, 6, 47, 343
university offerings on ethnic studies, 136

Racial Formation in the United States From the 1960s to the 1990s (Omi & Winant), 33

Racial harassment, 133–134

Racial identity, 337. *See also* Asian American identity consciousness; Critical Race Theory (CRT); Racial differences
Asian American Identity Development Model (AAID) and, 67. *See also* Identity development models
compared to ethnic identity, 64–65
student empowerment and, 57

Racism. *See also* Racial differences
appearance as factor in, 74, 77, 100–101
campus climate and, 133–134, 135, 218, 235–236
exclusion of Japanese Americans, 126–127
as external influence on Asian American identity consciousness, 76–77
Greek organizations, exclusions by race and religion, 127, 219–222
immigration history and, 75–76
social isolation and, 234–236, 256
stereotyping and, 67
student organizations fighting, 135–138

Redirection to Asian American consciousness, 67, 96

Reflection in Learning and Professional Development (Moon), 161

Religiosity and ethnicity, 81, 137

Renn, K. A., 97–99, 297

Reputation of student affairs administrators, 293

Research
on AAPIs, 4, 6
identity consciousness, 62–64
multiracial/multiethnic identity development, 100–105
recommendations, 23–24, 46, 63, 106, 225
scholarly personal narrative as, 110
on therapist-client ethnic or racial match, 242

Restrictive housing covenants, 221

Rho Psi, 214, 220

Risk taking, 184

Rodriguez-Patel, Daisy, 149

Role modeling by AAPI teachers, faculty, and administration, 6, 10, 303–305, 316, 330, 337

Roosevelt, Franklin D., 121, 127

Root, M. P. P., 97

Ross, Ian, 222

S

Samahang Pilipino, 223

Sandeen, Arthur, xxi

Sandhu, D. S., 63

San Francisco State University, 129

Sasaki, Windi, 149, 150

"Saving face," 233

Scholarship `Aha (traditional Hawaiian feast), 206

Schön, Donald, 170

Schools and Staffing Survey (NCES), 7